THE DARKNESS AND THE GLORY

His Cup and the Glory
From Gethsemane to the Ascension

Greg Harris

Kress Christian
PUBLICATIONS

The Darkness and the Glory
His Cup and the Glory from Gethsemane to the Ascension

Published by:

Kress Christian
PUBLICATIONS

P.O. Box 132228
The Woodlands, TX 77393
www.kresschristianpublications.com

Unless otherwise indicated, all Scripture quotations taken from the *NEW AMERICAN STANDARD BIBLE®*, © Copyright 1960, 1962, 1963, 1968, 1971, 1972, 1973, 1975, 1977, by The Lockman Foundation. Used by permission.

ISBN 978-1-934952-01-6

Editorial Consultants: Lauren Harris, Kevin McAteer, Rebecca R. Howard
Cover Design: Mario Kushner
Text Design: Valerie Moreno

To Dr. Imad Shehadeh,

founder and president of Jordan Evangelical Theological Seminary,

man of God and dear friend,

whose cup involves ministering

often in the midst of deep darkness

Jesus therefore said to Peter, "Put the sword into the sheath; the cup which the Father has given Me, shall I not drink it?"

—John 18:11

Now from the sixth hour darkness fell upon all the land until the ninth hour.

And about the ninth hour Jesus cried out with a loud voice, saying, "Eli, Eli, lama sabachthani," that is, "My God, My God, why hast Thou forsaken Me?"

—Matthew 27:46-47

And He said to them, "O foolish men and slow of heart to believe in all that the prophets have spoken!

"Was it not necessary for the Christ to suffer these things and to enter into His glory?"

—Luke 24:25-26

CONTENTS

FOREWORD

Jesus of Nazareth, the King of the Jews.

His name alone evokes powerful images in the minds of people. Some immediately think of Him as a baby in a manger, the Christ of Christmas. Others envision Him as a child, a boy growing up in the home of a carpenter and confounding the religious leaders in the Temple. Still more picture a bold and courageous preacher who amazed the crowds and angered the Pharisees, or a compassionate shepherd and teacher—the perfect model of goodness, justice, and trust in God.

But if there is one image that surpasses all of these, it is that of Jesus Christ on the cross. There—with His body beaten and torn, His head rimmed with a bloodstained crown of thorns, and His hands and feet affixed by nails to the rough timber—He was shamefully hung between two political revolutionaries, being mocked and scorned by the angry crowds until He died.

Yet, in spite of the horrific torments Christ endured, it was not His physical anguish that caused Him the greatest suffering on the Cross. What happened at Calvary was infinitely more profound than bodily pain and crippling torture. His suffering transcended far beyond either the physical or the temporal. His deepest agonies were spiritual and relational—as the full fury of divine wrath was cast upon Him and He felt, for the first time in eternity, the bitter loneliness of being forsaken by His Father.

As we look back on the cross after almost two thousand years, we stand in awe at all that was accomplished there for us. We see the cross of Jesus Christ as that act by which Christ provided salvation for us; by which He saved us from sin and death and hell and the power of the flesh; by which He delivered us from the kingdom of darkness and put us in the kingdom of His dear Son; by which He ushered us into that place where we're blessed with all spiritual blessings in the heavenlies; by which He delivered us from the wrath to come; by which He took us who were enemies and made us friends of God; and by which He granted to us eternal life and all that it involves. We see it from our viewpoint, and it is legitimate to do so.

But ours is not the only perspective worth considering. The disciples, for example, looked ahead to the cross, wondering what it meant and ultimately facing it with abject fear. When it finally came they could see nothing but the oppressive specter of tragedy, astonished that their Master had been suddenly taken away from them. The enemies of Christ, both human and demonic, came to the cross with the scornful smile of triumph. They had finally gained victory over their enemy the Son of God, or so they thought. But their momentary conquest was in actuality their ultimate defeat. There were others at the cross as well: Simon of Cyrene, a visitor chosen to help carry the cross; two criminals, one of whom was saved that day; and a Roman centurion who remarked in astonishment, "Truly this Man was the Son of God."

But what was Christ's perspective as He endured the cross? The physical pain, the emotional ridicule, the social rejection, and most significantly the spiritual reality of bearing sin and being forsaken by His Father. It was there that He endured the punishment for sin in His own body for all who would believe in Him; it was there that He cried out with excruciating heartache, "My God, My God, why have You forsaken Me?"

Our Lord's death was vastly unlike our own deaths, in which we will finally experience release from our sinful bodies. His death did not involve release from a body of sin. Rather His sinless body was ravaged and crushed as His infinite Person felt the full weight of God's wrath poured out upon Him for sins He did not commit. Nevertheless, He anticipated the cross with an eager heart. And He endured it faithfully on account of the joy set before Him and the glory that was planned for Him from before the foundation of the world.

By examining the cross from Christ's perspective, *The Darkness and the Glory* provides a compelling behind-the-scenes look at the profound spiritual and theological realities of Calvary—realities that transcend the physical, as the wrath of man was surpassed by both the wrath of Satan and ultimately the wrath of God. With theological acumen and pastoral insight, Greg Harris invites readers to join him on a journey to the cross they will never forget. Doctrinally sound yet warmly devotional, this Christ-centered book is highly recommended to all who desire a better understanding of the glories of the cross.

As you read the pages that follow, may the infinite suffering and ultimate triumph of Christ rekindle your heartfelt worship, praise, and thanksgiving.

John MacArthur

THE BEGINNING

HIS CUP

When I finished writing *The Cup and the Glory*, I knew that God had wonderfully ministered to me through His Word. The Good Shepherd had indeed Himself perfected, confirmed, strengthened and established me (1 Pet. 5:10). Yet after the book was written, I knew something was not quite right about it; however, I could not figure out what it was. I pondered this continually until finally it dawned on me that the problem was the fifth chapter. Those of you who have read the book know that the fifth chapter is entitled "The Fellowship." That, however, was not its original name or content.

The original chapter title was going to be either "The Counting" or "The Ledger," taken from Philippians 3:7-8: "But whatever things were gain to me, those things I have counted as loss for the sake of Christ. More than that, I count all things to be loss in view of the surpassing value of knowing Christ Jesus my Lord, for whom I have suffered the loss of all things, and count them but rubbish in order that I may gain Christ." Paul employed accountants' terminology in these verses: on one side of the ledger is the loss column; on the other side is the gain. Paul's counting in his ledger regarded the loss of all things; but even more so, he immeasurably gained the Lord Jesus Christ.

While there were other reasons to change this chapter (see "*The Writing of The Cup and the Glory*" in *The Cup and the Glory Study Guide*), besides God granting me no peace whatsoever about what I had written, the biggest reason this chapter did not fit was that it would have placed the emphasis on *me* counting the cost and *me* suffering loss (and gain). Philippians 3:10 is much more appropriate for the overall flow and focus of the book: "that I may know Him, and the power of His resurrection and the fellowship of His sufferings, being conformed to His death." Simply put, "The Fellowship" is about His suffering—not ours. When we even remotely understand what this verse teaches, we vastly more appreciate what Jesus endured for us. We compare His suffering with how small ours is/was, and it humiliates us into worshipful adoration of Him—or at least it should. Knowing that we fail and struggle and often whine in the midst of our trials, His sufferings vastly exceeded more than we can begin to conceive in our minds until we are home with the Lord. So "The Fellowship" chapter has two unique features: one, it became the only chapter of the book that was completely rewritten from beginning to end; and two, although its place is in the middle of the book, it was the last chapter written.

We can appreciate "The Fellowship" better when we return to the original text where I began my studies, Mark 10:35–41. When James and John ask Jesus that they may sit in His glory (10:35-37), Jesus replied with an answer that startled them—as it should startle us: "But Jesus said to them, 'You do not know what you are asking for. Are you able to drink the cup that I drink, or to be baptized with the baptism with which I am baptized?'" (Mark 10:38). As many of you know, this is where "The Cup" part of the title for *The Cup and the Glory* originated.

Perhaps it would be fitting to walk through more detail of what "drinking the cup" entails because it will be so significant in our present study. The cup of which Jesus spoke in Mark 10 is only for His disciples; no unbeliever ever qualifies for this. This is not the cup of salvation, but rather the one that true disciples drink in following their Lord after being saved. Furthermore, the cup that Jesus referred to is not just a one-time event. It incorporates whatever comes along during a lifetime of following Jesus: wherever that leads, whatever that means. For those who walk with Jesus, their cup ends either at their own death when they go home to be with the Lord, or—if they are alive—when the Lord returns for His own.

We can see the broad spectrum of what the cup entails by examining related Scriptures. For instance, in Paul's death row epistle, while not specifically using the word "cup," he still conveys the same concept. Just before his execution for the cause of Christ, the Apostle Paul wrote in 2 Timothy 4:7: "I have fought the good fight, I have finished the course, I have kept the faith." Paul's statements are similar to what Hebrews 12:1 teaches, "let us run with endurance the race that is set before us." Paul was finishing his fight, his course, his race—and his cup.

Second Corinthians describes some of the elements contained in the cup the Apostle Paul drank in his service unto the Lord:

Are they servants of Christ? (I speak as if insane) I more so; in far more labors, in far more imprisonments, beaten times without number, often in danger of death. Five times I received from the Jews thirty-nine lashes. Three times I was beaten with rods, once I was stoned, three times I was shipwrecked, a night and a day I have spent in the deep. I have been on frequent journeys, in dangers from rivers, dangers from robbers, dangers from my countrymen, dangers from the Gentiles, dangers in the city, dangers in the wilderness, dangers on the sea, dangers among false brethren; I have been in labor and hardship, through many sleepless nights, in hunger and thirst, often without food, in cold and exposure.

Apart from such external things, there is the daily pressure upon me of concern for all the churches (2Cor. 11:23-28).

In addition to all of these trials Paul listed in Second Corinthians — and whatever else he endured for Christ's sake that happened after he wrote these verses — they culminated with his death; this will be true for many others also, whether by natural death or martyrdom.

But let's go back to the Mark 10 account because there are many goldmines within this text that will show in more detail what we have seen. Mark 10:38 records these words, "Are you able to drink the cup that I drink, or to be baptized with the baptism with which I am baptized?" Jesus used the present tense — not the future tense — for His cup and His baptism. The present tense could rightly be translated, "The cup that I am currently drinking" and "the baptism that I am currently being baptized with." Jesus was already drinking the cup; it was not something reserved for Him exclusively at the cross, which was approximately a year away from the present time. In harmony with what we have already seen, drinking the cup is not a one-time event; drinking the cup consists of multiple and collective events. The cup for Jesus then consisted of *everything* about His life that was necessary for Him to be the Messiah. This included, among countless other things: living every second of every day in sinless perfection, enduring the forty-day temptation by Satan, qualifying as a Man of Sorrows, being victorious over the multiple attacks of His earthly opponents, as well as the weariness resulting from an unbelievably busy ministry, such as is especially detailed in the Gospel of Mark.

The culmination and by far the most horrendous part of His cup was yet to occur in Jerusalem. The parallel account in Matthew 20:22 puts the emphasis on this future climax: "But Jesus answered and said, 'You do not know what you are asking for. Are you able to drink *the cup that I am about to drink?'"* We do not have time to camp out at this rich section of Scripture now (perhaps we will come back to it in the future); but although the accounts are similar, the two Gospels emphasize different aspects of the person and work of Jesus. Matthew presents Jesus as the promised King, and the question presented asks about rank within His kingdom that the disciples were expecting to appear immediately (Luke 19:11). Jesus accordingly directs His answer in relation to the future entrance of the King—and the King's death—in Jerusalem. The Gospel of Mark presents Jesus as the Servant of Yahweh Who is presently drinking His cup and already is being baptized with His baptism by constantly serving God and others. Plus—note this well, beloved—James and John, who had previously witnessed the Transfiguration Glory in Mark 9:1-8, asked about sitting in His glory. Jesus responded appropriately to what they requested. There is more, but we must move on.

While James and John did not know what they were asking concerning what was required to sit in His glory or in claiming that they were able to do whatever was necessary, Jesus informed them that they would, indeed, drink the cup that He drank: "And Jesus said to them, 'The cup that I drink *you shall drink*; and *you shall be baptized* with the baptism with which I am baptized'" (Mark 10:39b). As was true for Jesus, the cups for James and John (and others) were an ongoing process. The cup that each was to drink would have several different portions along the way, diverging in various places for each one—each precisely determined by the will of the Father. The cup for James ended in Acts 12:1-2 when Herod beheaded him. John's cup consisted of decades more, some of which included working as a slave on the isle of Patmos, and ended when he died as an old man. Later, Jesus revealed to Peter in John 21:18-19 how his cup would end: death by crucifixion. But as was true for Jesus, the cups that these beloved followers must drink would include many other matters. For example, being flogged in Jerusalem (Acts 5:33-40) was a component of their cups, plus imprisonment, plus whatever else occurred that Scripture does not contain—all part of the overall means of drinking the cup that Jesus drank.

The cups that each true disciple were/are to drink may have similarities, but the cup that Jesus drank was unlike anyone else's who has been or ever will be born. Scripture repeatedly reveals this. To begin with, most of "the cup verses" are framed by some question or statement about "being able." In the Mark 10:38-39 passage, Jesus asks,

"Are you able to drink the cup?" James and John reply mostly in blissful ignorance, "We are able." It is vital to our understanding to note that the word "to be able" (*dynamai* in the Greek) has the sense of having the capacity or ability to do something. It is the root form for our word "dynamite."

You can read more about this concept in chapter six, "The Footprints," in *The Cup and the Glory*, but the restrictive nature of Jesus' cup is clearly seen in John 13:31-38. The passage begins immediately after Jesus dismissed Judas from the Passover meal: "When therefore he had gone out, Jesus said, 'Now is the Son of Man glorified, and God is glorified in Him; if God is glorified in Him, God will also glorify Him in Himself, and will glorify Him *immediately*'" (John 13:31-32). Remember that Peter, James, and John had seen His glory in Mark 9. If Jesus had not continued speaking, they most likely would have jumped up from their reclining Passover postures expecting the immediate display of the glory of God. Instead, Jesus revealed a truth that jarred those present—especially Peter: "Little children, I am with you a little while longer. You shall seek Me; and as I said to the Jews, I now say to you also, 'Where I am going, you cannot come'" (John 13:33). The phrase "you cannot come" is the same verb form used in the Mark 10 statements. It literally reads, "you are not able to come." As before, this is not lack of permission to go with Jesus; this is the utter lack of capacity to be able to do so. Jesus answered Peter with the identical statement in John 13:36, saying, "Where I go, you [singular, Peter] cannot [are not able; do not have the capacity to] follow Me now; but you shall follow later."

The original apostles did not have the ability or capacity to drink the cup that Jesus drank, but it is by no means limited to them. No one else ever has been or will be able to—ever. This is true throughout eternity. In Revelation 5:1-3 the Apostle John was transported to heaven and recorded these words:

> And I saw in the right hand of Him who sat on the throne a book written inside and on the back, sealed up with seven seals. And I saw a strong angel proclaiming with a loud voice, "Who is worthy to open the book and to break its seals?"
>
> And no one in heaven, or on the earth, or under the earth, was able to [*dynamai*—had the ability to; the capacity to] open the book, or to look into it.

John recorded his response and the subsequent statement of victory in

Revelation 5:4-5: "And I began to weep greatly, because no one was found worthy to open the book, or to look into it; and one of the elders said to me, 'Stop weeping; behold, the Lion that is from the tribe of Judah, the Root of David, has overcome so as to open the book and its seven seals.'" He—and He alone—was able.

Such a contrast in capabilities should not surprise us. When Paul wrote First Corinthians, he exposed a promise from God that is wonderfully comforting to us, especially in the midst of our own struggles: "God is faithful, who will not allow you to be tempted *beyond what you are able*" (1 Cor. 10:13). Paul employed the same word form as before: "beyond what you have the capacity" or "beyond what you have the ability." What a grace gift from God that He sovereignly measures and restricts—and obviously knows—how much each one is capable of enduring. That is why we marvel—or least we should—at Jesus. To what depths was this One able to be tempted beyond what we are able? Can it remotely be fathomed? Measured? Explained? What Jesus was able to receive infinitely surpassed the breadth of what the entirety of fallen man was able to receive. We simply cannot mentally grasp how much Jesus was able to be tempted and endure. Our only true means of comparison for the present time are our own woefully inadequate failures. As written in *The Cup and the Glory*, even if we had the opportunity to do so at our birth—which we do not—we would have long since disqualified ourselves from accompanying Him to where He was going based on our multitude of sinful failures. The cup that Jesus drank was uniquely His, uniquely alone—and unimaginably deep. He alone is able; He alone is worthy.

We see this truth developed elsewhere in Scripture. As noted in Mark 10:38, Jesus was already to a degree drinking the cup (present tense) the Father had given Him. Yet by far the unspeakably horrendous component was about to take place as He headed to His cross. He understood this completely; His prayers in Gethsemane reveal this. It was the removal of His cup that was the core of the immeasurably intense prayers of Jesus. On the three different segments of prayer Jesus implored Abba to remove, if possible, what lay before Him (Mark 14:32-41). Mark 14:36 records: "And He was saying, 'Abba! Father! All things are possible for Thee; remove this cup from Me; yet not what I will, but what Thou wilt.'" His cup was so unfathomable, so severe, that it greatly tormented and grieved Him as the wounded Son repeatedly called out to Abba. Luke 22:44 describes Jesus as "being in agony" in this prayer. We who love the Lord have no true base of comparison to such agony in prayer because we are protected by the Father; even beyond this, we are not able to begin to comprehend its weight.

We should note that, technically speaking, the cup could be removed from Jesus—but Scripture would be broken (which it cannot), and the Son would be outside the Father's will (which He could not). So in a sense, no, there was no other way. *No one* would ever be saved, Satan's domain would never end, and the Kingdom of God would never come—if Jesus had refused or failed to drink the cup set before Him.

Mark well, beloved, the change that occurs from the agonizing prayer sessions to moments later when He was arrested. Gethsemane had settled the issue for Jesus. The time for asking Abba was over; the Son would totally submit to the Father's will. Having awakened His three sleeping disciples, Jesus went forth from the Garden to meet His arresters (John 18:1-11). In John 18:10, Peter still attempted to keep the Messiah from going to His God-ordained cross: "Simon Peter therefore having a sword, drew it, and struck the high priest's slave, and cut off his right ear; and the slave's name was Malchus." Jesus responded immediately and majestically in John 18:11: "Jesus therefore said to Peter, 'Put the sword into the sheath; the cup which the Father has given Me, shall I not drink it?'"

Note how vastly the substance of what Jesus says differs from the Gethsemane prayers of just a few minutes before:

—"The cup"—not "a cup." The cup is uniquely His and uniquely defined.

—"which the Father"—Jesus used *pater* in the Greek, where we get our word "paternal" and the word Jesus routinely used when He referred to the Father. He did not employ *Abba* ("Papa" or "Daddy") in front of His enemies; He only used that endearment form in the Garden.

—"has given Me"—a perfect active indicative in the Greek. This denotes a completed action that points to ongoing results. The Father will not be defining the cup that the Son must drink as it unfolds; it has already been given by the Father. It is now up to the Son to drink what the Father has already determined.

—"shall I not drink it?"—Jesus used the strongest Greek negation available (*ou me*) that could be translated, "shall I by no means whatsoever drink of it?" It is the exact same negation that Peter used in Matthew 16:22 when Jesus first announced His pending death. Peter declared, "This shall never [by no means whatsoever (*ou me*) ever] happen to you."

Jesus stepped forward at His arrest to finish drinking the cup that the Father had given Him. He must drink it alone—every last bit of it. As we will see, and without any exaggeration whatsoever, Jesus drinking His cup vastly exceeds the sum of all the redeemed drinking their own combined cups.

Even without totally understanding what all of this means, we can still identify—and marvel at—some of the components that made His cup uniquely His. One way we can see this is through Isaiah 53. This wonderful portion of Scripture has long fascinated students of the Bible because it offers a vivid account of the ministry of Jesus centuries before He walked the earth. As with Psalm 22, the Trinity insists we view this chapter with Jesus in mind. For instance, the Ethiopian eunuch of Acts 8, after reading Isaiah 53:7-8, pondered this passage which speaks of One who was led to slaughter as a lamb. After prompting by an angel, Philip approached the chariot of the eunuch. In Acts 8:34 the Ethiopian asked simple, direct questions: "Please tell me, of whom does the prophet say this? Of himself, or of someone else?" The next verse states, "And Philip opened his mouth, and beginning from this Scripture he preached Jesus to him." Others, especially skeptics of the Bible, attempt to relate Isaiah 53 to some particular individual or group in history past or present. However, not only does no one else fit the description given in this passage, the Bible repeatedly points to Jesus as the prophesied Suffering Servant of Yahweh. Multiple Messianic truths exist in Isaiah 53, such as the prophecy that Jesus' burial would be associated with a rich man (Isa. 53:9; Matt. 27:57-60).

Beyond such detailed prophecies, Isaiah 53 presents a description of the Messiah's sacrificial role. Isaiah 53 is actually wonderful New Testament theology, as the Trinity so intended. Isaiah prophesied, "He has no stately form or majesty that we should look upon Him, nor appearance that we should be attracted to Him. He was despised and forsaken of men, a man of sorrows, and acquainted with grief; and like one from whom men hide their face, He was despised, and we did not esteem Him" (53:2-3). In summation of the sacrificial ministry of atonement the Servant of Yahweh alone could bring, Isaiah concluded, "By His knowledge the Righteous One, My Servant, will justify the many, as He will bear their iniquities. . . . He poured out Himself to death, and was numbered with the transgressors; yet He Himself bore the sin of many, and interceded for the transgressors" (53:11b-12).

But there is more. While often not realized by many readers of the Bible, Isaiah 53 actually begins with the three previous verses, namely Isaiah 52:13-15. Remember chapter and verse divisions are manmade inventions placed for our convenience. These last three verses of Isaiah 52 contain a summary of what follows in Isaiah 53:

> Behold, My servant will prosper, He will be high and lifted up, and greatly exalted. Just as many were astonished at you, My people, so His appearance was marred more than any man, and His form more than the sons of men.
>
> Thus He will sprinkle many nations, kings will shut their mouths on account of Him; for what had not been told them they will see, and what they had not heard they will understand.

Here is another example of a prophet of God predicting the sufferings of Christ and the glories that follow (1 Pet. 1:10-11). Once more we see the atoning benefits of His sacrifice in that "He will sprinkle many nations," using Old Testament terminology particularly associated with the High Priest and the Day of Atonement.

But consider for a moment: is Isaiah 52:14 a true statement, or is it a hyperbole—that is, is it merely an exaggeration for the sake of effect? Was Jesus' appearance actually "marred more than any man, and His form more than the sons of men"? To begin with, we should hope that this description is not an overstatement by God because if it is the effects of His sprinkling and accepted sacrifice might be exaggerated for the sake of effect as well—and consequently we might not be truly cleansed. We also should note that Isaiah 52:15 begins with the word "thus"—that is, it connects the promised high priestly sprinkling to whatever He received in Isaiah 52:14 that so altered His form beyond that of anyone else in history. Nothing other than someone's presuppositions indicate that Isaiah 52:14 is an exaggeration. The form and appearance of this One actually was marred vastly beyond that of any man who ever had or ever will live. We do not know exactly when this transpired; it may have been a progression that terminated at His death. Accordingly, the appearance of Jesus differed immeasurably from that of the two men who were crucified on each side of Him. This would have been evident to all the onlookers who viewed them, including the thief on an adjacent cross who was ultimately saved, as well as the centurion and those on duty with him. These soldiers had *never* witnessed anything like the death of Jesus before—nor had anyone else, then or ever.

So many artists who paint a depiction of either the crucifixion or of Jesus after they had taken Him down from the cross fail miserably in their attempts to paint this scene accurately. From many paintings, which seem to get locked into people's perception as biblical truth, all things considered, Jesus did not look all that bad at His death. Tired and exhausted—and dead—but at least you could recognize who He was. That would not be true, however, for those who were present for the crucifixion. If the head of Jesus had not been connected to His body and was discovered by someone in a field, it could have raised questions as to whether it actually was a human head.

But still, why? Millions have been savagely beaten; multitudes have been scourged; hundreds of thousands have been crucified. History indicates that it was not unusual for the ones crucified to linger in agony on the cross for several days before they eventually succumbed. What was it about His relatively short six-hour crucifixion that vastly exceeded what none of Adam's seed had ever—or would ever—or could ever endure? Is there any way to know even remotely what or why?

In addition to this, one other point must be considered. In John 19:31-36 the Jewish officials approached Pilate asking that the legs of those crucified be broken so that they might die and be taken from the cross on the Sabbath. The soldiers broke the legs of those crucified beside Jesus, but His they did not; He was already dead. The apostle John stated the importance of what he had witnessed (John 19:35-36): "And he who has seen has borne witness, and his witness is true; and he knows that he is telling the truth, so that you also may believe. For these things came to pass, that the Scripture might be fulfilled, 'Not a bone of Him shall be broken.'" This is a tremendously important revelatory nugget from God. Jesus was scourged (Matt. 27:26; Mark 15:15), and yet not one of His ribs was broken. Matthew 27:30 states, "And they spat on Him, and took the reed and began to beat Him on the head." Mark 15:19 puts the focus on the repetitive acts of violence against Him: "And they kept beating His head with a reed, and spitting at Him, and kneeling and bowing before Him." If the reed had been a rod or iron, such as the one He will wield against the nations (Ps. 2:7), it would not break one bone of this One who had set His face like flint (Isa. 50:7). Regardless of the savagery against Him, His jawbone was not broken; neither was there the tiniest fracture of His cheekbones. Still, even without any broken bones, "His appearance was marred more than any man, and His form more than the sons of men" (Isa. 52:14). *Something* beyond the normal physical trauma must have occurred.

Here then is the question before us: is there any way to know what the cup His Father had given Him contained? Or stated differently, is there any way to see—even in a mirror dimly—any of the elements that made Jesus drinking His cup so exceed all other cups combined?

Actually there is. God sets the answer before us in His Word. The Bible reveals that the cup that Jesus drank had at least three unique components that caused His death to be unlike any other and made His appearance to be marred more than any man. All three parts were hidden to humanity present at the crucifixion—and in many cases still remain hidden to modern readers of the Bible. All three items are the same type of "behind the scenes" spiritual truths (such as matters related to the birth of Jesus) that would not be known even to the elect unless God chose to reveal them in His Word. All three measures that made the cup Jesus drank so hideous are found within the pages of Scripture. We will identify each of them, but by no means will we even properly define nor describe them and by no means remotely exhaust their significance. In fact, it will take all eternity to understand the depths of what Jesus endured for us.

Come: let us observe—even as children, and from a distance—the cup which the Father had given to the Son.

And let us marvel at what He alone was able to do.

1

THE WAGER

In order to begin to understand how the cup of Jesus differed from all others, we need to go back in Scripture before coming to the cross. After all, if the cross was the pinnacle of the cup He was about to drink (Matt. 20:22), and yet He was already in some measure drinking the cup throughout His entire ministry (Mark 10:38), then it reasons that we should not go directly to the end. We would miss much of what He endured; but even more, we would miss very strategic truths within the Bible that are relevant to His cross.

Let us consider such an embedded truth within God's Word and then a question that results from it. In Matthew 16:21-23, after Jesus disclosed details of His pending death to His disciples, Peter rebuked Him for saying such a thing. To this Jesus replied, "Get behind Me, Satan! You are a stumbling block to Me; for you are not setting your mind on God's interests, but man's." Here Satan attempted to use Peter as a means of keeping Jesus from His divinely appointed destiny. Yet months later in Luke 22:3-4 we read that: "Satan entered into Judas who was called Iscariot, belonging to the number of the twelve. And he went away and discussed with the chief priests and officers how he might betray Him to them." Both passages contain important clues. Each has common characteristics: the presence of Satan, an apostle of Jesus, and Jesus Himself. The accounts are similar, yet they differ significantly—and this is important. In both cases Satan used an apostle of Jesus as the means to hinder or attack Him, but the task the evil one attempted to have them perform was different. Once the clues are set forth there emerges a simple (but often repeated) question: Why? *Why would Satan attempt to hinder Jesus from going to the cross by means of Peter in Matthew 16, but later in Luke 22 use Judas to help lead Jesus to the cross?* This is odd. It seems contradictory. In the first account Satan attempted to keep Jesus from ever directing Himself toward the cross; in the other Satan actively worked to bring about Jesus' death by crucifixion. Why the change in strategy? Why would Satan alter his tactics? What did Satan hope to accomplish in either case?

To ascertain a biblical solution to this mystery — and the many such related mysteries that will emerge — we first have to carefully examine. As with any good detective, we must drop down into the world of those present and consider all the relevant factors available. Simply put, we must observe the crime scene for clues. We will begin with Satan's first attempt to keep Jesus from ever arriving at His cross.

Matthew 16:16 is the biblical account of Peter's declaration: "You are the Christ, the Son of the living God!" Having taken approximately three years to lead Peter to this conclusion, Jesus — as virtually always — surprised those who heard the chief disciple's vocal proclamation. After Peter pronounced that Jesus was the divinely promised Christ, the Messiah Himself revealed the ultimate source of the statement, saying, "Blessed are you, Simon Barjona, because flesh and blood did not reveal this to you, but My Father who is in heaven" (16:17). After the declaration and the following attestation, Jesus then most unexpectedly restricted His disciples, warning them they should tell no one at that time that He was the Christ, the Son of the living God. Restraining those present from telling others of this foundational truth was an unexpected limitation placed on the apostolic preachers whom Jesus had previously commissioned to announce that the kingdom of God was at hand (Matt. 10:1-7). Yet He had so much more to teach them. Within the same chapter Jesus staggered His flock even further by predicting His own pending execution (Matt. 16:21). He had alluded to His death on previous occasions, but the Matthew 16 account was the first instance where Jesus openly spoke of it ("from that time"). Jesus' statement would have evoked a sickness in the pits of the disciples' stomachs. His prophecy was a tragic, horrible, bewildering announcement to the Messiah's chosen apostles.

Or perhaps what Jesus said was not true. By no means would they have considered Jesus to be a liar, but maybe what He just stated was simply another way of teaching His disciples. For instance, in a episode just months earlier, Jesus astounded the Twelve when they approached Him about sending away the five thousand men (plus the women and the children) because it was late, and they had no food. In

Luke 9:13 He instructed them, "You [plural] give them something to eat!" The parallel account in John 6:4-5 adds additional details and insight, including the unique role that Philip played in this: "Now the Passover, the feast of the Jews, was at hand. Jesus therefore lifting up His eyes, and seeing that a great multitude was coming to Him, said to Philip, 'Where are we to buy bread, that these may eat?'" John 6:6 reveals the strategic truth that Jesus used these impossible circumstances to educate Philip: "And this He was saying to test him; for He Himself knew what He was intending to do." Jesus knew Philip could not pass this impossible test by himself. He simply led Philip to make the obvious deduction that Jesus intended: he and the other disciples did not have sufficient resources to feed the multitude; God alone did. But fortunately, Philip was in the presence of Immanuel—God was indeed with them. So maybe what Jesus now said in Matthew 16 concerning His death was a similar test to see how the disciples would respond. After all, Jesus had previously instructed them, "A disciple is not above his teacher, nor a slave above his master" and, "he who does not take his cross and follow after Me is not worthy of Me. He who has found his life shall lose it, and he who has lost his life for My sake shall find it" (Matt. 10:24, 38-39). Perhaps what Jesus now spoke was the first test for the disciples after Peter's divinely inspired declaration concerning the Christ. *Who or what is the supreme love of their lives: Jesus or their own personal survival?* Jesus affirmed that He was indeed Christ the King, which would make those present His kingdom subjects. Would a "knight" in any elite guard stand idly by when the king abruptly warned of his pending doom and not offer any intervention in behalf of his sovereign? Would a knight in the King of Kings' service do any less?

One most certainly would not. Peter would have none of this nonsense about Jesus being killed. Jesus had given Peter (and the others) authoritative positions in the Church He Himself would build, promising, "and whatever you shall bind on earth shall be bound in heaven, and whatever you shall loose on earth shall be loosed in heaven" (Matt. 16:19). Having such authority given to him, the first thing Peter intended to "loose" was what Jesus had just predicted concerning His death—a death Jesus later revealed would be by means of crucifixion. Peter employed a double negative in the Greek when he rebuked Jesus, a stern response that could be translated, "by no means whatsoever shall this be to You!" (Matt. 16:22). Peter stated in the strongest means available to him that Jesus would never taste the death He had just predicted.

But note this: both Matthew (16:23) and Mark (8:33) report that Jesus had His back turned to Peter and the other apostles when Peter attempted to correct and instruct Him. Perhaps at this time Jesus could not enter into a face-to-face discourse with Peter, the pronouncement of His death still too fresh even to Him. Reasoning with a man as a Man may have been too burdensome. Jesus' cross was something He endured, despising the shame (Heb. 12:2), but nonetheless something to which He was faithful even unto death (Phil. 2:8). Regardless of the reason, Jesus was facing away from them when Peter prohibited Him from His Trinity-ordained destiny. Then Jesus turned. Something in the way Peter addressed Jesus jolted Him to respond. Jesus *knew*—He immediately discerned—*the source* behind Peter's statement.

In the previous verses Jesus had revealed that Peter's declaration about Him was not from flesh and blood: that is, not by means of human or earthly reasoning. Another source had inspired Peter, namely, God the Father. The other disciples who were present would not have necessarily made this same conclusion. This Divine proclamation was not like God's previous awe-inspiring revelation at Mount Sinai almost fifteen hundred years before. Neither did this resemble the Father's glorious attestation of His Son at Jesus' birth or baptism. A voice from heaven accompanied by the physical sign of the Holy Spirit descending as a dove is more in line with how the disciples would have expected God's revelation—not from the mouth of one of their associates, especially one who had exhibited his own share of stumblings. They would not have perceived that God was the source of Peter's declaration unless Jesus had revealed it as such. However, the same was true shortly thereafter when Peter spoke once more. Those present in Matthew 16—including Peter—would never have known that Satan was the ultimate source of Peter's second declaration unless Jesus had likewise exposed it as such. Satan's subtle deception was undetected to all present—except Jesus. While they would not have concluded that Peter spoke from God, the disciples certainly would not have considered that Peter would ever speak for Satan. Peter was for Jesus, not against Him, and they all knew this. Satan knew it too and used Peter's open love and allegiance to Jesus to his own advantage by making Peter an unwitting mouthpiece for his satanic scheme.

No doubt a major reason why Jesus properly identified the source of Peter's statement was because Jesus was born God incarnate and knew the inner thoughts of all men (John 2:24). But another reason exists: Jesus had encountered this same form of satanic temptation years earlier. Mark 1:12-13 and Luke 4:1-2 report that Satan continuously tempted Jesus for forty days, the present tense verb indicating the temptation did not occur only at the end of the forty days but in repetitive, never ceasing attacks. Satan's final temptation of Jesus during this segment consisted of shortcuts to His Messianic work and glory, any of which would have temporarily made Jesus' earthly life vastly easier — and His cup incomparably less torturous — but also any of which would have disqualified Him as the spotless Lamb of God who takes away the sins of the world (John 1:29). Each of the final three temptations Satan offered related to either Jesus' comfort or an alternative route to His ultimate rule. However, Jesus did not come with the purpose of attaining a life of ease. Jesus came as a Servant, as a Ransom, as a Redeemer — and it would cost Him all that He had to achieve this. In fact, it would require of Him more than anyone else ever born had ever paid for anything. When Peter rebuked Jesus and attempted to dissuade Him, it was a temptation disguised to cause Jesus to abandon God's eternal plan of redemption that required the only sinless, holy Sacrifice acceptable to God.

Years later the Holy Spirit would inspire Peter to write concerning our salvation that "you were not redeemed with perishable things like silver or gold from your futile way of life inherited from your forefathers, but with precious blood, as of a lamb unblemished and spotless, the blood of Christ" (1 Pet. 1:18-19). However, even the smallest step away from the will of the Father would equate to blatant disobedience and rebellion before God. The tiniest trace of blemish or imperfection would permanently disqualify Jesus as the spotless Lamb of God. In fact, if Jesus sinned even once throughout His entire life, then He Himself would have needed a savior — but no other savior would come for either Him or for unredeemed humanity because no other redeemer existed.

Matthew 16:22 reports that Peter began his rebuke by saying, "God forbid it, Lord!" or, literally in the Greek, "[God be] merciful to you, Lord." Yet being merciful was God's purpose, but only for those who truly needed the mercy He intended: namely, those contaminated and imprisoned by the effects of Adam's sin. Jesus embodied the mercy and grace God freely offered to the utterly defiled inhabitants of a putridly defiled world.

Perhaps because Jesus was facing away from Peter, this caused Him to hear the words by themselves, removed from any human trappings associated with them. Then in "turning around and seeing His disciples" (Mark 8:33), Jesus immediately discerned the ultimate source of the statement. As surprising as the revelation a few verses earlier had been that God was the ultimate source behind the Messianic truth spoken by Peter was this revelation of Satan now being the ultimate source of what Peter spoke. At the end of the temptation in Matthew 4, Jesus commanded Satan, "Begone!" (4:10) — *hypage* in the Greek. Jesus responded to the temptation Peter spoke by using the *exact* Greek word. "Get behind (*hypage*) Me, Satan! You are a stumbling block to Me; for you are not setting your mind on God's interests, but man's" (Matt. 16:23).

The last part of Jesus' response deals more with Peter personally because Satan never has man's interest at heart. Nevertheless, the satanic core was present, even though it did not accomplish Satan's desired result. Satan had floundered at this point in that he could not deter Jesus from heading toward His cross, but his failure was not caused by lack of effort. Satan attacked through a temptation culminating after a forty-day fast that had weakened Jesus. But the Living Word of God employed the written Word of God both to identify the temptation and to rebuke the tempter. The second temptation delivered by means of Peter similarly failed to cause Jesus to stumble. The first son of God, Adam (Luke 3:38), had fallen quickly and with relatively little effort by the deceiver in Genesis 3. No grandiose scheme by Satan. He had not offered the totality of the world's domain or beyond — just the simple temptation of choosing the creature over the Creator — and it worked to perfection. Yet this Son of God (Luke 3:22), the last Adam (1 Cor. 15:45), was different from the first Adam. Jesus had not fallen during the prolonged encounter with Satan. Neither had Jesus stumbled from the satanically inspired plea from a beloved friend. Jesus stood firm — *and* remained standing — after the temptation ended.

At the Matthew 16 account, Jesus had only about one year of His earthly life remaining. From that point onward the Messiah began a slow but steady procession toward the cross that had awaited Him even before God had established the foundation of the world (1 Pet. 1:17-21).

But exactly what did Satan desire? Why did he repeatedly attempt to ensnare Jesus? We know Satan attempted to divert Jesus from the cross, but what would Satan lose if Jesus went there? To understand this better, we need to go back in time to the initial contact between Satan and man: namely, the origin of this world's battle in the spiritual realm.

In Genesis 3, after sin marred Adam's race, God judged Satan by pronouncing that one from the seed of woman would bruise or crush the serpent's head (Gen. 3:15). That is to say, one who would be born of a woman would ultimately lead to Satan's eternal destruction. God could have immediately judged Satan in Genesis 3 and banished him to the hell originally prepared for him and his angels (Matt. 25:41). God needed no intermediary agents to bestow on Satan his justly deserved punishment. Instead, God chose to use some future, and at this time, undisclosed offspring of woman who would cause Satan's total demise. God did not say who would come; God did not say when. But He did declare that one would come. Consequently, from both a human and satanic perspective, from Genesis 3 onward through the ages came an endless stream of potential deliverers born from Adam's race. Yet all of the previous millions of candidates had failed miserably, beginning with the first two potential head crushers: Abel and Cain. All of the myriads of Adam's lineage had not come even slightly close to dooming Satan. Each was born and then, with the exception of Enoch (Heb. 11:5) and Elijah (2 Kgs. 2:1-11), each died, just as contaminated and bound by sin as his forefather Adam had been after the Fall. These were not the redeemer—they required a Redeemer—and Jesus alone was the One; or as Satan would reason, Jesus *could* be the one. Satan knew holiness when he was in its presence, and he had not encountered this in human guise since the Garden. Adam too had once exhibited this same undefiled holiness—but Adam had failed and had fallen quickly. So maybe the holiness of Jesus did not indelibly dwell within Him. Maybe the same temptation that tripped Adam would also cause Jesus to stumble.

Because of God's strict standard of holiness, Satan did not need to kill Jesus, although no doubt he would have done so if he could have because Satan was a murderer from the beginning (John 8:44). Satan would have killed Jesus at any opportunity, such as shortly after His birth (Matt. 2:1-18), but he had no authority from God to do so. In John 10:17-18 Jesus rebuked the unbelieving Pharisees by stating, "For this reason the Father loves Me, because I lay down My life that I may take it again. No one has taken it away from Me, but I lay it down on My own initiative. I have authority to lay it down, and I have authority to take it up again. This commandment I received from My Father." Perhaps because of this revelation from Jesus, killing Him was not

Satan's primary strategy. At this point Satan focused on keeping Jesus from ever going to the cross. He would try various maneuvers to force Jesus out of God's redemptive plan—and the smallest, fractional deviation would suffice. It did not matter to Satan what worked, as long as something did. He appealed to the physical senses. Satan offered Eve food; he did likewise with Jesus in tempting Him with bread (Matt. 4:1-3). Satan promised Eve she would be like God. Satan did this to an extent with Jesus, tempting Him to display His divine attributes in a boastful manner outside His obedience to the Father (Matt. 4:6). Adam and Eve had fallen by this time in their hour of testing—Jesus had not. Satan then added one more enticement he most likely would have offered to Adam, if he had not already succumbed: a panoramic view of world history. All the nations . . . all the glory of the world. All freely and gladly given to Jesus without the cross, without the brutality, without ever suffering—without the cup. All transferred to Him for the mere asking coupled with one simple act of worship (Matt. 4:8-9).

"Begone, Satan! For it is written, 'You shall worship the Lord your God, and serve Him only'" (Matt. 4:10). "Begone, Satan/Get behind Me! You are a stumbling block to Me; for you are not setting your mind on God's interests, but man's" (Matt. 16:23).

Now Satan knew—this One was different. This One was unique. This One kept standing. So far Jesus had withstood what all of the previous sons of Adam had not even come close to resisting. However, while this One had withstood only the trinkets of temptation, this One had not withstood *all* that Satan had to offer. Satan still had much more to employ against Jesus, but after Matthew 16 the battle necessitated a change in strategy.

The Bible often presents world events as having both a physical and spiritual reality. In other words, spiritual forces—both divine and evil—are operative, although the spiritual side remains hidden from human observation unless God chooses to disclose it. The events leading to the death of Jesus demonstrate this. Luke 22:1-2 describes the activities visible in the earthly realm: "Now the Feast of Unleavened Bread, which is called the Passover, was approaching. And the chief priests and the scribes were seeking [imperfect tense in the Greek— they repeatedly sought over and over again] how they might put Him to death; for they were afraid of the people." The next verse reveals a behind-the-scenes element of the spiritual world: "And Satan entered into Judas who was called Iscariot, belonging to the number of the twelve" (Luke 22:3). Two different realms existed; one that could be observed by mankind and one that could not—but both real and both extremely active. So even though the earthly component did not know of the other, Scripture actually presents both the earthly *and* spiritual enemies of Jesus as aggressively plotting against Him.

The religious leaders must have reveled in their abrupt change of fortunes. After their repeated councils and failed attempts to kill Jesus, then their opportunity sought audience with them. The irony of having one of Jesus' own apostles serve as their stooge must have likewise evoked a certain smugness. The Bible reveals that from that point onward Judas conscientiously "began seeking a good opportunity to betray Him to them apart from the multitude" (Luke 22:6). The earthly countdown to the crucifixion had begun.

Yet this brings us back to the original question and an apparent problem. *If the sacrificial death of Jesus meant the defeat and ruin of Satan, and if Satan had attempted to hinder Jesus from going to the cross all throughout His earthly ministry, such as in Matthew 16, then would Satan not make an even more exhaustive effort to keep Jesus from the cross the closer it got to the Passover?* Satan would by no means be an apathetic bystander. His reign, his dominion, his divine judgment—literally his eternal damnation—hung in the balance of causing Jesus to stumble, of making Him turn aside. It seems the absolute *last* thing Satan would desire would be to assist Jesus to the cross; yet Luke 22 records that is precisely what Satan did. At casual observation this appears absurd. However, we must consider this: Satan is many things, but foolhardy (other than not worshiping and serving the true God) is not one of them. He continuously plots; he schemes. He is always active and always works with purpose and intent—and he is quite adept at what he does—and never does the enemy do anything motivated by pure intentions. So at this most crucial of all junctures, Satan must have had a plan against Jesus—which he did—and he was wagering his entire domain and existence that it would succeed.

In addition to disclosing the plot to kill Jesus by both His physical and spiritual enemies, Luke 22 is also the account that records the last Passover supper and Jesus' warfare prayer in the Garden of Gethsemane. The chapter contains Jesus' revelation to Peter, "Behold, Satan has demanded permission [or "obtained permission by asking"] to sift you like wheat; but I have prayed for you, that your faith may not fail; and you, when once you have turned again, strengthen your brothers" (22:31-32). In these brief statements by Jesus we see Satan actively working behind-the-scenes in the events leading up to the crucifixion, as an aspect of his strategy would be targeted against Peter and the other disciples (the "you" in Luke 22:31 is plural, "to sift you [pl.] like wheat"). As before, neither Peter nor any future reader of Scripture would have known of Satan's hidden activities unless God chose to reveal them. We also have the disclosure that Peter's faith would indeed fail, but that he would later be restored after his failure; Jesus switched to the "you" singular when He addressed Peter in Luke 22:32. If the same were said about Jesus, then this divine drama would have ended before the curtain ever rose. God's standard of righteousness did not allow Jesus the option of failure and restoration. One minor slip in His Messianic duties, one slight blemish on an otherwise spotless life would require an additional Lamb of God. But no other Lamb existed in heaven or on earth; there was only One, and He was foreknown before the foundation of the world (1 Pet. 1:20). Literally the outcome of heaven, hell, earth, and the totality of humanity—the outcome of all history past, present, and future—would be decided in less than twenty hours.

The eternal clock of God was ticking. The scales of righteous judgment were being brought forth. The spotless Lamb is present. So are His executioners. His blood is ready to be poured out on the altar of God. Satan realized he had better act quickly if he had any hope whatsoever of defeating Jesus. In fact, Satan had already moved into action long before the silent Lamb arrived for His propitiatory slaughter.

Hours earlier, when Jesus informed Peter that Satan would sift him like wheat, Jesus did not reveal all He knew concerning what the Father had granted. Not only did God the Father grant Satan permission concerning Peter, but the Father had also granted the evil one permission regarding His own Son. Luke 22:52-53 notes that at His arrest Jesus revealed, "Have you come out with swords and clubs as against a robber? While I was with you daily in the temple, you did not lay hands on Me; *but this hour and the power of darkness are yours.*" Literally in the Greek Jesus said, "This is the hour of you [plural] and the power [authority] of the darkness." Three definite articles are used: the hour; the power; the darkness. Each is a very precise indication of some specific allotment permitted by God, not a reference to something in general. God had granted Satan *the* hour and *the* authority of *the* darkness to do all he desired to Jesus. The word "hour" can mean a determined segment of time that goes beyond the normal use of the sixty-minute framework, such as in Revelation 3:10 where God promises, "I also will keep you from the hour of testing, that hour which is about to come upon the whole world, to test those who dwell upon the earth." So God had granted Satan some specified segment of time in his authority of the darkness that would have both a definitive beginning and ending.

While sometimes we fail to make the connection, this actually is the second such occurrence in Scripture where God permitted Satan an authoritative designated time to inflict pain on someone. Job 2:4-6 reveals this rather startling truth:

> And Satan answered the LORD and said, "Skin for skin! Yes, all that a man has he will give for his life. However, put forth Thy hand, now, and touch his bone and his flesh; he will curse Thee to Thy face."
>
> So the LORD said to Satan, "Behold, he is in your power, only spare his life."

The word for "power" is the Hebrew word for "hand," and it is often used for the authoritative hold of someone or some possession. In the Song of Moses, God declares, "See now that I, I am He, and there is no god besides Me; it is I who put to death and give life. I have wounded, and it is I who heal; and there is no one who can deliver from My hand" (Deut. 32:39). Job 2:7 demonstrates what God permitted and what would be completely hidden from the human beings associated with Job: "Then Satan went out from the presence of the LORD, and smote Job with sore boils from the sole of his foot to the crown of his head."

Even though First Corinthians 10:13 had not yet been written, the biblical truth would already exist: in spite of the horrendous torment, God would not permit Job to be afflicted beyond what he was able (*dynamai*). In this second account of divine permission granted to Satan to torment, the Lamb of God possessed an entirely different capacity to be tempted beyond what Job—or any other descendant of Adam— would be able (*dynamai*) to endure.

So then with the exception of His death, *anything* Satan's evil mind and nature could contrive, *anything* within his entire arsenal of perverse malevolence could be fully and freely cast upon Jesus but only for a limited, designated period of time. This was an aspect of the cup that the Father had given the Son to drink—and what Satan desired to do during his God-given hour is inconceivable on a human level.

Meanwhile Simon Peter had his own scheme to enact. He remained intent on carrying out his previous declaration of months before, "This shall by no means happen to you, Lord" (Matt. 16:22). The gravity of the last Passover coupled with Jesus' warnings and predictions of his fall and failure caused Peter to be on guard on the physical level. Evil engulfed him; he must have sensed it. Peter had good reason to be alarmed. In Luke 22:35-36 a burdened Jesus warned the disciples of the pending change of their circumstances from what they had previously experienced during their ministry. Up to this point Jesus had led and protected them, teaching them and directing their activities. Soon hereafter, the disciples would become the ones persecuted. Jesus would still lead and protect them, but after His ascension He would do so from a heavenly perspective—and away from their visual vantage point.

Jesus needed to prepare His chosen ones for this most serious altering of their walk with Him. Such a change would not come easily to His confused disciples, especially with their expectations of the immediate advent of the kingdom and its glory. Only weeks earlier, after the rich young ruler refused to abandon his worldly pursuits to receive the treasure offered by Jesus, Peter asked the simple question in Matthew 19:27, "Behold, we have left everything and followed You; what then will there be for us?" Jesus responded with a remarkable answer saying to them, "Truly I say to you, that you who have followed Me, in the regeneration when the Son of Man will sit on His glorious throne, you also shall sit upon twelve thrones, judging the twelve tribes of Israel" (Matt. 19:28). What an answer Jesus promised them as He connected their reward with His own glory. Luke reveals details about the expectations of His disciples as they left Jericho, roughly fifteen miles away from where Jesus would be crucified only days later. Before the Messiah would enter Jerusalem with the crowds hailing Him as the promised Son of David, Jesus had to redirect His disciples' thoughts and expectations: "And while they were listening to these things, He went on to tell a parable, because He was near Jerusalem, and they supposed that the kingdom of God was going to appear immediately" (Luke 19:11).

So now, on the night of His betrayal and arrest, in the midst of His final Passover with His own, Jesus spoke of His approaching death.

Instead of Kingdom glory, the King announced again that He was about to die. Not only that, but the same enemies who persecuted Jesus would soon seek to destroy His followers as well. Rather than presently receiving high-ranking positions in the Kingdom, those loyal to Jesus would soon have to endure many of the same hostilities He Himself had suffered. The Kingdom would come with its full glory — and with the full glory of the King — but not at this time. Until Jesus returned for them, the disciples instead had to cultivate a warrior's mentality. Of course, all true warriors have weapons; the disciples would need theirs too.

Jesus started a lesson that He knew He could not currently complete. He still had so much yet to teach the Eleven, but the approaching hour of evil left little time to instruct them in detail. Jesus led His cowering flock into the subject of their pending change in status by reminding them of His previous care and provision. "When I sent you out without purse and bag and sandals, you did not lack anything, did you?" The disciples responded, "No, nothing." Jesus continued, "But now, let him who has a purse take it along, likewise also a bag, and let him who has no sword sell his robe and buy one" (Luke 22:35-36). "But now" — it was different; the times were about to change. So in the midst of their darkest hour, Jesus counseled His followers to obtain swords they would need even more than they would their own outer garments. However, in view of the restraints He later placed on the use of such physical weapons, Jesus referred to swords in a figurative manner. The disciples would eventually understand that the weapons of a believer's warfare consist of the Sword of the Spirit, which is the Word of God (Eph. 6:17) — the same sword Jesus had used to resist Satan in Matthew 4. They would learn by experience and divine discipleship what the Holy Spirit would inspire Paul to write decades later in 2 Corinthians 10:3-4: "For though we walk in the flesh, we do not war according to the flesh, for the weapons of our warfare are not of the flesh, but divinely powerful for the destruction of fortresses" — weapons such as battle-prayer wrought in the mighty name of Jesus. The weapons the disciples needed would be "in the word of truth, in the power of God; by the weapons of righteousness for the right hand and the left" (2 Cor. 6:7). On this night, however, each disciple played spiritual soldier, as a young child would attempt to mimic his warrior father — and each one deemed himself the greatest apostle (Luke 22:24), while the King steadily inched toward His God-determined hour.

"Lord, look, here are two swords," some of the disciples offered to Jesus. Jesus simply said in response, "It is enough" (Luke 22:38). The disciples' conclusions were incorrect, but no time currently existed to develop this teaching. Jesus had planted a seed lesson that night, leaving it to germinate until He taught them again after His resurrection.

Jesus' counsel to acquire swords was the first good news Peter had heard all night. *Finally!* Here was teaching from Jesus with which Peter could relate. His subsequent actions demonstrate how Peter interpreted Jesus' teaching. "Physical sword — physical warfare. We need our weapons to succeed. I'll prove my love and devotion for Jesus. He thinks I will deny Him, but I'll be ready. Let anyone come near my Lord — he will have to contend with me." So Peter followed Jesus to Gethsemane. He stood prepared: at least physically; at least by his own estimation. Yet two measly swords against the multitude of soldiers sent to arrest Jesus would hardly suffice. Nor would they be any use against the previously announced spiritual assault that awaited Peter and the others. When the multitudes approached to arrest Jesus, Peter attacked, cutting off the ear of the high priest's slave. On a human level Peter demonstrated bravery and loyalty to Jesus, but on a spiritual level he did not exercise a trusting, submissive obedience to his Lord.

In the John 18:11 passage Jesus ordered Peter: "Put the sword into the sheath!" After all, "The cup which the Father has given Me, shall I not drink it?"

In the parallel passage of the same event, Matthew reveals a crucial bit of information that ultimately helps explain Satan's strategy. After healing the wound that Peter inflicted with his sword, Jesus rebuked His disciples by asking, "Or do you think that I cannot appeal to My Father, and He will at once put at My disposal more than twelve legions of angels? How then shall the Scriptures be fulfilled, that it must happen this way?" (Matt. 26:53-54). Jesus was not instructing the disciples about the number of angels in existence. He simply reminded them no one took His life from Him; He gave it willfully. He alone had the power to lay it down — only He had the power to take it up again.

The number of angels that Jesus revealed were available to Him further demonstrates His inner strength and composure. Jesus possessed more than sufficient numbers to end His ordeal if such had been His intention. A Roman legion consisted of 6,000 men. Twelve legions would thus contain 72,000 soldiers. Jesus said the Father would readily send more than twelve legions of angels — at bare minimum, over 72,000 angels — to come to His aid, to rescue Him from His peril. However, escape was not Jesus' purpose, and He never summoned His attendant angelic multitudes. The very existence and readiness of warrior angels both willing and eager to help at a moment's notice only added to Jesus' temptation. It is one thing to be overwhelmed and helpless in a situation completely out of your control. It is quite another to have the means of escape readily available at your first call, but decline to use what is rightfully yours. Jesus possessed the Godhead's inner strength and composure encompassed in a frail human package—and Satan was about to deliver his full wrath against the designated Lamb of God.

We must note something important: while Jesus could call His angels, Satan could summon his angelic forces as well. Unlike his opponent, Satan had no hesitation whatsoever in calling his warriors into battle—and the numbers he brought against Jesus stagger us. But who are Satan's angels? How many are there? Where did they come from?

In order to answer this, we must examine various Scripture passages. Earlier in Matthew 25:41 Jesus revealed that hell consists of "the eternal fire which has been prepared for the devil and his angels." So it is evident Satan does have angels—and has them in large quantities. In Luke 8, when Jesus asked demons their name, they answered "Legion," for many demons had entered the man (Luke 8:30). Within this one man was one of Satan's legions, which if the words mean the same thing, then there were approximately 6,000 demons within this man. How many more demons exist is beyond our scope of understanding, unless God chooses to reveal more.

Fortunately, to a degree He does. Revelation 12:4 reveals that when God cast Satan out of His heavenly abode, "his tail swept away a third of the stars of heaven." This is most likely a reference to the angels who followed Satan in his insurgence against God, especially since Revelation 9:1 contains an account of a star descending from heaven who was shown to be an angel of God. So whatever the aggregate population of angels, one-third of them followed Satan in his rebellion and were instantly changed forever from angels of God to angels of the devil, becoming his servants. The Bible usually refers to such fallen angels as demons. No earthly source knows exactly how many angels God created, but their numbers are overwhelming. Some Bible scholars think that at least as many angels exist as there are people born throughout history. Yet beyond human speculation, certain Scripture references indicate the innumerable multitudes of the angelic host. In a vision that God gave to Daniel, the prophet describes God's abode in Daniel 7:9-10:

> I kept looking until thrones were set up, and the Ancient of Days took His seat; His vesture was like white snow, and the hair of His head like pure wool. His throne was ablaze with flames, its wheels were a burning fire.
>
> A river of fire was flowing and coming out from before Him; thousands upon thousands were attending Him, and myriads upon myriads were standing before Him; the court sat, and the books were opened.

The Hebrew could be translated as "ten thousand times ten thousands" or "hundreds of millions" — angelic multitudes innumerable to Daniel, but not to the omniscient Creator-God who made and knew each one.

In the same way, hundreds of years later, the Apostle John was transported to heaven in a vision. There he records virtually the same description of the angelic host that surrounds God's throne in Revelation 5:11-12:

> And I looked, and I heard the voice of many angels around the throne and the living creatures and the elders; and the number of them was myriads of myriads, and thousands of thousands, saying with a loud voice, "Worthy is the Lamb that was slain to receive power and riches and wisdom and might and honor and glory and blessing."

The same phrases "myriads of myriads" and "thousands of thousands" that occurred in Daniel, although written in Greek in the Book of Revelation instead of Hebrew, again show the innumerable number of God's heavenly host. So however many millions upon millions these myriads of myriads and thousands of thousands contain, one-third of the original number followed the deceiver and became his angels. One-third became the demonic hosts.

By simply restricting this to the number Jesus referred to at His arrest, at the very least more than twelve legions — over 72,000 angels — stood willingly ready to come to His immediate rescue. But the same math can likewise be applied to Satan's angels. The one-third who became demons would at the very least consist of over 36,000 demons (not one-third of 72,000 but the 72,000 equal the two-thirds that remained). As we saw, this is merely a fraction. While they do not equal God's numbers, the depth and design of Satan's demonic hosts are vastly beyond the comprehension and strength of the human world.

We do not know much about demons because God offers only

glimpses of them in Scripture. Perhaps God intends for believers to focus more on Him and His truth rather than on the seductive allurements of the kingdom of darkness. Still, the Bible reveals certain aspects about demonic activities. Ephesians 6:12 presents Satan's angels as being organized into specified categories, stating that "our struggle is not against flesh and blood, but against the rulers, against the powers, against the world forces of this darkness, against the spiritual forces of wickedness in the heavenly places." The Bible does not give much information to distinguish between the four categories, such as what the difference is between a ruler and a power. But it does show rank, authority, and organization. These demonic hosts actively work throughout the entire world, because 1 John 5:19 states, "and the whole world lies in the power of the evil one." In other words, no part of the world is off limit to their activity. Besides this, in some way, satanic activity occurs within the realm of the atmosphere, because the Bible depicts Satan as "the prince of the power of the air" (Eph. 2:2). We also know that demons are actively involved in disseminating false doctrine, especially inside what are considered Christian churches and institutions. First Timothy 4:1 states, "But the Spirit explicitly says that in later times some will fall away from the faith, paying attention to deceitful spirits and doctrines of demons." We will see in heaven how terribly effective these demonic beings were in propagating such false doctrines to many.

We need to consider more about demonic beings because this helps us understand better how they function. Demons continuously undertake only evil activities, being as completely evil and defiled as Satan. No good whatsoever exists in any of them. They have no mercy; their evil never becomes satiated. They have no conscience; they have no pity; they never repent. It should be especially noted that demons are immensely powerful. Daniel 10:11-13 gives the account of a holy angel commissioned by God to speak to the prophet Daniel. Yet even with God's instructions, an extremely mighty demon hindered this angel's mission for twenty-one days. Eventually, the archangel Michael had to be sent into battle against the demonic forces. Together they fought spiritual warfare completely devoid of human perception, a warfare that no human could have survived for even an instant—no one except the One headed for the Cross.

Demons have one crucial capability that we must recognize. In the fifth trumpet judgment in the Book of Revelation, God will unleash previously bound demons from the abyss and send them to the earth.

Though spiritual beings who will most likely be unobserved by those on earth, they will have the capacity to inflict severe pain upon human beings. Revelation 9:4-6 describes to a degree what they can do:

> And they were told that they should not hurt the grass of the earth, nor any green thing, nor any tree, but only the men who do not have the seal of God on their foreheads.

> And they were not permitted to kill anyone, *but to torment* for five months; and their *torment* was like *the torment* of a scorpion when it stings a man. And in those days men will seek death and will not find it; and they will long to die and death flees from them.

All of this will occur under the strict sovereignty of God. These select demons come only when summoned; they are restricted as to whom they can attack; they are restricted in how long they can attack: in this case, five months. By God's sovereign decree they will not be permitted to kill, but they will be permitted to torment "like the torment of a scorpion when it stings a man." The text does not say how they will accomplish this torment; it simply states that they will. In fact, the word "torment" occurs three times within these passages. What else God does or does not allow demons presently to do, we do not know. We see glimpses of what God at times permits in the sense of Job 1–2 and in spiritual warfare against Christians in Ephesians 6. Yet when authorized by God, demons can torment humans to the extent that death will be considered vastly better than life.

Interestingly, not only can demons torment others, they likewise can receive torment themselves. This was their great fear in encountering Jesus, as Luke 8:28 indicates: "And seeing Jesus, he [the demon possessed man] cried out and fell before Him, and said in a loud voice, 'What do I have to do with You, Jesus, Son of the Most High God? I beg You, do not torment me.'" In the parallel account of Matthew 8:29, the demons clearly understand that a specified divine judgment awaits them, asking Jesus, "What do we have to do with You, Son of God? Have You come here to torment us before the time?" Significantly, Satan's angels employ the same word for "torment" that is used to describe the demonic torment of Revelation 9. Demons have the capacity both to inflict and to receive torment.

Thankfully, Revelation 9 is still future. Thankfully, the time when Satan's realm will receive the proper judgment awaits the sovereign calendar of God. But the night Jesus was betrayed was different— immensely different from any other time in eternity past or present. It was their hour, and the power of the darkness was theirs.

Consider the evil magnitude of at the very least 36,000 demons, plus the added power of Satan himself. *All* would be summoned against Jesus. *All* would assemble over one hill in Jerusalem, *all* intent on one Individual. No other battle in the entirety of God's creation existed or mattered that morning. Calvary alone was the field of battle—Jesus was the lone Foe. The totality of Satan's strength and demonic force would muster their collective power of evil against one beaten, weakened, and scourged Man. All of Jesus opened and exposed to all of them. With the exception of killing Him, Satan and his angels could employ all that was within their power to torment Jesus with no threat of Michael or anyone else coming to His aid. The Legion whom Jesus had cast out in Luke 8 most likely would be there too. Who currently knows other than the Godhead, but He may even have permitted the demons currently confined in the abyss of Revelation 9 to be temporarily released and added to the assault against Jesus. We will find out when we get to heaven. However, this much is abundantly clear: whatever the totality of the arsenal Satan had available to him, not one member would be absent. It was their God-given hour to assemble.

By the time the final battle began, Jesus was already in a depleted condition, both physically and spiritually. Gethsemane was many times more strenuous than the physical scourging and beating He would receive thereafter. The physical torture certainly added to the limitless burden. A lesser man's resolve would have ended long before this time. Jesus still stood—but He would face His battle alone, as He had previously informed His own the night before, "Where I am going you cannot [are not able; do not have the capacity to] come" (John 13:33). Heavenly assistance would be given only if Jesus asked for it. But if He asked, if He cried out "Enough!" or "Stop!"—or simply stated, if He stopped drinking His cup before it was empty—then the battle would have ended as soon as His word left His mouth. Then Jesus and His angels would have returned to their rightful place with the Father in heaven—but they would have returned there alone. No one born of Adam's race would ever go there after them. Satan would maintain his worldwide dominion—and sin and death would continue to reign. All hope for future life would perish—and the Apostle John would not be the only one weeping that no one was found worthy to take the scroll from God's hand and to open its seals (Rev. 5:1-5).

So here in paraphrase form is the wager that Satan placed before

Jesus at Calvary: *"You, Jesus, withstood me throughout your life on earth, but our encounters were greatly restricted in their scope. Now the real battle begins. While it is true you refused what Adam and the countless failures since never could refuse, you are not through with me yet. You see your cross before you. I wager I can bring upon you such affliction, such torment, such agony of the soul that you will stop me long before my authority and hour are diminished. Before I am finished with you, you will gladly call for the heavenly assistance that stands so readily available to you.*

"Let him try to resist me! He thinks he knows the depth of my power. I am the Adversary! I reign over the dominion of the darkness! I am the god of this world — the ruler of this age! Your angels revere me and take due notice of my heightened power over them. But I have my angels too. Usually I strategically station them around the world, but today I have summoned them all to Calvary. They render service to me and me alone. Today I will bring the full force of my power and legions against you. Every evil ruler of the spiritual realm, every evil power, every world force of darkness, every spiritual force of wickedness in the heavenly places — all will assemble against you and you alone. You held out before with my lesser tactics. Let's see how you fare in open warfare — not as the Son of God — but as Son of Man wrapped in the same earthly garb as those idiot mortals you seem so intent on having.

"I had my way with Adam — and I will have my way with you. I have authority from the One to do so. No angels to minister to you now — unless you choose to give up and summon them. No divine strengthening or assistance will come your way either. You are alone with me and mine. You have a human body capable of receiving pain — and I possess the greatest spiritual power in heaven or hell to inflict upon you torment beyond description.

"And you will fail — and I will win. And all I possess shall be mine forever."

Here then, in reality, Satan still attempted to hinder Jesus from the cross, or stated better, from finishing His Messianic course that culminated with His death on the cross. In the previous encounters Satan had slipped into his temptation the pleasant enticements related to Jesus' physical survival or His earthly reign. Now events exposed Satan's scheme for the ugly horror it had always been. Satan purposed to torture and torment Jesus beyond the capacity of all previous human suffering combined. All he had to do was to cause Jesus to resign before He finished the course — and the cup — the Father had designated He must take, and Satan would be the victor. We who have suffered or have been tempted have never suffered like this — God would not permit it (1 Cor. 10:13). Even more to the point, we have long since disqualified ourselves from ever entering even the remotest confines of this restricted arena of battle. Furthermore, we who have suffered have never had the means or opportunity to remove ourselves from it as Jesus had. The question is, would He endure to the end?

Here was Satan's one God-granted hour of opportunity. He stood ready—as did his legions.

The wager had been placed—and literally the eternal destiny of both the human and spiritual worlds hung on its outcome.

2

THE VIEW

P salm 22 has fascinated students of the Bible since David first composed it. Nearly one thousand years before Jesus' death, David recorded a vivid account of his utter despair and misery before God. It is a psalm that begins with frustration as David repeatedly cried out to the God he knows can surely rescue him, but also to the God who had not yet acted on his behalf. He knew God was faithful; yet he was perplexed about why God did not answer him. In Psalm 22:2-5 David lamented, "O my God, I cry by day, but Thou dost not answer; and by night, but I have no rest. Yet Thou art holy, O Thou who art enthroned upon the praises of Israel. In Thee our fathers trusted; they trusted, and Thou didst deliver them. To Thee they cried out, and were delivered; in Thee they trusted, and were not disappointed." Beyond this, as many readers of the Word know, David—under the inspiration of the Holy Spirit—described many elements and events associated with the crucifixion of Jesus. God inspired the psalmist to reveal Messianic truths He intended for us to learn centuries beyond David's situation at the time of the psalm's composition.

Christians did not assemble and decide that Psalm 22 ultimately referred to Jesus Christ. Rather the Trinity insists we associate Psalm 22 with Jesus, especially in regard to His death. One of the last things Jesus did before yielding His spirit was cry out to His Father, "My God, My God, why hast Thou forsaken Me?" (Matt. 27:46)—a direct quote from Psalm 22:1. This famous phrase forever linked the original witnesses of Jesus' crucifixion with Psalm 22, as well as linking it with the millions of readers of God's Word since then. In addition to these, the Gospels contain two other quotes from Psalm 22 that relate to events associated with Jesus' death. Matthew 27:43 refers back to Psalm 22:8 in reference to the hostile crowds who jeered Jesus: "He trusts in God; let Him deliver Him now, if He takes pleasure in Him." Regarding the seamless tunic Jesus had worn, John 19:24 records how the soldiers reasoned, "Let us not tear it, but cast lots for it, to decide whose it shall be." John emphasized the importance of this event by concluding that such was done "that the Scripture might be fulfilled, 'They divided My outer garments among them, and for My clothing they cast lots,'" quoting Psalm 22:18.

One of the amazing aspects about Psalm 22 is that crucifixion was not invented when David wrote this psalm. Crucifixion would not become a means of execution until many centuries later. In fact, the description given in Psalm 22 is so accurate and vivid that critics of the Bible contend that some unknown author must have composed this psalm hundreds of years beyond the time of David. In other words, the psalmist offered such a trustworthy account that they conclude he must have written it *after* the invention of crucifixion, for according to them, the psalm is *too accurate* a description to believe a man could have written it on his own. Perhaps they are right. Perhaps Psalm 22 is a spurious fraud . . .

Or God could have given the world a preview of the most important event in all history.

What many people who study this psalm fail to notice is that Psalm 22 is not a description of someone viewing a crucifixion even when it later relates to Jesus on the cross. Instead it is written from the viewpoint of the one who is suffering. The author penned the psalm in first person ("I"), not third person ("he"). Among other items within the psalm, verses 14-17 demonstrate the self-perspective view of the author:

> I am poured out like water, and all my bones are out of joint; my heart is like wax; it is melted within me. My strength is dried up like a potsherd, and my tongue cleaves to my jaws; and Thou dost lay me in the dust of death. For dogs have surrounded me; a band of evildoers has encompassed me; they pierced my hands and my feet. I can count all my bones. They look, they stare at me.

Along these lines of personal vantage point, the psalmist also identifies his present enemies who stood against him. This was true for David in some real life situation where his enemies encompassed and persecuted him, most likely one of the many times that King Saul attempted to kill him. It would also refer to the ultimate Son of David, Jesus Christ, centuries beyond David's life. In verses 11-13 the psalmist calls to God for help because of the magnitude of his enemies: "Be not far from me, for trouble is near; for there is none to help; many bulls have surrounded me; strong bulls of Bashan have encircled me. They open wide their mouth at me, as a ravening and a roaring lion." Bashan was a fertile area east of the Jordan River. The bulls Bashan produced were famous throughout Israel for their enormous physical strength. The author of Psalm 22 employed this descriptive term to depict the massive power his enemies possessed: the brute strength they intended to use against him.

Still, because so much in this psalm relates to the crucifixion of Jesus, it would seem the description of the attending enemies would apply to His enemies. Other Scripture references may help us broaden our understanding. For instance, over a thousand years after David, the Apostle Peter, whom Jesus personally trained for over three years, would write a warning using similar terminology to that of Psalm 22. Peter cautioned his readers, "Be of sober spirit, be on the alert. Your adversary, the devil [not "your adversary the Roman Empire" or "your adversary the Jewish officials"], prowls about like *a roaring lion*, seeking someone to devour" (1 Pet. 5:8). God is so perfectly precise with His Word that it would be reasonable to conclude that this verse may describe the same enemies referred to in Psalm 22, especially because both passages use the term "a roaring lion" (Ps. 22:13). Also, Psalm 22:12-13 contains a strange mixing of metaphors. Most people do not fear the mouth of a bull; it is their strength and horns and hooves that cause dread.

Throughout the Gospel accounts, Jesus had demonstrated His knowledge of both the human and Satanic conspiracies against Him. He specifically did so in matters relating to His betrayal, arrest, and crucifixion, as we saw in Luke 22:1-3. Earthly forces acted, but so did spiritual ones. Because of such factors, here is a good question to consider: *Because Scripture closely connects Psalm 22 with the crucifixion of Jesus, do the enemies referred to in this psalm describe the earthly enemies of Jesus, or is it a reference to Jesus' spiritual enemies — namely, Satan and his legions?*

Perhaps the best answer is Psalm 22 refers to both human and spiritual enemies. Yet if one enemy received notice, Satan and his agents would be designated because the Bible places much more emphasis on their role in Christ's death. The physical enemies of Jesus were genuine partners in the crime, but the spiritual enemies were the driving force; they were the "brains behind the operation." If such is the case, then Psalm 22 reveals that the One crucified saw more than the physical agents who actually carried out the crucifixion. In some way Jesus almost certainly viewed His spiritual enemies as well.

This brings us to an unanswerable question, but one whose simple pondering, even in our limited understanding, should make us appreciate Jesus more: *What did Jesus view from the cross?* A few biblical examples show that this is a question worth considering. For instance, in the days of Elisha the prophet, the king of Aram warred against the northern kingdom of Israel: "And he sent horses and chariots and a great army there, and they came by night and surrounded the city [of Dothan]" (2 Kgs. 6:14). The next verse shows the response by Elisha's servant as he beheld the physical enemies: "Now when the attendant of the man of God had risen early and gone out, behold, an army with horses and chariots was circling the city. And his servant said to him, 'Alas, my master! What shall we do?'" (2 Kgs. 6:15). God's prophet then made an extraordinary prayer request:

> So he answered, "Do not fear, for those who are with us are more than those who are with them."
>
> Then Elisha prayed and said, "O LORD, I pray, open his eyes that he may see." And the LORD opened the servant's eyes, and he saw; and behold, the mountain was full of horses and chariots of fire all around Elisha (2 Kgs 6:16-17).

Many truths can be deduced from this account. First, the spiritual side, in this case God's angels presented in warrior motif, was hidden from virtually everybody present; nonetheless, these mighty angels were still attendant and quite active. Second, even Elisha's servant, whom we assume to be redeemed, had no capacity on his own to see the hidden spiritual agents. In other words, it was not merely the physical enemies who were unable to see this assemblage of holy angels. Third, the spiritual side, both good and evil, remains completely out of view unless God chooses to reveal it. Out of view does not mean out of existence. Elisha's prayer was that God would open the servant's eyes to see what was already there, not that God would send angelic help. We should also note that the prayer request is singular—"his eyes," not "our eyes." Elisha either already knew that the angels were present or that God had already granted him the same spiritual capacity to see. Would these same angels (and/or others) also have been present at Calvary? After all, if God saw fit to have His angels present during this relatively obscure battle at Dothan, tucked away in the Book of Kings, how much more would their presence be expected at the death of God's Son? Would these warrior angels be the same type that Jesus could "appeal to My Father, and He will at once put at My disposal more than twelve legions of angels" (Matt. 26:53)? There is no way to know for sure, but we definitely can glean from this text that the spiritual agents must have been present for this unheard of exhibition of God's grace that was about to be demonstrated.

Also worthy of consideration is this: just before Stephen became the first martyr of the newly founded Christian Church, he exclaimed, "Behold, I see the heavens opened up and the Son of Man standing at the right hand of God" (Acts 7:56). What did Jesus see as He lay on His back when the soldiers began nailing His hands and feet? He would be looking straight up toward heaven. Did He too see heaven opened? If so, He would have seen His rightful place by the Father unoccupied. He and the Father would reunite not many days hence, but before His ascension home the Son must drink the cup the Father had determined.

On a more sinister note, by being nailed to the cross while He lay on His back, not only would Jesus be looking straight up toward heaven, but also He would be looking straight into the domain of "the prince of the power of the air" (Eph. 2:2). Later in the same epistle, Paul explained, to a degree, the realm of Satan's wickedness with which Christians have to wrestle: "For our struggle is not against flesh and blood, but against the rulers, against the powers, against the world forces of this darkness, against the spiritual forces of wickedness in the heavenly places" (Eph. 6:12). Did Jesus see any of "the spiritual forces of wickedness in the heavenly places," or literally translated, "in the heavenlies"? Significantly, this same word is used five times in Ephesians (1:3, 20; 2:6; 3:10; 6:12) with each reference referring to a spiritual realm beyond earth, some referring to God's domain and others to Satan's. Would Jesus view the myriad of demons actively hovering or swirling over Calvary, perhaps being the ones centuries earlier prophesied as part of the enemies who would encircle Jesus (Ps. 22:12)? The demons came prepared to battle for their domain and existence. Did Satan manifest them to Jesus as a means of intimidation? Did Satan even need to manifest them? Jesus may have seen them without any manifestation necessary. Conversely, did Jesus see His legions of warrior angels assembled in their ranks, standing ready for summoning—if their summons came?

We do not know what Jesus saw for the simple reason that God chose not to reveal this to us for the present time. Still the concept is compelling: *What did Jesus view while He endured the cross?* While God did not disclose all the truths concerning Jesus' death, He did establish key clues that we often overlook in His Word. Contained within Scripture are priceless gold veins and nuggets that help us gain a broader composite picture — and a better appreciation — of our Savior's victory, but we must go mining to uncover these deeper treasures.

One thing Jesus certainly saw from the cross was the human agents who executed Him. Even then the Savior showed forth His fathomless love beyond the deep darkness of man's hatred and ignorance. Although Jesus' earthly antagonists played a major role in killing Him, these people were not His true enemies — Jesus was dying for the world that God loved (John 3:16). In fact, some of the same religious leaders who once opposed Him would eventually believe that Jesus was the Christ, and they would find their salvation in Him (Acts 6:7; 15:5). But even beyond the present enemies, anyone who ever has been or ever will be saved was in a way at the cross also. Romans 5:6 states, "For while we were still helpless, at the right time Christ died for the ungodly." Romans 5:8 continues, "But God demonstrates His own love toward us, in that while we were yet sinners, Christ died for us." Romans 5:10 indicates the degree of our hostility before salvation: "For if while we were enemies, we were reconciled to God through the death of His Son, much more, having been reconciled, we shall be saved by His life." Christ died for us, the ungodly, while we were still sinners — and more than that, while we were His enemies.

What grace Jesus manifested in the midst of His agony! Contrary to roaring threats of God's wrathful revenge that one would expect at such a heinous sin, the first recorded words Jesus spoke from the cross convey just the opposite reaction: "Father, forgive them; for they do not know what they are doing" (Luke 23:34). Here then is Jesus' view of the lost He was dying to save, and it offers us insight into His perspective. According to Jesus, the human agents did not know intellectually what they did. They knew what they were doing by crucifixion; they did not understand the significance of their crime nor especially to Whom they were doing it. Those who played any sort of role in bringing about Jesus' illegal death would still be held accountable by God for *all* their sins, including this one — unless they repented and received eternal salvation through Christ's blood. However, at the deep core of what they did, they acted out of ignorance: vain, rebellious, inexcusable ignorance, but ignorance nonetheless.

Jesus' request for forgiveness for those who did not know what they were doing could not be said in regard to all parties involved. Satan and his minions most assuredly knew what they were doing—and to Whom. The collective forces of darkness fully knew who Jesus was: at His birth, during His life, at His death. Satan would know the prophecies, would see the star announcing the Savior's birth, would observe the angels manifesting themselves to shepherds outside Bethlehem. He would have previously heard the stirring of the people as they conversed about the unusual circumstances surrounding the birth of John the Baptist, one whom God's Holy Word had prophesied would become a forerunner to the Messiah. Satan always knew who Jesus was, and most likely, always knew where Jesus was at any point in His life. Would ever an instant exist where Satan would turn his thoughts away from Jesus? Jesus was the promised Seed of Woman of Genesis 3:15 who would lead—or as Satan concluded, *could* lead—to Satan's downfall. The evil one would vigilantly watch over the Christ child who grew into the Christ man. Scripture is silent on any personal contact Satan attempted with Jesus until He grew into a man, so it is best not to delve into areas that God has not chosen to reveal. Yet Satan's nature would not permit him to sit idly by without any intent of attack. He would have done anything he could against Jesus from His birth onward, but it seems that God the Father restricted Satan from attacking, perhaps similar to God placing a hedge around Job (Job 1:10). The Father may have protected His Son from Satan until He decided the time was right—and the time the Father chose came immediately after Jesus' baptism, at the beginning of His public ministry.

The baptism of Jesus is one of the most momentous events ever recorded in Scripture. It publicly marked Jesus as the promised Messiah of God. Messiah or Christ means "the anointed one," and the baptism was the time of His anointing. It is at this time that the Holy Spirit empowered Jesus for His Messianic ministry. In fact, only after His empowering by the Holy Spirit do the Scriptures make reference to Jesus performing any miracles. It would seem that with the willful emptying of Himself and the voluntary setting aside of the independent use of His divine attributes (Phil. 2:5-8), Jesus would have to be empowered by another source. This point is even made by Jesus when arguing against the Pharisees, stating, "But if I cast out demons *by the Spirit of God . . .*" (Matt. 12:28). God's Anointed One was thus empowered, as the Godhead had planned, as the Holy Spirit descended on Jesus to enable Him to do all that was necessary to achieve Messiah's ministry. The baptism of Jesus also marks the reduced prominence of John the Baptist. Jesus must increase; John must decrease (John 3:30). Jesus also began gathering disciples to Himself at this time: Andrew, Simon Peter and Philip, (John 1:35-43), each of whom would each eventually assume the office of apostle (Matt. 10:1-4).

Yet far beyond these very important factors stands one simple fact that accompanied Jesus' baptism: God the Father bore open testimony that Jesus was His beloved Son. Just in case any doubt existed in Satan's realm as to who Jesus was—but it is most unlikely that they would fail to know Who the incarnate second member of the Godhead was—God audibly bore witness from heaven, something that rarely had occurred in Scripture. Matthew marked this important pronouncement with the exclamatory word, "Behold!" The Greek text is very emphatic in presenting what God said. Matthew 3:17 could be translated, "This is My beloved Son" [or "the Son of Mine the Beloved"] using two definite articles within this designation. Jesus is *the* Son; He is *the* beloved—unique, unparallel, without equal. God would later offer this same testimony about Jesus on the Mount of Transfiguration, but now a different purpose was at hand.

Satan no doubt heard God's declaration as well. God's pronouncement was in a way a call to battle, as Jesus would soon begin His earthly ministry. Not only did God publicly announce the identity and advent of Messiah, He also initiated Jesus' ministry of restitution and reclamation of that which was lost. Having anointed Jesus, the first thing the Spirit did after His baptism was to lead Jesus "into the wilderness to be tempted by the devil" (Matt. 4:1). Mark's account is succinct yet highly descriptive, stating that after the baptism of Jesus, "immediately the Spirit impelled Him to go into the wilderness" where He would be tempted by Satan (Mark 1:12-13). Mark employed the same verb for "impel" that he would later use to describe when Jesus cast out demons. A strong moving by the Spirit cast the Son into the wilderness. Unlike mankind's initial episode where Satan approached Eve in the Garden, this time God specifically led the Son of Man into Satan's presence, bringing about their first earthly encounter in the spiritual war of the ages. The battle for sovereign rule of the world—and beyond—had begun. Only one would depart as victor. The winner took all, including its inhabitants; the loser lost everything.

A direct relationship exists between the baptism of Jesus and Satan's temptation of Jesus that immediately followed. In this account of the temptation, we see another hint that Satan fully understood who Jesus was by how he addressed Jesus. Twice Satan employed the same designation the Father had used at Jesus' baptism: "If you are *the Son of God*" (Matt. 4:3, 6). Yet contained within the Greek text is a glimpse into Satan's mentality. Actually what Satan said is a subtle rephrasing of God's statement, but one substantially different at its core. In both cases Satan used no definite article in front of "Son." English translators often add "the" to make it smoother (i.e., "the Son of God"), but the original text does not contain this. What Satan literally said was, "If Son of God you are . . ." or "If you are *a* Son of God. . ." It was a twist, a distortion, of what God said—as it is Satan's base nature to do—as he had done earlier with Eve. A few years later the disciples who received Jesus into the boat after He had walked on water said virtually the same thing: "Of truth Son of God [or 'a Son of God'] You are" (Matt. 14:33). As with Satan's words, no definite article is present. For the disciples, theirs was an extended education. Jesus gradually brought them to an understanding as to His identity, culminating with Peter's divinely-inspired declaration of Matthew 16. In Matthew 14 the disciples collectively grew closer to the Messiah's true identity, but they had not fully grasped it yet. Peter's latter proclamation in Matthew 16:16 contrasts with what the disciples previously concluded about Jesus: "You are *the* Christ, *the* Son of *the* God *the* Living One!" God Himself made sure that four definite articles were included as He inspired Peter to say what He wanted said in the exact way that He intended. What the disciples gradually learned about Jesus, Satan already knew.

At this point in the confrontation, Satan may not have believed or accepted that Jesus was *the* Christ. The Christ—or Messiah—is a title, an office. As far as Satan was concerned Jesus had not fulfilled this function yet. Perhaps He never would. At this stage in His life Jesus was not yet fully qualified to be Messiah. Hebrews 2:10 gives an indication of some of the means that God chose to accomplish completely all that He intended in Jesus: "For it was fitting for Him [that is, God the Father]. . . . in bringing many sons to glory, *to perfect* the author of their salvation through sufferings." "To perfect" is used in the sense of fulness or completion, not as correcting something that has defects. The sufferings of the Messiah were only now beginning in earnest, as

God perfected into maturity His Messiah who would not only redeem the lost from their sin but also would identify with their sufferings (Heb. 2:14-18). Such was part of the cup that Jesus was drinking throughout His entire Incarnation.

Satan hated Jesus with abhorrence unrivaled by any human hatred. Satan's approach to Jesus demonstrates this. Unlike the demons who throughout the Gospels always cowered in Jesus' presence, Satan never did. Satan, who deems himself worthy of all worship, honor, glory, and praise, was not about to acknowledge Jesus' title or status without a fight—and the fight was just beginning during this initial temptation of Jesus. Even how Satan addressed Jesus was an insult, a prod. He did not acknowledge Jesus' unique status; he simply tempted Him by acknowledging He was a son of God. But Jesus was not the first so designated. Adam had originated as God's son (Luke 3:38)—and Adam had been no match for Satan.

It should be noted that the reference to Adam as God's son in Luke 3:38 is the last verse before Luke presents the temptation of Jesus in 4:1. Matthew, Mark and Luke each record that the temptation immediately followed the baptism. Luke presents the baptism of Jesus (3:21-22), ending with God's declaration declaring Jesus as *the* Son of God, and then adds a genealogy. When you read Luke's account, it seems almost absurd to have "a dull genealogy" interjected at this point in such a tremendous event in the Gospel. Yet Luke's placement of the genealogy has its purpose. Unlike Matthew's genealogy of Jesus in Matthew 1, which presents Jesus' connection with the Davidic ancestry and right to rule, Luke traces Jesus' lineage all the way back to Adam. Also differing from Matthew's account, Luke wrote in descending order, beginning with Jesus and working backward to Adam. Luke concludes with the significant statement, "Adam, the son of God" (3:38)—very similar to what God had just announced at Jesus' baptism. The next verse, Luke 4:1, shows that Jesus was led by the Spirit into the wilderness to be confronted by Satan. The first son of God—Adam—faired poorly in his conflict against Satan. Their contest was short and decisive. This next Son would have to stand much more firmly; otherwise, He would join the endless list of Adam's defiled and disqualified lineage.

Satan baited Jesus by saying in effect, "If you are a Son of God"—not *the* Son of God. "You are a One, not the One. You are no different than the first one, Adam."

But this Son was different.

So when He prayed, "Father, forgive them, for they do not know what they are doing," Jesus referred only to the ignorant agents of His crucifixion, those of the human realm. Satan knew (to know intellectually; to understand) what he did better than any human did, including Judas, Caiaphas, Herod, or Pilate. The demons also were totally cognizant of their actions. Before Satan and his demons rebelled against God, they had been holy angels who communally beheld the Second member of the Godhead with the glory He shared with the Father "before the world was" (John 17:5) — and they all had at one time individually and collectively worshiped Him. Ignorance did not lie at the heart of their attack — only evil. They did not need to wait until the death of Jesus to say with the centurion, "Truly this was the Son of God!" (Matt. 27:54) — they knew that before and during the Incarnation of Jesus.

As we saw in the previous chapter, Scripture often presents major events in the human realm while also exposing the hidden spiritual source involved, both good and evil. In other words, often what occurs in the human realm has an irreplaceable spiritual element that is just as important, if not more so, than the earthly activities. Without the spiritual base, many times the human element never would have transpired. Eve's temptation by the serpent is such an example. Physical characters played a part, but the spiritual side (in this case an evil one) also was present. Peter speaking with God as the source and then later with Satan as the source is another instance. Many other examples could be cited, especially several matters relating to the birth of Jesus.

Yet we often skip over these markers in Scripture, not fully appreciating their significance. John 14 contains such an example. This chapter records some of the last words of Jesus to His disciples before His arrest. Together they "celebrated" the Passover Supper — or stated better, they partook of the Passover meal. Celebration would have been an alien term to the somber disciples that night, especially to the Man of Sorrows who announced He was "troubled in spirit" (John 13:21). Jesus used this very Passover feast to instruct His disciples about deeper spiritual truths concerning Himself and what He was about to accomplish. The atmosphere of their assemblage would have been permeated with great sadness and confusion. In His Upper Room Discourse (John 13–17), Jesus gives us a glimpse of how matters that were transpiring at that time related to His pending suffering.

Much had happened by the time Jesus was finishing the Last Supper with His apostles. The humble Servant of Yahweh had already washed their feet. He had predicted and identified the traitor, and then expelled Judas from their presence. Jesus informed the disciples of His pending return to the Father as well as His subsequent return for them (John 14:1-3). He promised the magnificent advent of the Holy Spirit, Who would reside in them forever, filling the void His absence would cause. Then in John 14:29, Jesus summarized why He had spoken on so many different topics: "And now I have told you before it comes to pass, that when it comes to pass, you may believe." Jesus knew His disciples had little faith—and little faith, though not mature, vastly surpasses no faith. Little faith can be multiplied and grown; the total absence of faith cannot. While they possessed little faith, at this time great consternation and confusion swallowed the disciples whole. Jesus would still teach them many more truths before His ascension, but now was not the appropriate time—an enemy rapidly approached.

Jesus knew the total extent of what was transpiring even as He spoke to His disciples. This was true regarding the activities of both the spiritual beings and of those in the human realm. From the view of Jesus, however, the spiritual realm lay at the heart of the earthly events. In a few moments He would reveal to Peter that Satan had received permission from God to sift him like wheat. He also would explain that the Father had given Satan and the forces of darkness a specified time of open hostility against Him. Later, when He stood before Pilate, Jesus informed the Gentile ruler that he would have no authority whatsoever unless it had been given him from above (John 19:11). Even at this point, in some of His final teachings during the Passover meal, Jesus disclosed how He viewed the pending events of His betrayal, arrest, and crucifixion. In John 14:30 Jesus explained, "I will not speak much more with you, *for the ruler of the world is coming*, and he has nothing in Me." From Jesus' view Judas was not coming; neither were the chief priests and scribes, nor the temple police; the Roman soldiers were not coming; nor were even Herod or Pilate. "The ruler of the world" was coming, and he remained at the forefront of Jesus' thoughts, the designation occurring three times in this section of Scripture (John 12:31; 14:30; 16:11). Just as Jesus identified the ultimate source when Satan tempted Him by means of Peter, Jesus again disclosed the real power behind the earthly activities. Jesus was fully aware of who was coming—and why. Taking His disciples with Him, He later rose after His prayers in Gethsemane to meet the foe in the arena of battle the Father had predetermined (John 18:1).

At this hurried time and in their confused state of mind, the disciples may have concluded Jesus' earlier statement concerning the ruler of the world referred to Pilate, because he was Caesar's representative. King Herod could not rightfully be considered the ruler of this world—or if so, only in the most restricted sense. A Jewish zealot's view would envision Israel as the center of the world and as the pinnacle of the nations, and whoever ruled Israel would, in theory, rule the world. It mattered not that Rome reigned over a conquered Israel at that time; the Jews rightly viewed themselves as God's covenanted people from whom their promised Messiah would arise and exercise worldwide rule (Ps. 2). That Jesus had repeatedly referred to His pending glory would not clarify anything for those disciples present; it would only confuse them further. While Israel benefited from eternal covenants and promises from God, it was not their duly appointed time of world supremacy during Messiah's reign. They lived instead in the designated "times of the Gentiles" (Luke 21:24). Rome was the world power of the day; whoever ruled Rome, in a sense, ruled the world.

It is feasible that the disciples understood Jesus to refer to Satan as the ruler of the world who was coming, but at this point all they could do was attempt to maintain their rational minds as best they could, and they were rapidly losing the battle. They were on a spiritual white water rapid ride already beyond their capacity to lay moorings—and the turbulence would greatly intensify before it slackened any. Each revelation and explanation that Jesus made gave rise to only deeper and more serious questions. The disciples had to assimilate repeated couplets of apparent contradictions: glory yet crucifixion; Jesus hailed but rejected; the King standing in their midst, yet no kingdom now; the declared Son of God, yet smitten by men; promised thrones of honor in the kingdom, yet Jesus returns to His Father—alone. These concepts, plus several more, would make no sense whatsoever to the Shepherd's little flock until after the resurrection, and only after Jesus breathed into them the Holy Spirit (John 20:22) and opened their mind (singular in the Greek) to understand the Scriptures (Luke 24:45).

Yet the account in John 14:30 gives another nugget of truth vital in gaining more insight into Messiah's person. Jesus encouraged His followers that although the ruler of the world was coming, they should not fear for "he has nothing in Me." Regardless of how the disciples would have understood this statement, Jesus referred to Satan and the pending confrontation. Satan would find absolutely nothing in Him: no avenue of entrance, no defect that would lead to sin and destruction. This doctrine we can conceive in our minds, as much as we can perceive on a child's level the expanse of God's creation: Jesus was perfect and holy through and through. No spots, no blemishes—the totality of divine holiness encompassed in humble human garb. Let Satan have ten thousand years to probe and seek to bring failure, he still would find no weakness. Let the adversary offer Christ world upon world and kingdom upon kingdom; no temptation would take root. If twelve thousand legions of Satans existed, they collectively would find no hole, no glitch, no imperfection. Pure gold is pure gold; a diamond is a diamond, as much at its core as it is on the surface.

A thousand years before the advent of Jesus, David wrote, "The commandment of the LORD is pure, enlightening the eyes. The fear of the LORD is clean, enduring forever; the judgments of the LORD are true; they are righteous altogether. They are more desirable than gold, yes, than much fine gold; sweeter also than honey and the drippings of the honeycomb" (Ps. 19:8b-10). Centuries before Christ walked the earth the psalmist would write, "Thy word is very pure" (Ps. 119:140). In this same psalm he also wrote, "Those who love Thy law have great peace, and nothing causes them to stumble" (Ps. 119:165). No one knew and loved God's written Word as much as God's incarnate Living Word, Jesus. No stumbling would take place for this One. It was His very nature not to do so.

Satan could not know or understand this, neither intellectually nor experientially. The holiness which once embraced him had long been shattered and completely stripped from him at his initial rebellion and subsequent banishment from heaven, replaced instead with a total embodiment of evil from stem to stern. We of the human realm do not experientially understand pure holiness, ourselves so deeply marred by the effects of sin. But in the same way, because we are created in God's image, neither do we understand the full capacity of evil containing no goodness or grace whatsoever. Christ's holiness only magnified the utterly defiled wickedness of Satan—Jesus' very presence would have repulsed Satan as much as it caused him fear.

That Satan would find nothing in Jesus by no means reduced the intensity of Satan's attack—quite the contrary. We do not know exactly how Satan and the demons tormented Jesus; we only know that they did. It seems as with virtually everything in comparison between the physical and spiritual worlds, that of the spiritual is much stronger. The first element of the cup of Jesus that He alone was able to drink and why His crucifixion vastly exceeded all others was about to begin. The Lamb of God was about to endure the torment caused by the combined attack of satanic forces during their God-given hour of darkness. When we get to heaven we will understand completely what we now only comprehend in part, as we presently see in a mirror dimly (1 Cor. 13:12).

We previously saw in Revelation 9:4-6 that demons, when permitted by God, possess the capacity to inflict tremendous torment on their victims. Such torment will be inflicted during the Tribulation that "in those days men will seek death and will not find it; and they will long to die and death flees from them" (Rev. 9:6). The source for this torment, of course, will be unobservable to the world at large and would have remained unknown to even the elect unless God chose to reveal this in His Word.

Even in their designated hour of darkness, however, it would seem that the demons would approach the crucified Christ quite cautiously. Throughout His earthly ministry, whenever Jesus came in contact with demonic beings, the demons acknowledged who He is and expressed fear regarding their punishment. "What do I have to do with You, Jesus, Son of the Most High God? Have You come here to torment us before the time? (Mark 5:7; Matt. 8:29). Further, "And they were entreating Him not to command them to depart into the abyss" (Luke 8:31) — that is, a place where God has already confined some subset of demons in a place of torment. Demons greatly feared Jesus as He walked on His earth. James 2:19 indicates they still do; demons believe and tremble. Both verbs are present tense verbs in the Greek, not past tense. They continuously believe; they continuously tremble.

At the crucifixion, the demons initially would have most likely approached Jesus very cautiously. Sinless holy seraphim cover their face in the presence of God (Isa. 6:1-3), a chapter the Holy Spirit later reveals that especially relates to the person of Jesus. After a quote from Isaiah 6, John 12:41 explains, "These things Isaiah said, because he saw His glory, and he spoke of Him." Would fallen defiled angels do any less? Besides, Jesus had spoken freely even in the midst of His crucifixion. Demons feared the spoken word of Jesus in the Gospel accounts. Jesus did not need to lay hold of the satanic realm or to be standing in a particular position ready to retaliate. The absolute authority of His verbal command would render the demons confined and tormented in the abyss, waiting for the final punishment that would come if Christ were the victor.

Perhaps the legions and ranks of the demonic world initially moved in by their designated ranks, with the lesser demons ordered in first. Any volunteers to be the first to torment the second member of the Trinity?

We know some of Satan's nature and tactics simply by contrasting these to God and His attributes. For instance, 1 John 4:16 states, "God is love" — not that God loves (which He does), but rather that love is an attribute of His being. The opposite is true of Satan. It is not only that Satan hates (which he does), but rather that hate consumes him to such a degree that it becomes part of him and his domain. Consequently, since no love exists in Satan's realm, demons serve Satan out of fear; they do not love him or one another. Demons have no friends. Hatred, envy, distrust and jealousy are all normal working conditions in the demonic regime. Although by no means subservient to him, the holy angels of God respect Satan's power (Jude 9); would demons under his authority do any less? The demonic masses may have faced a severe predicament at Christ's crucifixion, having two unenviable options: attack the Son of God or be subject to Satan's wrath. Regardless, if they did at first hesitate, either through Satan's authority or merely as a natural consequence of their totally evil nature, the demons would eventually attack. To their surprise, however, the Messiah never responded; He never fought back. Jesus refused to use His authoritative Word that He had repeatedly spoken against them throughout the Gospel accounts. Maybe their fears were unfounded. As evil permeated the area, a herd mentality most likely would take hold, similar to the account where demons caused the swine to drown themselves (Mark 5:13). Faster, stronger, harder — a flurry of demonic gathering previously unknown to the world was taking place, but was completely hidden from the ignorant masses gathered at Calvary. Still, through the composite sum of Satan's assault, the Son stood firmly — and faithfully. It was His very nature to do so — as He willingly drank this first element of the cup the Father had given Him.

Satan could not win — in a billion years he never could have won. However, while his utterly evil nature had in the past given him false hope that he would triumph, at some point during the crucifixion he must have realized he would not prevail. For nearly three hours Satan would pour upon Jesus the full force of his evil power and authority.

Nothing had worked. Although obviously physically weakened by this time, Jesus' resolve and determination had not diminished even by a trace. As defeat approached, Satan still attacked, but most likely for a different reason. Revelation 12:12 reveals what Satan will eventually do in the Tribulation once he has been thrown out of heaven: "For this reason, rejoice, O heavens and you who dwell in them. Woe to the earth and the sea, because the devil has come down to you, *having great wrath*, knowing that he has only a short time." In the final part of the Tribulation, Satan's wrath will be poured out in a previously unknown intensified manner, and the end result is "woe to the earth." If Satan had not done so already, if by chance he kept anything back (which he most certainly would not have), he would likewise pour out the entirety of his wrath on Jesus during his designated hour of darkness. Is it any wonder that Jesus would tell His closest followers the same thing that He would His enemies: "Where I am going, you cannot [you are not able to; do not have the capacity to] come" (John 13:33). He alone was able.

So like a spoiled child who breaks toys simply because he wants no one else to play with them if he cannot, Satan, too, would also vent his hatred toward Jesus, pouring out the entirety of his wrath on the Lamb. Would enduring this wrath not result in a large degree so that "His appearance was marred more than any man, and His form more than the sons of men" (Isa. 52:14)? It would seem Satan most likely reached a point in his savagery against Jesus when his attack changed from efforts to keep Jesus from completing His Messianic course to a tantrum-like barrage consisting of evil for evil's sake—pain for pain's sake. It would be his very nature to do so.

How utterly frustrating it must have been for Satan to throw his entire arsenal against Jesus during his hour of the darkness and have nothing accomplish what he had expected. Not only did Jesus refuse to summon His angelic host, but He even demonstrated acts of divine grace and goodness in the midst of His own agony. Satan furiously attacked; Jesus prayed for forgiveness for the ignorant human masses who crucified Him. Legions of demons raged against the Lamb in warfare; Jesus extended grace to one on a cross adjacent to Him, promising him that day they would be together in Paradise (Luke 23:43). The declaration of Jesus was a promise of victory for the Lamb and His followers—a spoken reminder of defeat for the demonic world; Jesus would be in Paradise *that very day*. Satan and his demons had no authority to go there, that day or ever. If Jesus made it to Paradise, He would go only as the total Victor. So hate raged—but divine love reigned. Even amid the intensity of the battle, instead of looking at His own misery, the Son lovingly placed the earthly care of His mother into the trusted hands of His beloved disciple John (John 19:25-27). Satan's plot was unraveling. He was losing his grand wager. His one opportunity grew shorter. Still the Christ, the Son of the Living God, stayed the course. How much longer did Satan have? He may not have known for certain, but he did know God's eternal clock progressively ticked—as his divinely permitted hour of darkness neared its termination.

―――――――――――

The angels of God viewed this spiritual carnage as well. Myriads and multitudes of divine warrior angels stood by—armed, ready, witnesses to a grace displayed that they themselves could never begin to comprehend. Certain Scripture passages allow us a limited peak inside angels' minds to see how they would have viewed Jesus at Calvary. For instance, some of the most telling verses occur in 1 Peter 1:1-12. In his first epistle, Peter wrote to persecuted and discouraged Christians about the greatness of the believers' salvation. He described the salvation given by God as "an inheritance which is imperishable and undefiled and will not fade away" (1:4). Peter encouraged the churches in his care that their active faith is more precious than gold (1:7). With point after point Peter exhorted and reminded his readers of the depth of God's gift in salvation. Such salvation is so wondrous, is so grand in its magnitude, it continually interests and intrigues angels. In reference to the divine revelation in the Old Testament, 1 Peter 1:12 explains regarding the prophets that God used to communicate His Word: "It was revealed to them that they were not serving themselves, but you, in these things which now have been announced to you through those who preached the gospel to you by the Holy Spirit sent from heaven." Then Peter adds one vitally important element: "things into which angels long to look." What the holy angels of God longingly desire ("desire" being the same Greek word for "lust," but used here in a good sense) are matters relating to salvation: not physical beauty, not world power or dominion, not wealth—but salvation. Angels have witnessed everything throughout history: Satan's fall, creation, Adam and Eve, earthly kingdoms rising and falling. Yet salvation is what angels desire to explore. They have good reason for being so fascinated. Despite all they know and have viewed concerning God and His glory, they have stood only as spectators in regard to salvation—never as recipients of

God's imputed grace.

One reason angels do not know God's grace through salvation is that the Word did not become an angel—the Word became flesh. The author of Hebrews states in reference to Jesus, "For assuredly He does not give help to angels, but He gives help to the descendant [seed] of Abraham" (Heb. 2:16). Not one angel has ever experienced God's grace and forgiveness, primarily because they have no sacrificial replacement, no substitutionary atonement. When considered from the angels' perspective, it makes sense that salvation would fill their thoughts. One sin at one point in history past, and one-third of their fellow holy angels became angels of Satan, eternally transformed into demons, awaiting the hell that was originally prepared for them (Matt. 25:41). The change occurred instantly; it required no process. Immediately these demons became as evil as they ever would be, as evil as their new master Satan. Instead of belonging to the realm of the God of Love, the demons became inhabitants—*and* participants—in Satan's realm.

Those who may be reading this and think that this is too presumptuous in its conclusions should consider a few matters from the Book of Colossians. For one thing, regarding our salvation, Jesus "delivered us from the domain of darkness, and transferred us to the kingdom of His beloved Son" (Col. 1:13). How striking and fitting that the phrase "the domain of the darkness" is the same wording used in the Luke 22:52 account with the arrest of Jesus. He endured the totality of that domain so that we could be delivered out of it. The reverse is obviously true as well: if He had not endured, we would never have been delivered out of it.

But there is more. In Colossians 2:13-14, Paul wrote:

> And when you were dead in your transgressions and the uncircumcision of your flesh, He made you alive together with Him, having forgiven us all our transgressions, having canceled out the certificate of debt consisting of decrees against us and which was hostile to us; and He has taken it out of the way, having nailed it to the cross.

Three things were actually nailed to the cross that day, two visible to those present and one hidden: Jesus Himself, the placard above the cross, and the certificate of debt consisting of decrees against us. This is some of the most awe-inspiring and richest sections of Scripture, but we must move on.

Paul continues his thought in the next verse. Connected with what he wrote about being nailed to the cross, something else transpired that day that was totally hidden from the world at the time: "When He had disarmed the rulers and authorities, He made a public display of them, having triumphed over them through Him" (Col. 2:15). The vast majority of Bible-believing scholars writing about this verse hold that "the rulers and authorities" include *all* the hostile demonic hierarchy available to Satan, such as the same ones referred to in Ephesians 6:12. But the disarming occurred *after* their hour of darkness was complete—not during it.

The Greek word for "disarmed" occurs only twice in the New Testament, here and in Colossians 3:9 ("since you *laid aside* the old self with its evil practices") so there are no other examples to see how this word is used. It is interesting, however, that many scholars understand the middle voice of this word in Greek as indicating "stripping off from Himself." Some even add that this is though the demons had somehow affixed themselves to Jesus in an attempt to cause Him intense pain or destruction. Others see this phrase as depicting a wrestler who has thrown off his foe in utter defeat. Perhaps this is more accurate than people realize in describing what Jesus accomplished on His cross. Again, we would have no idea that this occurred unless God saw fit to show it in Scripture. In order to strip the demons away from Himself, they had to be in some way (for lack of better words) "attached" to him. But before Jesus disarmed them, they were allowed to bring about the full authority granted them in their hour of darkness, which is a component of the cup that He alone was able to drink.

Note this well, beloved: while we currently do not know the exact extent of what Jesus endured, an aspect of what He accomplished that day was to disarm from Himself the rulers and authorities of the demonic realm. This would never happen again throughout eternity because there was no need; only one hour of darkness was granted to the evil one and his collective forces—and they severely lost.

The holy angels of God most likely had known, and perhaps even befriended, many of the angels who had been transformed into demons. These disobedient angels had sinned, becoming permanently defiled with no hope whatsoever of forgiveness of their sin or salvation. From their one sin of disobedience they entered into a state of constant enmity with God. For the redeemed of Adam's lineage, however, a different scenario exists: sin upon sin, millions and millions of times over, and yet we receive God's complete cleansing forgiveness. Grace upon grace repeatedly replaces sin upon sin—all covered by the divine magnitude of the Lamb's perfect sacrifice. Even beyond this, Paul informed the Corinthian church that they (and other Christians) would ultimately judge angels in some ruling capacity (1 Cor. 6:3). Here stands a concept too vastly bizarre for us to appreciate fully; redeemed sinners, with multitudes of sins, will be granted authoritative positions over angels who have never sinned even once. It is no wonder that angels take such interests in things related to our salvation. They do not fully understand it any more than we can currently know experientially their holy status. We know of it, but we do not know it. Angels accept the role God the Father has given them without murmur and complaint, and they do so with sparkling obedience.

Contrary to some artists' renditions, angels are not pudgy infant beings with wings, lazily contemplating the substance of puffy clouds. Every instance recorded in Scripture, whenever a human encountered an angel manifested as an angel, the result was always the same: terrifying, dreadful fear. *Everyone*—from Old Testament encounters to Mary to the soldiers who guarded the tomb of Jesus—responded in like manner. They had ample reason to fear. We have already seen the 2 Kings 6:17 reference where the eyes of Elisha's servant were opened to see "the mountain was full of horses and chariots of fire." The Bible further describes God's attending angels as "mighty angels in flaming fire" (2 Thess. 1:7), holy warriors who execute His judgments, such as the two angels that destroyed Sodom and Gomorrah in Genesis 19. Scripture depicts angels as flame of fire (Heb. 1:7), sent out by God Himself to render service for the sake of those who would inherit salvation (Heb. 1:14). So even though man is currently made for a while a little lower than the angels (Ps. 8), angels maintain a service ministry to the elect. Consequently, no one throughout the total expanse of God's creation would they be more desirous to assist than the One whom they worship, Jesus Christ: "And when He again brings the first-born into the world, He says, 'And let all the angels of God worship Him'" (Heb. 1:6). But during the God-given hour of the darkness, the One they worship was being brutalized. Was there any way that they could witness Christ's crucifixion and not have it produce great internal agitation within these holy ones whom the Bible likewise refers to as "sons of God" (Job 1:6; 2:1; 38:7)?

We find out later in Scripture that, among other things, God had angels in view with what occurred on the cross and its subsequent ongoing results:

> To me, the very least of all saints, this grace was given, to preach to the Gentiles the unfathomable riches of Christ, and to bring to light what is the administration of the mystery which for ages has been hidden in God, who created all things; in order that the manifold wisdom of God might now be made known through the church to the rulers and the authorities in the heavenly places.
>
> This was in accordance with the eternal purpose which He carried out in Christ Jesus our Lord, in whom we have boldness and confident access through faith in Him (Eph. 3:8-12).

Although we often like to think about salvation in terms of what we receive, Ephesians 3:10 reveals a totally different understanding of why God permitted the death of His Son: "in order that the manifold wisdom of God might now be made known through the church to the rulers and the authorities in the heavenly places." We would not know this unless it was stated in Scripture; God specifically showed forth His wisdom that it might *now* be made known to—in this case not to humanity—but rather "to the rulers and the authorities in the heavenly places" (3:10). Yet even beyond this, it was "in accordance with *His eternal purpose* which He carried out in Christ Jesus our Lord" (Eph. 3:11). We are not even sure if "the rulers and the authorities in the heavenly places" in this verse refer to the holy angels or the fallen angels. Many scholars conclude that it refers to both, which seems more likely. This offers even more biblical support that with the death of Christ, God was making known to the angelic world His manifold wisdom in accordance to His eternal purpose. Such angelic beings *must* have viewed the crucifixion in progress.

The attending angels had a mental comprehension of what God was doing, but they had no experiential base to connect it. Never before in all eternity had angels seen any member of the Godhead subjected to such brutal audacity from evil powers. It reasons that left to themselves, God's angels would have instantly leapt into the battle, the same way a mother would leap in front of a speeding car to save her child caught in its path. But the Father did not permit them; they were divinely restrained from intervening. In their confirmed state of holiness, the angels had no temptation to disobey the Father's command. However this very state of holiness would have caused them deep consternation as they stood witness to horrendous evil manifested in a way previously unknown to them. Similar to when the Lamb will eventually break the seventh seal during the future Tribulation (Rev. 8:1), there may very well have been complete silence in heaven as God the Son was dying.

From the holy angels' view, the death of Jesus would most likely seem to be an extremely long ordeal; the time would not go quickly. However, the angels did not simply stand by idly; they stood in active obedience to God, even standing against their own inclination to intercede. This was something Peter had not yet learned at the arrest of Jesus. The holy angels of God stood by without intervening as they watched Jesus suffer, but apart from the Father's command, it was not their very nature to do so.

Finally—with the beloved Son on the cross for hours, having endured what one fallen son of Adam was not able to endure for even a fraction of the speed of light—at the very height of Satan's wrath, the Father stirred to action. Even the human agents present at the crucifixion understood something tremendous and terrifying was about to transpire, but they did not exactly know what. Even less would they understand why.

God's attending angels would have noticed this movement immediately, such as seen throughout Ezekiel 1. Satan and his forces may or may not have readily taken note. Eventually they too understood that God Himself was approaching Calvary. Did the Father come to rescue His wounded Son? Was Satan's hour of authority over? Was this the end of the battle and the torment? Soon every spiritual entity, both holy and evil, realized that all the previous activities had been only the preliminary rounds. Now began the final assault in this epoch battle— and the next half would be so much more brutally horrible that the first half would forever pale in comparison to this new episode.

The totality of both the heavenly and demonic realm watched as God the Father approached God the Son.

3

THE DARKNESS

Darkness, at its base definition, is the absence of light. Darkness by itself is an absolute. No degrees of darkness exist; the only variable is the amount of light present, if any light is present at all. Only light, not heat, affects darkness. Hell is both hot and dark (Matt. 8:12; Luke 16:22-24).

Light is the antithesis of darkness. Light always wins. A simple match in a subterranean cave still breaks through the deepest darkness it encounters. Ironically, deep darkness simply offers light an opportunity to manifest itself more fully. Darkness resumes its dominion whenever light ceases to shine, but darkness itself is not the reason the light is extinguished.

Truths in the physical world often correlate to the spiritual realm as well. In reality, the reverse is true. What is true in the spiritual realm, which existed before the world began, is often illustrated in the physical world. These same truths regarding light and darkness are true about Jesus Christ, the Light of the world, especially when contrasted with Satan, leader of the forces of darkness. Jesus would incarnate the prophecy of Isaiah 9:2, "the people who walk in darkness will see a great light"—and they did. This Light shone in the midst of deep spiritual darkness. As is true in the physical world, so again is true in the spiritual; the smallest light illumines the deepest darkness. How much more would the Light of the world shine into a world so desperately in need of light? Deep spiritual darkness offers the best background to manifest the Light. The Apostle John understood these concepts. In simple language he wrote these immensely deep truths concerning Jesus: "And the light shines in the darkness, and the darkness did not comprehend [overpower] it" (John 1:5). In reference to John the Baptist, the Apostle John stated, "He was not the light, but came that he might bear witness of the light. There was the true light which, coming into the world, enlightens every man" (John 1:8-9). That true Light shines just as brightly today, although diffused differently since Jesus has returned to heaven.

Light shining in darkness also divides between that which is illumined and that which remains dark. However, such an advent of light in the midst of darkness is not always welcomed because its very presence forces one to choose with which sector one will align. Instead of relishing in the glory of the Light, some prefer darkness instead. John wrote of this in John 3:19-21: "And this is the judgment, that the light is come into the world, and men loved the darkness rather than the light; for their deeds were evil. For everyone who does evil hates the light, and does not come to the light, lest his deeds should be exposed. But he who practices the truth comes to the light, that his deeds may be manifested as having been wrought in God." The advent of the Light of Christ then becomes either the greatest truth one ever encounters—or the most horrendous. The Light remains the same for both; the response of the recipient to the Light becomes the core issue.

With so many Scriptural analogies between light and darkness (and there are dozens more), a simple but confounding question stands before us: *Why did darkness cover the land at Jesus' crucifixion?* Three Gospels record this phenomenon, so it must be important theologically. But still, what does God intend for us to learn from this?

As with many issues of Scripture, by far the most repeated response by laity and scholars is, "Well, I don't know. I never really thought about it." For instance, many commentaries note that the darkness occurred but offer nothing regarding its significance. This may be appropriate. God certainly may choose to reveal matters in Scripture without giving any additional explanation, such as in Daniel 12:1-9, where God's own prophet does not understand the meaning or significance of what has just been revealed to him.

However, after some thought, various attempts to explain the darkness at the crucifixion emerge. One answer identifies the darkness with the vast assemblage of satanic forces present. With Satan exercising his rule in the domain of the darkness (Col. 1:13), especially during his God-granted hour of authority (Luke 22:53), it reasons that darkness would occur when he gathered his forces in an unprecedented manner. This would especially be true regarding his presence during the crucial activities at Calvary. Another view sees the darkness as God's testimony to individuals such as the attending Roman centurion. The darkness alerted those who had no known interest in the things of God that this was not merely another crucifixion of some condemned criminal. If those present did not understand what was transpiring or the claims of Jesus concerning Himself, God the Father bore witness to the gravity of the event by sending darkness over the land, perhaps extending over the entire world—such was the magnitude of Christ's death. Yet another approach places more emphasis on the presence of the Light at the cross. In other words, the darkness appeared because the Light of the world was dying. Jesus Himself bore witness to the multitude that the Light would not always be in their presence. Just a few days earlier, in John 12:35-36 Jesus warned, "For a little while longer the light is among you. Walk while you have the light, that darkness may not overtake you; he who walks in the darkness does not know where he goes. While you have the light, believe in the light, in order that you may become sons of light." The cross would be the departure of which Jesus cautioned. By using a simple analogy of nature, if the light is removed, darkness must manifest itself.

One answer has many advocates. Those who receive the Bible as God's truth understand that a divine separation transpired. The basis for this answer holds that a holy God cannot bear to look upon sin and must turn away His face. Therefore, as Jesus became sin for us (2 Cor. 5:21), God turned away from the Son. The explanations for how God's turning away from His Son relates to the darkness over the cross (if it relates at all) vary considerably. Many see the turning away as occurring at the end of the crucifixion when Jesus cried out, "My God! My God! Why have You forsaken Me?" (Matt. 27:46; Mark 15:34). Others, somewhat by default or by not addressing it, infer that the separation from the Father lasted the entire crucifixion. Galatians 3:13 is such a verse that views the crucifixion as a whole and how God viewed Jesus: "Christ redeemed us from the curse of the Law, *having become a curse for us*—for it is written, 'Cursed is everyone who hangs on a tree.'"

Obviously, something vastly significant occurred at the end of the crucifixion. We will get to this in the next chapter. But we need to consider other matters first. To begin with, no Scripture explicitly states that God cannot bear to look upon sin and therefore must turn His face from it, yet it is often quoted in sermons. The Bible contains many references to the judicial act of God turning His face away or hiding His face from people involved in blatant, rebellious sin but none that He cannot look on the sins they commit. Some people hold that Habakkuk 1:13 supports the fact that God cannot look on sin: "Your eyes are too pure to approve [look on] evil." Yet the context indicates this verse deals with the idea of God looking on evil without responding to it—not that God must turn His face away from sin. Adam and Eve would not have made the same conclusion of God not being able to look at sin (Gen. 3). Consider also just a very small sampling of multiple biblical references of God's capacity to look on sin: Genesis 6:5: "Then the LORD saw that the wickedness of man was great on the earth;" Exodus 3:7: "And the LORD said, 'I have surely seen the affliction of My people who are in Egypt, and have given heed to their cry because of their taskmasters, for I am aware of their sufferings;'" and centuries later in condemning the heinous sins that were done in His very own temple, God, by means of his prophet, both asks and answers: "'Has this house, which is called by My name, become a den of robbers in your sight? Behold, I, even I, have seen it,' declares the LORD" (Jer. 7:11). These are just a few examples. After all, He truly is the God who sees (Gen. 16:13).

Actually, just the opposite occurs. Instead of God not being able to look at sin, man cannot stand to see his own sinfulness in light of God's holiness. Isaiah saw the glory of God and concluded, "Woe is me, for I am ruined! Because I am a man of unclean lips, and I live among a people of unclean lips; for my eyes have seen the King, the LORD of hosts" (Isa. 6:5). After Jesus taught the multitudes and then blessed Peter's fishing endeavor, a greatly convicted Peter pleaded, "Depart from me for I am a sinful man!" (Luke 5:8). When the Apostle John beheld the, glorified Christ, he described Him as the One whose "eyes were like a flame of fire," denoting the penetrating gaze of the all-knowing, all-powerful God (Rev. 1:14). Jesus did not look away from John. This beloved disciple who lovingly rested his head against Jesus during the last Passover (John 13:23) later fell as a dead man at the One who looked upon him with the holy, fierce, flaming eyes of God (Rev. 1:17). All these references describe the reactions of beloved servants of God. How much more would the turning away response be from someone like Judas, Nero, or Hitler?

God must retain the capacity to look at sin. After all, the Judge of this world needs a sense of reference in order to judge properly. Everyone must give an account to God for every word uttered (Matt. 12:36). The Great White Throne judgment of Revelation 20 depicts the damned standing before Jesus as the divine accounting books will be opened, and they all will be judged "according to their deeds" (Rev. 20:12). God certainly will not turn His face away from these sins. In addition to this, if God could not look upon sin, then He could never converse with Satan whenever He chose, especially since the Bible repeated depicts Satan as "the evil one" (John 17:15; Eph. 6:16; 2 Thess. 3:3; 1 John 3:13-14). Scripture indicates that God has interacted with the evil one in the past (Job 1-2; Zech. 3), and most likely continues doing so because at this present time Satan remains the accuser of the brethren (Rev. 12:10). Nothing whatsoever in these accounts indicates that God has to turn His face away from this thoroughly evil one. Finally, if we take this logic to its extremity, God would never save anyone. The Good Shepherd would never seek the lost sheep because, after all, lost sheep are notoriously sinful. From these points it seems that we need to find a more substantial explanation for what occurred on the cross—especially at its conclusion. But before doing this, we need to address why darkness covered the land while Jesus hung on the cross.

As always, in-depth Bible study requires that we drop back into the world of those present and try "to see with their eyes and hear with their ears." We also must examine the evidence embedded in Scripture before making our conclusions. The issue is not so much, "Why do you think darkness covered the Cross?" as much as, "What does God's Word say about it?" In other words, we hope to determine relevant information that God has unveiled in His Word. We are mining out of God's written treasure house—and what His goldmine contains about the darkness may surprise you.

The Bible presents some information concerning Christ's death, but not an abundance. The crucifixion of Jesus lasted approximately six hours, from 9:00 A.M. to 3:00 P.M. (Mark 15:25, 33). This was not an unusually long crucifixion. In fact, it was just the opposite. The relatively short time Jesus agonized on the cross before He died surprised Pilate (Mark 15:44-45). It is important to note that the six hours of Christ's crucifixion divide into two distinct three-hour segments, with the main division beginning with the advent of the darkness. Matthew, Mark, and Luke specifically place the darkness at about the sixth hour, that is, at noon (Matt. 27:45; Mark 15:33; Luke 23:44). Luke gives additional details of how the sun was "obscured," literally translated "failing" (23:45), a point we will pick up later. So the darkness arrived at noon and resided during the last three hours of Jesus' crucifixion. There is one important observation we must make; with the exception of the "My God!" cry of Psalm 22:1 and a few brief statements at the end, all the recorded words of Jesus take place within the first three hours of the crucifixion—that is, before the advent of the darkness. Before the darkness, Jesus prayed, "Father forgive them" (Luke 23:34), interacted with the thief on the cross who ultimately believed, and charged John to care for His mother. After the darkness arrived, Jesus spoke no more until only moments before His death.

We must further note all three Gospel writers add a specific time marker in regard to the darkness. Matthew, Mark, and Luke each employ the same word "until" in describing the darkness. For instance, Matthew 27:45 states, "Now from the sixth hour darkness fell upon all the land *until* the ninth hour." The darkness had a definitive beginning and a definitive ending. Also, it is significant to note the "My God! My God! Why have You forsaken Me?" (Matt. 27:46; Mark 34) scream occurred at the end of the darkness, not during it. So by means of eliminating possible solutions, the darkness could not have been present because the Father turned away from the Son; the darkness occurred for three hours before this final event took place.

So the darkness resided over the cross, and the Son became silent. Again the simple question: why?

———————

Scripture presents God connected with light from Genesis through Revelation. Add such correlated words as "glory," "brilliance," "shining," or "burning," and the references would approach a thousand. James 1:17, which refers to the good gifts God gives, depicts God as "the Father of lights"—that is, the originator of all "good lights," whatever those lights may be. The final phrase of James 1:17 shows God's light is a constant, "with whom there is no variation or shifting shadow." First John 1:5 simply states, "God is Light, and in Him there is no darkness at all." In His essence and attributes, no trace of darkness whatsoever resides within God. Pure, perfect holiness: no faults or defects. Couple this with God's self-description "I, the LORD, do not change" (Mal. 3:6) and the eternality of His light shows forth. God does not attempt to shine—He is Light. The shining brilliance of His glory exists simply because God is Who He is.

Yet with all these references and hundreds more, the Bible also occasionally associates God with darkness, and surprisingly enough, connects darkness with God's very presence—not His absence. Herein is the key: God may use darkness as He sees fit, and may have it near

Him as He chooses, but it is not part of His essential nature or divine attributes. For instance, David wrote in reference to God: "He bowed the heavens also, and came down with thick darkness under His feet" (2 Sam. 22:10; cf. Ps. 18:9). Also, "He made darkness canopies [or pavilions] around Him, a mass of waters, thick clouds of the sky" (2 Sam. 22:12; Ps. 18:11). Perhaps the darkness surrounds God to conceal His glory. God presently exhibits His glory in greatly diminished degrees because His full glory would consume His creation, much in the same way God had to restrain His exposed glory before Moses in Exodus 33.

Beyond these examples two more scriptural accounts exist that associate God with darkness. In both passages darkness definitely indicates God's special presence, not His absence. Both instances establish a foundation that would again manifest itself when the darkness at Calvary covered the earth more than a thousand years later.

Abram lived in Ur of the Chaldeans when God called him to go to a land that God would show him (Gen. 12:1-2). This story, however, is not so much about Abram as it is about God. From the fall of man onward God had gradually unfolded His plan of redemption. Man stood marred and defiled before Him. Sin wedged into man—and ultimately all creation (Rom. 8:20-22)—creating an unrelinquishing strangle grip. Numerous centuries after the Fall, God raised up a people from whom ultimately the Christ would come, namely, the Jewish people who would become the nation of Israel. They would be His unique people, particularly blessed in their origin, their relationship with God, and their spiritual privileges (Rom. 9:1-5). Also, as they repeatedly learned by firsthand experience, the massive amount of divine light given them made the Jews unique in their accountability before God. Biblical and secular histories bear witness of countless tragic stories of the Hebrew people not living up to the Light's standard of righteousness and the dreadful consequences that resulted.

When God called Abram there were no such things as Jews. No one would have understood what was meant by the word. Abram would become the first. Jewish multitudes would follow, but they all would come forth from a most extraordinary origin. God wanted the world to know it was not the normal course of human affairs that led to Israel's existence. God raised up this people into being, but He would do so in a way that would both demonstrate His faithfulness as well as produce deep faith in the progenitor of the Jews (Deut. 7:6-8).

Abram, whose name means "exalted father," would later have his name changed by God to Abraham, "father of a multitude." God meant Abram's name change to be an encouraging promise—which it was—but difficult times lay ahead for Abram before he received the initial fulfillment of this divine prophecy. Both names became painful reminders of the fact that Abram and his wife remained childless. In Genesis 12:4, Abram was already seventy-five years old, and he was not growing any younger. This most unlikely candidate for fatherhood would be one hundred years old when his promised heir eventually arrived (Gen. 21:5). Abram would have his faith stretched considerably during this twenty-five year wait for the promised birth of Isaac.

In Genesis 12:3 God declared to Abram, "In you all the families of the earth will be blessed." How odd to make a promise to a seventy-five year old nomad who wandered—and wondered—through a land promised him, but a land he never fully received (Heb. 11:8-13). God repeatedly made promises to Abram that he would have offspring of countless magnitude. Yet these very promises of future generations troubled Abram. How could he be the father of multitudes when he not yet fathered his first child? How can all the nations of the earth be blessed in him? Abram had wealth as far as the standard of the day went, but who would ever hear of him in the countries that surrounded his hometown of Ur, several hundred miles away from his present dwelling, let alone to the unknown countries beyond the horizon? This greatly puzzled Abram. He had many questions, but he never was defiant before God (Rom. 4:19-21).

As year gave way to year in Abram's life, one constant remained: no child, no seed, no heir, no lineage. Abram contemplated his condition and responded as we so often do; he offered to help God with His solution. The context is as follows: God appeared to Abram in a vision in Genesis 15:1 announcing, "Do not fear, Abram, I am a shield to you; your reward shall be very great." God knew Abram's heart as well as the deep aching of his soul. God opened the avenue for Abram to pour out his painful perplexity before Him. Genesis 15:2-3 reports Abram responding, "O Lord GOD, what wilt Thou give me, since I am childless, and the heir of my house is Eliezer of Damascus?. . . . Since Thou hast given no offspring to me, one born in my house is my heir." This conclusion makes sense on a human level. God had promised future generations, but no present generation existed at that time. If Abram would have any future generations, he reasoned the only solution was to adopt his servant as heir—and it deeply troubled him to think he would have to do so.

God responded to Abram's prayer with a most specific promise. Taking Abram outside the tent, God said, "This man will not be your heir; but one who shall come forth from your own body, he shall be your heir. . . . Now look toward the heavens, and count the stars, if you are able to count them. . . . So shall your descendants be" (15:4-5). The following statement, Genesis 15:6, is a monumental Scripture verse: "Then he [Abram] believed in the LORD; and He reckoned it to him as righteousness." Both Paul and James later used this verse as evidence to New Testament readers of the utter necessity of approaching God through faith, even in the Old Testament (Rom. 4:1-3; Gal. 3:1-6; Jas. 2:21-23).

God used this context to unveil a tremendously important aspect of His progressive revelation. Along with the seed blessing, God had also promised Abram a land blessing (Gen. 12:7; 13:14-17). In Genesis 15:7 God reminded him, "I am the LORD who brought you out of Ur of the Chaldeans, to give you this land to possess it." Abram responded, "O Lord GOD, how may I know that I shall possess it?" (15:8). God then instructed Abram to prepare designated animals for a special event; God Himself was about to enter into a binding covenant with Abram. After Abram prepared the animals, a deep sleep fell upon him (15:12). God did not rebuke Abram for sleeping, such as Jesus later did in Gethsemane with Peter, James, and John (Mark 14:32-40). Instead, the sleep was God's design. So unchangeable did God intend His covenant with Abram that He alone wanted responsibility for its fulfillment. This was not a two-way covenant, conditioned on the behavior of both parties, such as the covenant later made between Jacob and Laban in Genesis 31:43-49. Every covenant made has to be ratified, that is, to have an officially designated and recognized starting point, and so did this one. Genesis 15:18 succinctly states, "On that day the LORD made a covenant with Abram." We should note that God alone ratified His covenant; He alone bore the task of bringing the covenant into fullness. Abram was a human instrument of this covenant, but the promises were of such magnitude, God alone could secure them. On his own Abram could not secure any of the promises of the covenant—the land, descendants, or a blessing to all the nations of the earth—only God could. Without God's active intervention and blessing, the Abrahamic Covenant never would find any of its fulfillment.

So as Abram lay sleeping, God approached to ratify His covenant. Genesis 15:12 contains a most unusual description of God's presence. The phrase begins with the tiny word "behold," a word so often overlooked but nonetheless so crucial. Without exaggeration, one could translate the word, "Now, look! This is important! Pay attention!" — but we rarely do. Perhaps the reason that the "behold" occurs within this verse is that the description of God's presence is so different from most of the other descriptions in Scripture. Genesis 15:12 states, "behold, terror and great *darkness* fell upon him [Abram]." A literal translation of the Hebrew is, "behold! a terror of great darkness," or "behold! a terror, even great darkness, falling upon him." In other words two separate entities of terror and darkness did not occur — the terror *was* the darkness. So here, in this special pronouncement of God's presence, on the day when God ratified the eternally important Abrahamic Covenant, He did so by means of darkness. God could have manifested Himself with light, such as when His glory filled His tabernacle and later His temple, but He chose not to. In this case God revealed Himself by means of darkness. This does not fit our understanding of God — and for good reason — but it is true nonetheless. In fact, the Bible presents another instance where God's presence is accompanied by darkness, and it is almost as surprising as the Abrahamic Covenant of Genesis 15.

Moses wrote to the generation poised to enter the Promised Land. The original Exodus generation had died in the wilderness because of their disobedience and lack of faith in God. The new generation stood ready to receive the land God had promised Abram more than four hundred years earlier (Gal. 3:15-17). Much of Deuteronomy is Moses' eyewitness account, and in some cases he gives more specific information than Exodus, Leviticus, or Numbers contain. But the primary reason for the book was to present a charge to the second generation. Had the new generation learned anything from the failures of their fathers and mothers? God had shown Himself strong and faithful, but also that He would most assuredly judge sins committed against Him. Would the response of the present assemblage differ from that of their parents? Would they go forward in faith to the good promises of God, or would they, too, stray from God and receive a similar punishment? Throughout Deuteronomy God issued warning after warning to fear and obey Him, to keep His commandments, to walk humbly before Him — and above all, never to forget that He alone is God. For the most part this generation would obey, having the noble Joshua as their human leader. Although they were far from perfect, they were vastly better than most of the subsequent Hebrew generations.

After the Exodus out of Egypt, God brought His physically redeemed people to Mount Sinai (Exod. 19:1). God further instructed and prepared the nation of Israel for another covenant He was about to make with them. This covenant is often called the Mosaic Covenant, the Mosaic Law, or simply the Law.

Exodus 24:1-7 gives the account of the ratification of Mosaic Covenant:

> Then He said to Moses, "Come up to the LORD, you and Aaron, Nadab and Abihu and seventy of the elders of Israel, and you shall worship at a distance. Moses alone, however, shall come near to the LORD, but they shall not come near, nor shall the people come up with him."
>
> Then Moses came and recounted to the people all the words of the LORD and all the ordinances; and all the people answered with one voice, and said, "All the words which the LORD has spoken we will do!"
>
> And Moses wrote down all the words of the LORD. Then he arose early in the morning, and built an altar at the foot of the mountain with twelve pillars for the twelve tribes of Israel.
>
> And he sent young men of the sons of Israel, and they offered burnt offerings and sacrificed young bulls as peace offerings to the LORD.
>
> And Moses took half of the blood and put it in basins, and the other half of the blood he sprinkled on the altar. Then he took the book of the covenant and read it in the hearing of the people; and they said, "All that the LORD has spoken we will do, and we will be obedient!"

Thus the nation of Israel entered into a binding covenant with their covenant-making and covenant-keeping God. This covenant differs from the Abrahamic Covenant in that there were specific obligatory requirements by God that would result in the nation being either blessed by God or cursed by Him.

As stated, the account in Deuteronomy offers details omitted in the Book of Exodus. After the retelling of Israel's history beginning with the sending out of the spies at Kadesh-barnea, Moses once more gathered the nation of Israel to remind them of their binding obligations stipulated in the Mosaic Covenant of which the Jews had previously already entered. At the original giving of the Law, God had manifested Himself to the people. Though not limited to this, God once more employed darkness as an aspect of His presence before the people. Moses told how the people came near Mount Sinai, "and the mountain burned with fire to the very heart of the heavens: *darkness,* cloud, and thick gloom" (Deut. 4:11). In the next chapter Moses again made note of the darkness, saying, "And it came about, when you heard the voice [of God] from the midst of the darkness . . . " (Deut. 5:23). Like Abram hundreds of years earlier, the entire nation responded to God's presence with terrible fear (5:25-27). In ratifying the Mosaic Covenant, the standard by which God would judge His covenanted people Israel, God once more employed darkness as an aspect of His special presence. Darkness was not the only means recorded in Deuteronomy that God chose to reveal Himself, nor was it the only venue available to Him. But in two Old Testament instances where God ratified eternally significant covenants, He did so surrounded by darkness.

The author of Hebrews likewise used this same description centuries later. In Hebrews 12:18-21 God's author reminded his readers how terrifying the advent of God at Mount Sinai had been: "For you have not come to a mountain that may be touched and to a blazing fire, *and to darkness* and gloom and whirlwind, and to the blast of a trumpet and the sound of words which sound was such that those who heard begged that no further word should be spoken to them. For they could not bear the command, 'If even a beast touches the mountain, it will be stoned.' And so terrible was the sight, that Moses said, 'I am full of fear and trembling.'" God displayed His presence at Sinai, but a major portion of it consisted of a terrible darkness, gloom, and fear.

But the author of Hebrews did not want to dwell on the awesome display of God demonstrated in the past. Instead, his main interest was that God had instead ratified another covenant. In contrasting the change from the Mosaic Covenant to the present age, the author of Hebrews wrote in 12:22-24:

> But you have come to Mount Zion and to the city of the living God, the heavenly Jerusalem, and to myriads of angels, to the general assembly and church of the first-born who are enrolled in heaven, and to God, the Judge of all, and to the spirits of righteous men made perfect, and to Jesus, *the mediator of a new covenant,* and to the sprinkled blood, which speaks better than the blood of Abel.

Only hours before His death, when Jesus was alone with His disciples, He strayed from the normal Passover celebration and disclosed to them this eternity-altering truth: "This is My body which is given for you; do this in remembrance of Me. . . . This cup which is poured out for you is the new covenant in My blood" (Luke 22:19-20; 1 Cor. 11:25).

What Jesus said stunned His disciples who were present that night. They very well may have audibly gasped — such was the magnitude of Jesus' pronouncement. The Eleven with Jesus knew exactly of what He spoke; they needed no extended information. We, however, so often casually read over tremendously significant statements in God's Word without comprehending their significance. Let's drop down into their world to see how His disciples would have responded in abject amazement at what Jesus had just said.

Part of the stipulation of the Mosaic Covenant was that if the nation of Israel obeyed God, He would bless; if they disobeyed, He would repeatedly and progressively discipline them with more intense judgments. For example, Leviticus 26 and Deuteronomy 28 laid out specific blessings and consequences directly related to Israel's behavior before their God. One of the last things God promised was that after repeated punishments for their sins, if the nation still rebelled, eventually God would send the people into exile into a strange land (Lev. 26:27-33; Deut. 28:63-65). As the Old Testament frequently bore witness, although there were generations of obedience, God's own people time after time rejected both Him and His Word. Much of the ministry of God's Old Testament prophets consisted of calling the sinful nation back into obedience to the Mosaic Covenant stipulations they had made with God at Sinai. However, while occasionally the nation would repent, such as during the reigns of King Hezekiah (2 Kgs. 18) and King Josiah (2 Kgs. 22-23), the revivals were short-lived and deeper sin and disobedience would follow. God, being true to His Word, was about to send the nation out of the Promised Land and into exile to Babylon, culminating with the destruction of Jerusalem and the temple in 586 B.C.

The prophet Jeremiah lived in Jerusalem for the last few decades before the Babylonian exile. He faithfully called Judah back to covenant obedience to their covenant-making God — but few paid any attention. God had revealed to Jeremiah and others that He had raised up the Babylonians to be used as an instrument to punish His people. The Book of Jeremiah expresses the blatant sinfulness of Judah and the warnings of the coming destruction of Jerusalem. It includes a brief account of the fall of the city, and then of the miserable situation after the exile. Yet in the midst of the denouncement and promised pending doom, immediately before the pagan invaders arrived, God furnishes four chapters that point to the future restoration and blessing on the nation of Israel (Jer. 30-33). The same God Who was about to bring severe judgment also promised that He Himself would bless, rebuild, and restore what

He had so severely judged (Jer. 31:27-28). Before the first rape, murder, and plunder of the Holy City, God pointed beyond the present chastising to a future time of blessing for the nation. It is in this context that God revealed something startling that was absolutely an act of grace: God would make a New Covenant with the house of Israel and the house of Judah (Jer. 31:31). The future aspect of this is seen in that three times in this context God begins with the prophetic phrase, "Behold, days are coming" (Jer. 31:27, 31, 38). God contrasted the New Covenant He will make with the present covenant the nation lived under and repeatedly did not live by — that is, with the Mosaic Covenant:

Here is what God promised His soon-to-be exiled people in Jeremiah 31:31-34:

> "Behold, days are coming," declares the LORD, "when I will make a new covenant with the house of Israel and with the house of Judah, not like the covenant which I made with their fathers in the day I took them by the hand to bring them out of the land of Egypt, My covenant which they broke, although I was a husband to them," declares the LORD.

> "But this is the covenant which I will make with the house of Israel after those days," declares the LORD, "I will put My law within them, and on their heart I will write it; and I will be their God, and they shall be My people.

> "And they shall not teach again, each man his neighbor and each man his brother, saying, 'Know the LORD,' for they shall all know Me, from the least of them to the greatest of them," declares the LORD, "for I will forgive their iniquity, and their sin I will remember no more."

What awe-inspiring covenant promises of God! He will write His law on their heart; He will forgive their iniquity; their sins He will remember no more. However, we should note God repeatedly used the future tense ("I will make," "I will write," etc.) in reference to this covenant. God had promised He would make a New Covenant. This is just as much a divine prophecy and promise as is any of the Messianic prophecies such as Isaiah 9:6-7. God promised that He would make a New Covenant with the house of Israel and the house of Judah, but He did not disclose in the Book of Jeremiah when He would do so.

Over six hundred years had transpired since Jeremiah 31 was written, and still God had not ratified the New Covenant. The nation was exiled and returned: but no New Covenant. The promises stayed future tense—and unfulfilled. John the Baptist heralded the arrival of the Messiah—but at least as recorded in Scripture, he never included the New Covenant in his teaching. The Messiah began His promised ministry on earth. The New Covenant did not appear in any of the extended teaching sections of Jesus.

Never did the Christ refer to this eternally important promised covenant of God *until*—alone with His Eleven, shortly before Gethsemane—Jesus altered the sacred Passover ceremony. As Luke 22:20 unveils, having just partaken of the bread, He revealed a divine revelatory bombshell: "And in the same way He took the cup after they had eaten, saying, 'This cup which is poured out for you is the new covenant in My blood.'" Decades later the Apostle Paul, in describing the account he received from the Lord about that night, wrote in 1 Corinthians 11:25, "In the same way He took the cup also, after supper, saying, 'This cup is the new covenant in My blood; do this, as often as you drink it, in remembrance of Me.'" We must note two important matters. First, both references have the definite article "the" in front of it: it is *the* New Covenant—the specified, promised one by God, not merely some new covenant of God in a generic sense. Second, Jesus employed a present tense in describing this. Future references would no longer be fitting in awaiting the covenant. Simply put, the New Covenant now becomes an "is"—not a "will be."

The other covenants of God required ratification to become effective; God's New Covenant did also. But it would not be during the Passover meal. The ratification of the New Covenant did not transpire the night Jesus was betrayed. What Jesus stated would happen the next day with the slaying of the true Passover sacrifice from God (1 Cor. 5:7). The blood of the New Covenant would be poured out within hours; or stated differently, the ratification of the New Covenant would occur the next day as Jesus offered the cup of the New Covenant in His blood during the crucifixion.

God used darkness to manifest Himself when ratifying the Abrahamic and Mosaic Covenants. Darkness is not required in order for a covenant of God to be ratified. For instance, when God ratified the covenant with Noah in Genesis 9, there is no mention of darkness. Yet, as we have noted, God may choose to have darkness with Him. Consequently, it should not surprise us to find darkness associated with the ratifying of the New Covenant as well. After noting that the darkness fell upon the land, Luke wrote of "the sun being obscured" (Luke 23:45). This is a translator's attempt to harmonize this verse with either modern science or to attempt to convey it properly in English. Literally the phrase reads, "the sun failed," or "the sun utterly failed." The sun had good reason to fail. As the glory of God illumines any darkness, so would the darkness of God overcome any source of light—the sun or anything else. What occurred was not due to an absence of light; rather it was because of the advent of the darkness of God's presence. This is the only recorded example in Scripture of darkness conquering light, and God intended that we mark its uniqueness. Something extraordinary occurred within the darkness at the cross, and that particular aspect would never happen that way again.

In answer as to why the darkness was over the cross comes this best biblical response: in the same manner by which the Abrahamic and Mosaic Covenant had darkness when they were ratified, so too did God employ darkness as He ratified His New Covenant in the blood of Jesus. This obviously requires God's presence at the cross. Could God possibly be absent from a covenant that He Himself ratifies?

We have previously noted Isaiah 53 and how it offers insight into what happened while Jesus hung on the cross. As a reminder, Isaiah 52:13-15 begins and is a part of this tremendously important chapter. But there is more. Something else occurred at the cross that the world would never have known without God's revelation. Part of what made the cup that Jesus drank differ from all others and also added to torture that marred His body beyond measure was this second element unique to Him: *God the Father struck and smote God the Son.* Satan and rebellious man each had his role in the crime, and God held each party accountable for his actions. However, the Father played a unique role in Jesus' suffering. Isaiah 53:4 states, "Surely our griefs He Himself bore, and our sorrows He carried; yet we ourselves esteemed Him stricken, *smitten* [or literally, "struck down"] *of God.*" Those in Isaiah 53 whose griefs were borne clearly understood that God was divinely judging this One, but erroneously concluded at that time that it was due to His own iniquity. Isaiah 53:6 shows that it was, in fact, God smiting Him, but for an entirely different purpose: "All of us like sheep have gone astray, each of us has turned to his own way; *but the LORD has caused* the iniquity of us all to fall on [literally, "to encounter"] Him." The language employed in this verse is strikingly similar to events related to the Day of Atonement. Isaiah 53:10 succinctly states, *"But the LORD was pleased to crush Him, putting Him to grief."* This is more than divine permission; this is divine activity. The second part of this verse offers the theological reason for God's action toward His Son: "If He would render Himself as a guilt offering, He will see His offspring [literally, "seed"], He will prolong His days, and the good pleasure of the LORD will prosper in His hand." God would bless the Son for His obedience even unto death, but the blessing would be at some designated time in the future. The cross was the time of striking, not uplifting. The Holy Word requires it—in some unique way that *only* God can do it—and does so even beyond what Isaiah 53 reveals.

After singing a hymn to close the Passover meal, Jesus left for Gethsemane with His eleven (Matt. 26:30). The next verse, Matthew 26:31 (also Mark 14:27), states the following, quoting a Messianic prophecy from Zechariah 13:7: "Then Jesus said to them, 'You will all fall away because of Me this night, for it is written, "I will strike down the shepherd, and the sheep of the flock shall be scattered."'" The Greek word for "strike down" does, in fact, mean to strike or to strike down. While it can have a milder sense of "touch" or "tap" (such as when the angel strikes Peter's thigh in Acts 12:7), it is generally used for a strong striking or striking down. For example, the same word is used for Moses "striking down the Egyptian" in Acts 7:24. John also uses the same word in reference to the return of the King, where the Messiah's sword will be the means by which "He may smite the nations" (Rev. 19:15). When Jesus was about to be arrested, the panicking disciples cried out, "Lord, shall we strike [same word] with the sword?" (Luke 22:49). One did not wait for permission: "And behold, one of those who were with Jesus reached and drew out his sword, and struck [same word] the slave of the high priest, and cut off his ear" (Matt. 26:51; also Mark 14:47; Luke 22:50). John 18:10-11 identifies the assailant as Peter.

But we need to look closely at what Jesus said. The Messiah used a first person singular "I," not the plural "they:" "I will strike down the shepherd," not "*They* will strike." Who is the "I" of whom Jesus spoke? The full quotation of Zechariah 13:7 uniquely requires God the Father's active involvement: "'Awake, O sword, against My Shepherd, and against the man, My Associate,' declares the LORD of hosts. 'Strike the Shepherd that the sheep may be scattered; and I will turn My hand against the little ones.'" While human and satanic agents all had a part, the Word mandates a specific and deliberate striking of

God's Messiah by the Father—a fact that we would never know unless God revealed it. Somewhere in the crucifixion narrative, in order for Scripture to be fulfilled, there must be a divine striking of God's own Shepherd by God Himself. Many commentators who have written on Zechariah 13:7, while not discussing its ramifications, observe that in the same way the worthless shepherd of Zechariah 11:17 will be struck down, now it will be God's Shepherd who is struck. Somewhat surprised at what the verse reveals, yet desiring not to deviate from God's Word, many conclude that apparently the One who wields the sword against the Son is God Himself.

And so it was. The arrest set the stage for the wielding of God's sword, but there was much more to come.

Movies depicting the events with the crucifixion focus primarily on the physical pain caused by human agents because that is what even unbelievers understand about the horrors of a crucifixion. The physical brutality receives the emphasis because often it is all they can comprehend. The spiritual side—to which Jesus had repeatedly referred— remains hidden to the world at large, but it is true nonetheless and very much a part of the pain Jesus endured on the cross. Even more to the point, the agony of the spiritual pain was the primary reason His image was marred more than any man's as the Son endured this portion of the cup that the Father had given Him in eternity past, the one He alone was able to drink.

So stepping back to view the six-hour crucifixion, this scenario emerges. Satan and his forces assaulted Jesus for the first three hours. Then, in the very midst of their savagery, God the Father approached God the Son. Satan and his legions would not know exactly why the Father had come to the cross. If holy angels had a difficult time understanding what God was about to do (1 Pet. 1:12), how much less the totally defiled demonic world would know. Having always feared the Son even in His humility, how much more would demons tremble in the presence of God Almighty? They may have concluded that the Father came to revenge His Son. Fearing God they most likely would have rapidly dispersed in terror, even as they repeatedly had done when encountering the Son in His humility throughout the Gospel accounts.

It seems best to understand that Satan had completed his God-granted hour of authority at this point. He would no more play a major role in the crucifixion from this point onward; Scripture makes no more reference to him again regarding the crucifixion. What would transpire now lay only in the Father's hands. Jesus had endured so much by the midpoint of His crucifixion, yet the two most horrific aspects of His suffering were only now beginning. No one needed to explain to either the angelic or demonic realm the key question at hand: what would God the Father do once He approached His Son?

To the perplexed astonishment of the holy angelic world and to the utter disbelief of Satan and his angels, the Father began striking the Son with wrath — violent, divine wrath poured out in vengeance upon the only Guilt Offering worthy to receive it (Isa. 53:10). Approximately two thousand years earlier in Genesis 22, God had instructed Abraham to sacrifice Isaac by his own hand. He did not instruct him to have someone else perform the offering. In a command that resonates of another Father and beloved Son later revealed in John 3:16, God commanded the father Abraham to "take now your son, your only son, whom you love, Isaac, and go to the land of Moriah; and offer him there as a burnt offering on one of the mountains of which I will tell you" (Gen. 22:2). In the Genesis account the Angel of the Lord intervened to stop Abraham's sacrifice; later with His own Son the Father would not stay the execution. In keeping with the prophetic picture established by Abraham and Isaac, God would raise His own hand against His Son, His only Son whom He loved.

Jesus remained silent during this phase of His suffering — the Lamb silent before the Chief Shearer (Isa. 53:7). For three hours Jesus endured unspeakable torment, matched only by the Father's holy capacity to strike so severely the One He loved so infinitely.

Jesus accomplished so much the day He died, most of which God reveals later in the epistles. One vital certainty that we know occurred; the Son bore the full wrath of God to the extent necessary to satisfy God's standard of holiness. We of limited perspective can understand neither the loftiness of God's holiness nor the amount of sacrifice necessary to atone for even *one* solitary sin which, by the way, was sufficient for the resulting death, curse, and dismissal from God's presence in the Genesis 3 account. Only Jesus experientially understands what is required to bear the weight of sin to the degree necessary to appease the holy God. How much less can we comprehend the cumulative sins of one's entire life, let alone including anyone else's sin as part of the task? Perhaps this is an aspect of Paul's desire in Ephesians 1:17-19, "that the God of our Lord Jesus Christ, the Father of glory, may give to you a spirit of wisdom and of revelation in the knowledge of Him. I pray that the eyes of your heart may be enlightened, so that you may know what is the hope of His calling, what are the riches of the glory of His inheritance in the saints, and what is the surpassing greatness of His power toward us who believe." Part of this understanding comes in perceiving more in depth the Father's selfless giving of the Son, as well as the Son's selfless giving of Himself—and what the Son received in our place vastly surpasses any adequate description we could muster.

That God Himself poured out wrath on His own Son may seem either impossible or absurdly cruel to some when initially considered. After all, this hardly sounds like a loving God. Part of the reason this concept sounds so strange is that many churches and much of what is considered to be Christianity have virtually eradicated the wrath of God from their teachings. Natural man never understands such deep doctrinal truths, nor properly appraises them (1 Cor. 2:14), because such a concept originates in the Person and mind of God—not in the mind of fallen man. The fact that God indeed does evoke holy wrath is quite often either purposely or ignorantly removed in Word-starved churches with a watered-down doctrine, but it never has been erased from the Person of God or His Word—and that is all that matters.

The wrath of God has properly been defined as His deep-seated, burning anger against sin when contrasted with God's perfect holiness. Scripture indicates the scope of God's wrath is vastly broad and encompassing, as Romans 1:18 indicates: "For the wrath of God is revealed from heaven against all ungodliness and unrighteousness of men." This is a concept we should by no means pass over lightly; the wrath of God stands against *all* ungodliness and *all* unrighteousness. This wrath is not just against what we consider heinous acts by the vilest of the vile, but against *all* ungodliness and *all* unrighteousness. This includes our sinful thoughts and deeds: every one of them—our worst and even our smallest. In contrasting the spiritual standing of the saved and the unsaved, John wrote, "He who believes in the Son has eternal life; but he who does not obey the Son shall not see life, but the *wrath of God abides on him*" (John 3:36). John employed a present tense verb in the Greek; the abiding wrath is a continuous and perpetual condition that does not and cannot change by its own initiative. At this point the lost usually do not understand—or believe—that God's wrath currently abides on them. Nevertheless it does. Unless this status is drastically altered through new life in Christ, the condition changes from positional abiding wrath to the experiential abiding wrath of God. In other words, the wrath that is already abiding but not manifested then becomes the experiential torture of their eternity, which they will most certainly know forever and ever.

The wrath of God may involve a cataclysmic death of those on earth, but it does not end there. Death is not an escape from God's wrath; on the contrary, those who were not saved during their earthly life enter into the eternal abiding and active wrath of God. Scripture supports this. For instance, after only the first six seals, the terrified lost of the Tribulation will cry out to the mountains and rocks in Revelation 6:16-17, "Fall on us and hide us from the presence of Him who sits on the throne, and from the wrath of the Lamb; *for the great day of their wrath has come;* and who is able to stand?" Stated differently, the pouring out of God's wrath is not just an event but rather an entrance into an eternal condition. The everlasting fate of the lost can be seen in Revelation 14:9-11:

> And another angel, a third one, followed them, saying with a loud voice, "If anyone worships the beast and his image, and receives a mark on his forehead or upon his hand, *he also will drink of the wine of the wrath of God, which is mixed in full strength in the cup of His anger;* and he will be tormented with fire and brimstone in the presence of the holy angels and in the presence of the Lamb.

> And the smoke of their torment goes up forever and ever; and they have no rest day and night, those who worship the beast and his image, and whoever receives the mark of his name."

The context of the previous passage relates to the beast worshipers in the Tribulation, but this description need not be restricted to this group since they will not be the only ones who will drink the full strength of God's wrath and be tormented forever. Revelation 19:15 describes the return of Jesus as follows: "And from His mouth comes a sharp sword, so that with it He may smite the nations; and He will rule them with a rod of iron; *and He treads the wine press of the fierce wrath of God, the Almighty.*" An aspect of this divine wrath follows later with the Great White Throne judgment (Rev. 20), which culminates with eternal damnation as the unredeemed are cast into the lake of fire.

We who are saved should note this to our core: *every* reference to the wrath of God being poured out on the unredeemed, we deserve. *Every* reference about receiving the full wrath of God was once true for us — and once abided on us — and would be just as true for us now unless we had a satisfactory Sacrifice accepted by God to remove His wrath from us. How great then our salvation for those who are in Christ Jesus! Having begun Romans 5 declaring that the redeemed currently possess peace with God (5:1), Paul further developed the enormous privilege that God grants His redeemed: "But God demonstrates His own love toward us, in that while we were yet sinners, Christ died for us. Much more then, having now been justified by His blood, *we shall be saved from the wrath of God through Him*" (Rom. 5:8-9). True children of God never have to worry about the wrath of God as it pertains to either their eternal identity or to their eternal destiny; it is a biblical impossibility for the wrath of God to abide on a true child of God. First Thessalonians 1:10 states it is Jesus "who delivers us from the wrath to come." Later in the same book Paul wrote, "For God has not destined us for wrath, but for obtaining salvation through our Lord Jesus Christ" (5:9). However, the wrath of God should remain in a believer's focus because of two important reasons: first, in thankfulness to God for removing His wrath away from them, and second, by presenting intercessory prayer for the lost on whom the wrath of God presently abides.

An immeasurable exchange takes place whenever anyone is saved. How vast the transition is for one who, literally in the Greek text, "delivered us out of the domain of the darkness and transferred us into the kingdom of His beloved Son" (Col. 1:13). Redemption is not restricted merely to the escape of hell. Salvation includes the bringing into a right relationship between putridly defiled sinners and a pure and holy God. Simply put, at the point of salvation one is totally reconciled to God, as He forever removes His wrath from His child. Second Corinthians 5:14–20 so beautifully proclaims this eternal truth:

> For the love of Christ controls us, having concluded this, that one died for all, therefore all died; and He died for all, that they who live should no longer live for themselves, but for Him who died and rose again on their behalf.
>
> Therefore from now on we recognize no man according to the flesh; even though we have known Christ according to the flesh, yet now we know Him thus no longer.
>
> Therefore if any man is in Christ, he is a new creature; the old things passed away; behold, new things have come.
>
> Now all these things are from God, who reconciled us to Himself through Christ, and gave us the ministry of reconciliation, namely, that God was in Christ reconciling the world to Himself, not counting

their trespasses against them, and He has committed to us the word
of reconciliation.

Therefore, we are ambassadors for Christ, as though God were entreating through us; we beg you on behalf of Christ, be reconciled to God.

God replaced His abiding wrath with *total* reconciliation between
Himself and the redeemed. The contrasts between the two conditions
continuously shout their differences throughout eternity: death—now
life; abiding divine wrath—now peace; utter condemnation—now
reconciliation.

The truth of 2 Corinthians 5:18, however, should not be something
that we casually read and then set aside in our thoughts: "Now all
these things are from God, who reconciled us to Himself through
Christ." We need to understand this better and appreciate what took
place at the cross. Our sins did not go away by themselves; they did
not evaporate. Our sins did not disappear because of some sort of an
imaginary sweep of God's divine eraser. Our sins were borne by the
One of whom the Scripture speaks. As we have previously seen,
Colossians 2:13-14 support this: "And when you were dead in your
transgressions and the uncircumcision of your flesh, He made you
alive together with Him, having forgiven us all our transgressions,
having canceled out the certificate of debt consisting of decrees against
us and which was hostile to us; and He has taken it out of the way, *having nailed it to the cross.*" Our sins were nailed to the same cross to
which Jesus was nailed. *He* was there; and in a way recognized only to
the Godhead, so were our sins.

Scripture repeatedly states that Jesus bore our sins on His cross.
Again, the Isaiah 53 passages reveal this: "Surely our griefs He Himself
bore" (Isa. 53:4). In the same chapter: "As a result of the anguish of His
soul, He will see it and be satisfied; by His knowledge the Righteous
One, My Servant, will justify the many, as *He will bear their iniquities.*
Therefore, I will allot Him a portion with the great, and He will divide
the booty with the strong; because He poured out Himself to death,
and was numbered with the transgressors; yet *He Himself bore the sin* of
many, and interceded for the transgressors" (Isa. 53:11-12). The
Apostle Peter referred to this same concept when he wrote his first
epistle, stating, "and He Himself [emphatic in the Greek] *bore our sins
in His body on the cross,* that we might die to sin and live to righteousness; for by His wounds you were healed" (1 Pet. 2:24).

Jesus bore our sins on the cross—not only at the end of the crucifixion when He died. All throughout His crucifixion He bore them, but in a unique capacity the last three hours of the cross were by far the heaviest. We must remember: "The wrath of God is revealed from heaven against all ungodliness and unrighteousness" (Rom. 1:18). So how did the Holy God inflict His wrath on Jesus for all our ungodliness and unrighteousness? Scripture states it best with one sentence that will take us all eternity to grasp fully — if we ever can at all. The last sentence in 2 Corinthians 5 summarizes what Paul has been arguing. The reason that we are reconciled to God comes down to this one eternally sublime revelatory truth: "He made Him who knew no sin to be sin on our behalf, that we might become the righteousness of God in Him" (2 Cor. 5:21).

We often casually sing songs or read about "the wrath of God completely satisfied" in Jesus, often without considering the magnitude of that statement. But we must pause and consider this because it is so vital to our reconciliation with God. Was the wrath of God actually completely satisfied through the blood of Jesus? Obviously this is true as is evident from the multiple references we have seen. But consider this: in order for Jesus to satisfy God's wrath, at some point He had to receive God's wrath. In order *to receive God's wrath*, God had *to pour out His wrath* on His Son. So here is the question before us: When did Jesus receive God's wrath? By whom did He receive it? The wrath *of* God must come *from* God. This must be some direct act from God; it *cannot* be some subsidiary by-product. While God can use angels to administer His wrath (Rev. 15:1), it is still His wrath. No other beings possess the wrath of God. Good angels cannot. Satan's wrath by no means equals God's wrath. Fallen humanity? Hardly. The wrath of God comes only from God.

Consider then the sheer absurdity of this question: Will those who ultimately receive the wrath of God notice it, feel it, or respond in any way when it occurs? Will those on whom the wrath of God currently abides (John 3:36), but do not yet have its full consequences, change in any way when they finally do fully receive it? Matthew 25:30 describes those who are tormented as enduring in a place where "there shall be weeping and gnashing of teeth." We saw in Revelation 14:10-11 that the worshipers of the beast "will drink of the wine of the wrath of God, which is mixed in full strength in the cup of His anger; and he will be tormented with fire and brimstone in the presence of the holy angels and in the presence of the Lamb. And the smoke of their torment goes up forever and ever." Interestingly, the Revelation 14 passage uses the same terminology of drinking God's wrath from a cup given them by God.

Fully alive and fully aware—and fully tormented—when the wrath of God is poured out. Would it be any less true for Jesus? Would He notice it? Would He feel it? Eternally more than we have the capacity to comprehend would the Lamb of God know and feel when God poured out His wrath on Him.

Jesus bore our sins, but He also bore the wrath of God for all believers.

The Bible does not disclose the exact means by which God poured out His wrath on His Son. We only know from the Word that He did because we see that His sacrifice was sufficient and accepted. The Son exhausted God's wrath for the redeemed. Whatever God required for His wrath to be received and satisfied, *He* had to pour out, just as He will in Revelation 14 and elsewhere. Whatever God required for His wrath to be received and satisfied, Jesus accomplished fully, wholly, completely in the cup of the New Covenant in His blood—as part of the cup that He alone was able to drink.

God did not make Jesus a sinner; God did not treat Jesus as sinful.

"[God] made Him who knew no sin . . ."

We have such a high priest, holy, innocent, undefiled,
Separated from sinners and exalted above the heavens (Heb. 7:26).
Tempted in all things as we are, yet without sin (Heb. 4:15).
Who committed no sin, nor was any deceit found in His mouth (1 Pet. 2:22).
And in Him there is no sin (1 John 3:5).

" . . . to be [or "become"] sin on our behalf . . ."

For the wrath of God is revealed from heaven
Against all ungodliness;
Against all unrighteousness (Rom 1:18).
For the wrath of God once abided—on Him—who became sin in our behalf (John 3:36; 2 Cor. 5:21).

". . . that we might become the righteousness of God in Him."

God's wrath poured out on Jesus made Satan's previous tormenting minuscule in comparison. What Satan inflicted on Jesus in no way compares with what the Father could do—and, in fact, what the Father did do.

God required appeasement for sin—not Satan.
God alone has a divine standard of righteousness—not Satan.
God alone possessed the capacity to pour out *divine* wrath—not Satan.

God alone cared about the atonement for the sins of the redeemed — not Satan.

God laid the totality of the world's sin on His Son; Jesus bore the totality of the sin of the world (John 1:29). We know this concept in principle, but we must stop there. Our present limitations force us to wait until we get to heaven to have Jesus explain it to us personally because no one other than Jesus experientially knows what is required to appease the righteousness of God and absorb His wrath for even *one* of our own sins, much less for our accumulated sins of our lifetime. We who are redeemed have had this done for us; angels have never experientially received grace and pardon. Those that will endure eternal hell will be no step closer to appeasing one sin they committed even after being there for a thousand years. Only Jesus experientially knows what is required.

The mere thought of the aggregate burden of one's own sin — let alone the weight of every sin ever committed from Adam onward — overwhelms us. At least the vilest offender who will receive God's wrath, perhaps with the exception of Satan, will not have the wrath deserved by others laid on him. For those who hold that the death of Jesus was only for the elect, still the magnitude of what He bore goes beyond our capacity to comprehend: "Worthy art Thou to take the book, and to break its seals; for Thou wast slain, and didst purchase for God with Thy blood men from *every* tribe and tongue and people and nation" (Rev. 5:9). We possess neither spiritual nor mental capacities to understand it completely. We could more easily fathom numbering the sands of all the beaches in the world, giving each granule a specific name, and then recalling each grain of sand by name. Multiply this by billions, and you will begin to understand some of the depth of God's love through Jesus Christ. We cannot even begin to seize it in thought — the magnitude of such a proposal rests only within the Godhead. No wonder angels fervently desire to look into the things related to salvation. No other event in history past or present even remotely compares to the divine love demonstrated that one dark day — as the Servant of Yahweh had His form altered and His appearance disfigured more than anyone who ever has or ever will live.

God did not look away from Jesus as the Lamb atoned for sins. During the darkness the Father looked fully on the Son. Each knew what the Other was doing during this unique second aspect of the cup that the Father had determined that His Son must drink. Is it any wonder that He was marred more than any Son of Adam ever had been

(Isa. 52:14)? How could He possibly not be?

For three hours—divine wrath inflicted and received by the One alone able to do so.

For three hours—silent, willful submission by the Lamb of God, the Servant of Yahweh.

For three hours—Jesus bore the full burden of sins past, present, and future.

For three hours—the Father smote the Son with the full wrath He alone could render.

And then—He stopped.

4

THE SEPARATION

T his is the shortest chapter I have ever written. I do not state this as a complaint; sometimes a profound truth projected by itself stands in greater contrast than it would if related truths surrounded it. Often people pay closer attention to a diamond solitaire set against a dark velvet backdrop more than they would to several diamonds clustered together among other displays of jewelry. Hopefully the bittersweet nugget of God's truth within this chapter will likewise stand alone. It may stand in isolation, but it will not be forgotten. In fact, I hazard to predict that you will ponder this truth many times throughout the rest of your life.

We begin the third and final phase of what made the cup for Jesus uniquely what He alone was able to drink, as well as what made His appearance different from that of any other. The previous two elements have been completed; first, enduring the full wrath of Satan during his God-ordained hour and authority of the darkness, and second, and vastly beyond the first, the Son enduring the full wrath of God to a degree sufficient to atone for sins. Yet as unspeakably horrendous as these two were, there remained one more aspect. The third part of His cup was the last; the third part was the shortest—and yet the third part was by far the most unbearable.

Matthew, Mark, and Luke all record that the darkness over Christ's cross covered the whole land from about noon until about the ninth hour, that is, 3:00 P.M. As we have previously seen, all three authors employ the word *until* in describing the darkness: the darkness lasted *until* the ninth hour (Matt. 27:45-46; Mark 15:33; Luke 23:44). It is at the ninth hour that Jesus cried out, "My God! My God! Why hast Thou forsaken Me?"

(Matt. 27:46: Mark 15:34). The inference that each Gospel writer gives is the darkness ceased just before Jesus cried out to God the Father. From the information given in Scripture it seems that the darkness had a specific advent and departure; it approached, resided, and then withdrew. Perhaps its arrival was instantaneous; perhaps it arrived slowly but noticeably. Perhaps the darkness was observable from a distance as it approached; perhaps it was even the darkness that was felt as in Exodus 10:21: "Then the LORD said to Moses, 'Stretch out your hand toward the sky, that there may be darkness over the land of Egypt, even a darkness which may be felt.'" We do not have enough information provided for us to be certain, but the darkness had a definite beginning that would have been quite noticeable to the witnesses of the crucifixion. Observers also would have noticed the departure of the darkness—and it was just that, a departure. The darkness did not fade into light; the darkness removed itself from the scene. The advent of a previously unknown darkness would have alarmed all the people of the land. The disappearance of such unexplained darkness would likewise have caused great bewilderment to those present. The overall effect that this would have on people would never leave them, even if they had no comprehension of what was occurring. Luke 23:48 indicates: "And all the multitudes who came together for this spectacle, when they observed what had happened, began to return, beating their breasts." Obviously they knew something unique had taken place in their very midst.

Jesus' cry unto God the Father was His first recorded words in three hours. His shout would have jolted the somber witnesses and bystanders. The arrival of the darkness no doubt frightened some who earlier had been blaspheming and ridiculing Jesus. Perhaps thinking a violent storm approached, many most likely returned to the protective shelter of their homes. After all, Jesus was not going anywhere.

Then, after the prolonged silence, after the darkness, the Light of the world cried out in agony unto God the Father, "My God! My God! Why have You forsaken Me?" A departure had transpired—a divine separation never before experienced, and one that never could possibly take place again. Since this unique moment in history, scholars have debated the meaning and significance of this forsaking of the Son by the Father. As with virtually everything else in biblical studies, various answers emerge as possible solutions. Based on the findings of the previous chapters, we may consider a logical and biblical explanation.

Adam knew separation from God and the resulting contamination after the Fall of man. With the first sin of humanity, man entered into a disjointed relationship with the heavenly Father. Adam recognized this altered state immediately, having an experiential base from which to make a comparison. He did not undergo a total separation from God, but then again, neither did Adam ever again enjoy the pure, undefiled fellowship with his Creator while living on fallen earth. Eventually in heaven Adam would renew what he once possessed with God—and infinitely beyond what he had previously experienced. Yet while living on earth, Adam enjoyed only a fractured fellowship. Fellowship with God existed, but sin marred its capacity to manifest itself fully, as it still does for us today. In the same manner, we who are saved currently enjoy fellowship with God (1 John 1:3), but it stands in stark contrast to what we will share in heaven. One day we will see Jesus face to face (1 Cor. 13:12), and even be like Him (1 John 3:2). In one sense we have it better than Adam because of our spiritual ignorance: we do not experientially know the richness of full fellowship with God without any trace or effect of sin, and then the gnawing agony of having it extracted from our life on earth.

But Jesus knew. John 1:1 states, "In the beginning was the Word, and the Word was with God, and the Word was God." In writing "the Word was *with God*," John used a more developed Greek phrase that depicts a face to face, intimate fellowship. Throughout eternity past, the Trinity basked in reciprocal fellowship. At the point of Mary's conception with Jesus, however, a separation of this heavenly fellowship took place. Sin played no part in robbing Jesus of His fellowship with God the Father and God the Holy Spirit; His separation from the full glory of God emerged out of grace and love. Salvation required the necessary sacrifice, and the Lamb of God who takes away the sins of the world uniquely possessed this capacity. But in order to accomplish mankind's deliverance, Jesus had to lay aside His status of face to face fellowship with the Father and the Holy Spirit. While on earth Jesus freely fellowshiped and communed with the Father as no other man had since Adam—and vastly beyond what Adam had known. Yet the full breadth of the Godhead's divine fellowship could not be enjoyed as long as Christ walked the earth as a man.

In Philippians 2:6-7 the Apostle Paul described what a tremendous step downward from glory the Incarnation was for Jesus: "Who, although He existed in the form of God, did not regard equality with God a thing to be grasped, but emptied Himself, taking the form of a bond-servant, and being made in the likeness of men." When Jesus emptied Himself, He abandoned His full, intimate fellowship with the Father in their domain of glory, surrounded by the worshipful heavenly host, choosing instead to walk among—and even become part of—His own creation. Although He communed with His Father throughout His earthly ministry, Jesus yearned for the deep fellowship the Trinity had previously enjoyed throughout eternity past. Just hours before His death, in His high priestly prayer of John 17, Jesus offered His perspective that we would never have known unless He had disclosed it: "And now, glorify Thou Me together with Thyself, Father, with the glory which I had with Thee before the world was" (17:5). Christ shared joyous fellowship with the Father during His humiliation, but with the exception of the Transfiguration, He did not share His glory. Forty days after His resurrection (Acts 1:3), Jesus would once more receive the glory rightfully due Him; in fact, glory even beyond that which He set aside when He came to earth, returning to heaven as Divine Conqueror (Rev. 4–5).

But before the resumption of reflective divine glory and the bliss of their reunited fellowship—fellowship we cannot comprehend until we are absorbed by it in heaven—Jesus faced a moment of complete separation from God the Father.

Ask any number of people their thoughts about hell and many would say that hell is the place where bad people go to be punished by the devil. Yet Scripture does not contain this. Actually, just the opposite will occur. God originally prepared hell for Satan and his angels (Matt. 25:41). Satan is not the sovereign master of hell; hell is the ultimate destiny of Satan, the place where he will be tormented throughout eternity (Rev. 20:10). Satan fears hell; he has good reason to do so. Others who are questioned about hell will describe the flames and the agony, which Scripture does support (Mark 9:43-49). While these aspects are true of hell, other biblical references offer another perspective that we may not have considered.

Jesus presented a different description that generally is neither noted nor used by most people when they describe hell. On three different occasions in Matthew, Jesus referred to hell as "the outer darkness." Matthew 8:12 records Jesus saying, "but the sons of the kingdom shall be cast out into *the outer darkness*; in that place there shall be weeping and gnashing of teeth." Matthew 22:13 and 25:30 state virtually the same thing and use identical wording to describe the darkness. Each of the three references in the Greek text has a definite article in front of the word *darkness* and in front of the word *outer*, describing it as *the* outer darkness. Each reference is followed by the word "there" or "in that place" ("*in that place* there shall be weeping"). Each reference has the preposition "into" in front of it ("they shall be cast out *into* the outer darkness").

Jesus' threefold reference to the outer darkness is an intriguing description. "Outer" or "outmost" is a term of specificity. The word occurs only within these three verses of the Greek New Testament, so we cannot look elsewhere for comparison or clarity. Yet the very description gives rise to points to ponder. If outer darkness exists, by default there must be something with which to compare it. In other words, something makes it the *outer* darkness. Otherwise only darkness would exist.

Possibly the outer darkness is the place where those residing in inner darkness go at their deaths. In writing to the Ephesians, Paul cautioned the readers not to live their lives as they had lived before receiving Christ: "that you walk no longer as the Gentiles also walk, in the futility of their mind, being darkened in their understanding, excluded from the life of God" (Eph. 4:17b-18a). Even more to the point, Paul reminded the Ephesians, "you were formerly darkness" (5:8). Paul wrote of a condition or an identity, not an environment. They formerly *were* darkness—not merely *in* darkness. Before receiving salvation everyone existed in this state of spiritual darkness. If this condition is not remedied by salvation through the Light of the world, those who die with inner darkness will exist forever, tormented in the outer darkness.

Still, another possibility exists as with what the outer darkness should be contrasted, which may offer a better solution. As always, nuggets embedded in God's Word require some digging to get to them.

One way to approach defining the outer darkness is to contrast it with what it is not. Because of their opposing natures, the best description of hell would be the differentiation between hell and the glory of God, since the glory of God is an aspect of God's dominion (such as in Isaiah 6). As we saw in John 17:5, the Son earnestly longed for reuniting in glory with the Father. God's glory extends infinitely beyond earth, because earth is only a small part of God's creation — or even possibly, God's creations. Psalm 19:1 states, "The heavens are telling of the glory of God; and their expanse is declaring the work of His hands." Every aspect of the heavens that God created — however many and however majestic they are — tell of His glory.

God's glory extends to wherever He is, and wherever God is consists of everywhere. God's glory is massively immense; we currently only partially witness it. While God currently displays aspects of His glory, such as in the heavens, for the most part He cloaks or hides His glory at the present time for the simple reason that God's full glory would be too overwhelming for mortals to endure. Also, God calls the righteous to live by faith and not by sight. Part of this faith entails believing God's glory exists, even when we cannot fully see it and believing that God is worth pursuing, even when He seems removed from us. God calls us to believe the glory He will one day reveal to us vastly surpasses any hardship and darkness of this present age (2 Cor. 4:17-18). We will eventually behold and experience the full glory that God longs to reveal to us when we enter into His presence in heaven: overflowing, uninterrupted fellowship between the redeemed and the Redeemer. No sin, no factions, no jealousy, no human limitations, no defilements from Satan — just the unadulterated fellowship the Trinity now shares in fullness and multiplied billions of times over.

Yet somewhere in His great expanse God prepared an extremely small portion where He chooses to remove His glory. While hell will have flame and torment, 2 Thessalonians 1:9 gives perhaps the best description of hell in all of the Bible. Writing about those who do not come to obey the Gospel of Jesus, Paul wrote, "And these will pay the penalty of eternal destruction, *away from the presence of the Lord and from the glory of His power.*" This then is the simple, but profound, description of hell: the eternal separation of the damned from God's presence and glory of His power. Heaven is heaven only because of the presence of God. Remove God's presence from heaven and all that is left is a blissful amusement park consisting primarily of children's rides. One does not have fellowship with things — one has fellowship with living beings. And since heaven is heaven because of God's presence, then it would reason hell is hell because of God's absence — or at least, the perception of God's absence. Actually God will still in some way be present even within this outer darkness. Revelation 14:10 explains that those in hell "will be tormented with fire and brimstone in the presence of the holy angels and in the presence of the Lamb." While the outer darkness is in full view of God, He nonetheless will remove any indication or demonstration of His presence or glory. For those imprisoned in hell, the resulting effect will be eternal separation from God and His glory — perpetually tormented throughout eternity in the outer darkness.

As noted, the Bible states that hell was originally prepared for Satan and his angels (Matt. 25:41). We need to consider what the word "prepared" means. This aspect of God's creation differs from His creation of the heavens and the earth depicted in Genesis. Technically speaking God did not create hell — He prepared it, employing the same word that Jesus spoke of in John 14:3 where He told His sullen disciples, "I go to prepare a place for you." God did not say in reference to hell, "Let there be darkness! Let there be torment! Let there be fire! Let there be punishment!" Instead He simply selected a relatively small sliver of His infinite expanse and purposefully removed any evidence of His presence and glory. The end result is hell. The darkness, torment, and fire — which are assuredly there — are merely effects of the absence of God's glory, much in the same way one does not create darkness; one removes the light. Perhaps the varying degrees of punishments for those in hell correlate with how far removed from God's glory one will be in the outer darkness. The farther the removal, the greater the agony.

Separation from God, then, best describes what Jesus experienced on the cross in this third spiritual component of the cup He must drink: the total separation and removal from God's presence. His separation was only temporary, but a separation uniquely agonizing for One so pure, for the One who knew in the deepest measure what it meant to have fellowship with God. We too will have this same fullness of God's presence one day in heaven. In the meanwhile we can no more comprehend this future blessing any more than we can fully understand God's holiness and love. Our fallen human perspective simply limits us. The spotless Lamb, the holy Son, who once fully enjoyed the glory reserved only for the Godhead (John 17:5), would understand better than anyone else ever born the depth of pain resulting from God's turning away from Him. Not even Adam in his pre-Fall state knew the agonizing depths of this type of separation. Momentary separation from God may not sound so bad to us; however, we have not known the divine fellowship Jesus knew — we do not currently possess the capacity to view this as He would. The absence of the Father would be the most unspeakable agony our Savior would encounter. Perhaps even the thought of this caused Jesus the greatest pain in His spiritual wrestling in Gethsemane. In some way on Calvary, in some manner reserved uniquely for the One alone able, Jesus experienced total separation from the Father.

The intensity of the progression that Jesus endured staggers us.

The physical assault of the beatings, scourging, and crucifixion was horrendous, especially to the unblemished Lamb of God. Yet as bad as those were — and certainly not to make light of them — it was relatively mild when contrasted against the full arsenal of Satan's authority thrown against the Son during their God-given hour of the darkness. Spiritual pain always vastly overrides physical pain, such as we saw with the agony Jesus endured in Gethsemane. Then as horrific as the satanic assault was, it too diminishes when weighed against the full wrath of God that Jesus received for three hours. We bow in abject wonder at what He endured — and even more so for whom He endured. Yet even with the totality of the physical pain and the satanic torment, and then the wrath of God poured out on Him, not through all of these did Jesus ever cry out. The final aspect — the separation from God — was by far the most unbearable. Mark this well, beloved: in all that He had previously endured, only in this last remaining portion of His cup did Jesus scream in untold agony.

This separation from God gives us a better idea of what Christ accomplished in His atoning sacrifice, but sadly it also gives us a better idea of what hell is like. Take away any love, goodness, joy, peace, hope — and this starts to describe hell. Add flames of torment in a lake of fire, and hell seems more real to us because we can perceive of roaring, violent flames on earth — and they frighten us. But make sure you add to your definition of hell the separation from the presence of the Lord, away from the glory of His power. When we do so we hit a wall in our thinking. We cannot fully perceive such separation even in principle since we who are saved are eternally secure in Christ. Simply put, it is a biblical impossibility for the redeemed to be separated from God. In a magnanimous gesture the Apostle Paul wrote concerning His kinsmen Israel in Romans 9:3, "For I could wish that I myself were accursed, separated from Christ for the sake of my brethren." Of course, Paul knew that this could never happen. Paul simply showed by means of hyperbole his great love for his fellow Jews. Paul knew even if he could wish it, no possibility whatsoever existed for those in Christ to be separated from God. A few verses earlier in Romans 8:35-39 he wrote,

"Who shall *separate* us from the love of Christ? Shall tribulation, or distress, or persecution, or famine, or nakedness, or peril, or sword? . . . For I am convinced that neither death, nor life, nor angels [the bad ones], nor principalities, nor things present, nor things to come, nor powers, nor height, nor depth, nor any other created thing [and that includes us], shall be able to *separate* us from the love of God, which is in Christ Jesus our Lord." As before, no wonder angels frequently converse about matters pertaining to salvation; it is matchless in its active demonstration of God's grace and love.

The last agony Jesus experienced before His death was literally hell on the earth. He experienced "the outer darkness" as God the Father removed Himself from God the Son. This darkness need not have flames; it necessitated only the removal of God's presence and glory. Jesus had to experience separation from God only temporarily; He did not need to remain within its confines. However, *every* other human or spiritual being who will endure this eternal separation will have either a resurrected body or a spiritual body (such as demons have) capable of enduring the outer darkness. *He* did not. *He* alone in all history partook of the outer darkness within the frailty of a human body. As we have seen so many times before, is it any wonder "His appearance was marred more than any man, and His form more than the sons of men" (Isa. 52:14)? How could it not be?

This concept of hell should strongly motivate believers to share the Light of the Gospel actively as they prayerfully intercede for the lost who are currently headed to the outer darkness. While we cannot fully grasp the concept of eternity in heaven, even less can we begin to conceive of eternity in hell.

We of the Christian world grow soft, myself at the forefront. Our nice relatives, good neighbors, friends, and acquaintances await a destiny of which God has given us a preview. Even a momentary encounter caused Jesus to cry out in torment to God the Father. How long will those cry out who are eternally damned? Help us Lord, to be light to Your Light. Burden our hearts for those who do not know You—and most likely do not know of or believe in the eternal separation that awaits them in the outer darkness.

5

THE BOUNDARIES

"It is finished!" Jesus released His victory shout only seconds before He yielded up His spirit unto God the Father. Indeed it was finished: the Servant of Yahweh had given His life as a ransom for many—the Christ crucified. Behold! The Lamb of God who takes away the sin of the world! The Father's righteous standard of justice had been met as God poured out His wrath in the cup of the New Covenant. The Son had crushed the serpent's head. Divine reconciliation was accomplished. Indeed, the most stupendous day in the history of mankind had ended.

Those involved in any way with Jesus and His crucifixion, both friend and opponent, had every indication that Jesus had in fact died, leaving this world behind Him. Still, regardless of people's various assessments of Him, the death of Jesus was not merely another execution of some political malcontent. The Gospels present a series of unique events associated with the crucifixion, many of which would cause heated conversation and debate for decades among those present. The temple veil that concealed the Holy of Holies—and access to God Himself—was torn from top to bottom (Matt. 27:51). A mammoth earthquake shook the land. A few days later, several Old Testament saints, centuries dead, "coming out of the tombs after His resurrection . . . entered the holy city and appeared to many" (Matt. 27:53).

Some of Jesus' grief-stricken followers made hastily arranged burial preparations. Likewise the chief priests and Pharisees concerned themselves about the burial, but for entirely different reasons. Matthew 27:62-64 explains their intent:

> Now on the next day, which is the one after the preparation, the chief priests and the Pharisees gathered together with Pilate, and said, "Sir,

> we remember that when He was still alive that deceiver said, 'After three days I am to rise again.'
>
> "Therefore, give orders for the grave to be made secure until the third day, lest the disciples come and steal Him away and say to the people, 'He has risen from the dead,' and the last deception will be worse than the first."

At their request Pilate dispatched a guard to seal and keep watch over the tomb of Jesus. How ironic that the enemies of Jesus understood His predictions of rising from the grave more than did the totality of His beloved disciples. None of His followers, neither men nor women, waited near the tomb in order to witness this frequently prophesied return of Life.

While offering additional details to fill in some sections, in essence the Bible limits itself to a three-part emphasis of the death of Jesus: the sacrificial Lamb of God had been slain; the dead Messiah buried; the resurrected Lion of Judah had been brought back to life three days later. Then came the subsequent appearances. This is the same order that Paul presented in 1 Corinthians 15:3-5: "For I delivered to you as of first importance what I also received, that Christ died for our sins according to the Scriptures, and that He was buried, and that He was raised on the third day according to the Scriptures, and that He appeared to Cephas, then to the twelve." We also know that after the resurrection Jesus "presented Himself alive, after His suffering, by many convincing proofs, appearing to them over a period of forty days, and speaking of the things concerning the kingdom of God" (Acts 1:3). At the end of the forty days of teaching, Jesus ascended into heaven where He currently dwells (Ps. 110:1; Acts 1:9-11; Heb. 8:1), and from there He will soon return (Phil. 3:20-21).

While the Gospels offer insight into certain events and personalities following the death of Jesus, extensive gaps in the account remain. A most important topic, as repeatedly demonstrated in the previous chapters, relates to the spiritual enemies of Jesus. While Satan and his legions were so active in bringing Jesus to the cross and wrought a tremendous amount of His torment, they receive virtually no mention after Jesus' death. Considering how much the Bible reveals about Satan's hour and the power of darkness before Jesus' death, one would think that at least some explanatory statement would be included — but the Gospels present none. This is odd. The Gospels interweave the human and satanic elements involved in bringing about Christ's death, and then shift to focus only on the earthly persons and activities. Satan had witnessed all the events of the Cross. What did he do when Jesus died? Did Satan cry out in triumph, or did he stand by in abjectly perplexed silence? Did he flee the cross in fear or rage as God the Father approached, or after Jesus' shout of victory? Did Satan comprehend the significance of what had happened? Did he think he had won by default, or did he conclude that he had utterly lost? Did Satan anticipate the resurrection, and if so, did he attempt to keep Jesus in the grave? Scripture does not give information into most of these matters, so while dwelling on them may spark interest, they will not lead to fruitful study. Human speculation never equates with "thus says the Lord."

Nevertheless, we do know that Jesus stayed active before His physical resurrection — His spirit remained alive, as is true with the spirit of everyone who dies. Jesus had informed the dying thief next to Him, "*Today* you shall be *with Me* in Paradise" (Luke 23:43) — not "three days later at My resurrection." We also know that Jesus had not yet ascended to the Father when Mary Magdalene first saw Him after the Resurrection: "Jesus said to her, 'Stop clinging to Me, for I have not yet ascended to the Father; but go to My brethren, and say to them, "I ascend to My Father and your Father, and My God and your God"'" (John 20:17). So while not restricted only to these matters, Scripture indicates that Jesus went to Paradise after His death, alive in His Spirit, waiting for the Resurrection to reunite soul and body. Here then is the core question we must consider: *does Scripture reveal anything else that Jesus did between His death and His resurrection?*

The Bible contains much humor, but, as is true for any humor, one has to understand the culture, the people, and the setting in order to appreciate it. One of the most amusing biblical statements is the one Peter made in reference to Paul in 2 Peter 3:15-16: "Just as also our beloved brother Paul, according to the wisdom given him, wrote to you, as also in all his letters, speaking in them of these things, *in which are some things hard to understand.*" Peter acknowledged Paul's revelation originated from God, considered Paul's writing as part of Scripture, and yet confessed that Paul wrote concepts so deep that one must carefully study them in order to grasp them mentally. The humor is that while Peter spoke of having a hard time understanding some of what Paul wrote, Peter himself wrote one of the — if not *the* — most controversial passages in all the Bible. In 1 Peter 3:18-20, having noted

Christ's sacrificial death, Peter revealed one activity that Jesus accomplished after His death but before His resurrection: Jesus was "made alive in the spirit, in which also He went and made proclamation to the spirits now in prison, who once were disobedient, when the patience of God kept waiting in the days of Noah, during the construction of the ark . . . ." *Everything* within these verses is controversial, leading to volumes of writings discussing them. Who are the spirits now in prison: are they human spirits or demonic beings? Did Jesus Himself or someone else do the preaching? What was the content of the message preached? Why preach to these particular spirits but not to others? When we think of preaching, we often think of salvation opportunities. Was this the thrust of the message? If so, and the imprisoned beings are human, does this suggest people (or at least some people) received a second opportunity for salvation after they have died? In addition to this, what does Noah have to do with anything related to Christ's death? Paul certainly wrote sublimely complex theology in his epistles, but Peter surely matched him in complexity by penning 1 Peter 3:18-20.

When considering the circumstances of the ones to whom Peter wrote, this passage becomes even more confusing. While Peter's statement about Christ's proclamation to the spirits intrigues us, its placement in Scripture is not where we would expect it. Peter wrote his first epistle to a group of churches who currently suffered and faced the distinct possibility of intensified persecution—perhaps even dying for their faith in Jesus. The tenor of the times had changed. No longer were Christians tolerated as some odd religious sect. Instead they had become enemies of the State. Thousands of Christians faced severe persecution. The wretched Roman emperor Nero would slaughter masses, often making Christians his spectacles at games or using their corpses as torches to illumine his garden party orgies. The barbarous nature of Nero's sins sickens us. What would you pray if you saw a friend or loved one impaled on a stake, doused with olive oil, and set afire so the perverted Roman emperor could entertain his equally perverted associates? Would it not cross your mind as to where God was during this godless carnage? How could God allow such hostilities against those who looked to Him as their Lord and Savior—and especially looked to Jesus as their Protector?

In the very midst of this time, Peter wrote to various Christian churches in Asia Minor about Jesus dying and making proclamation to the spirits now in prison. *Why?* Why write about spirits now in prison to believers who presently suffered and faced the distinct possibility of dying a martyr's death? Even if these Christians did not suffer person-ally, they nevertheless would suffer the trauma of watching many they loved become the pariah of the Roman Empire. They also endured the fear of suffering—that burdensome dread that people live under when their circumstances are so overwhelming. The likelihood that their greatest fears would soon materialize stifles all hope. What would you write to such believers if you had the opportunity? What would you say to believers today who may not have the Roman Empire persecuting them, but who remain engulfed in their own multifaceted suffering? Would you go to a hospital room of a friend who knew death would most likely arrive in only a few days and say, "Before I go I just want to remind you that Jesus went and made proclamation to the spirits now in prison?" Usually one picks his words rather carefully when ministering to those who are overwhelmed with fear or sorrow. Would the statement regarding spirits now in prison of 1 Peter 3:18-20 be part of your comfort theology?

It was for Peter. He wrote this spiritual truth to hurting and per-plexed believers as a means of comforting them and bolstering their faith. Still its placement within 1 Peter seems to be out of place—and there is no other correlating reference in the rest of the Bible to this particular activity of Christ. Since the passage is so controversial, befuddlement of the readers would seem the likely result instead of comfort. Peter was an aged apostle when he wrote this passage—he himself only months or weeks away from his own martyrdom. Being strong in the grace and knowledge of the Lord Jesus Christ, inspired by the Holy Spirit, Peter deemed it essential that he inform his perse-cuted readers about Jesus making proclamation to the disobedient spirits now in prison.

Again the simple question: *why?*

Both Peter and Paul described the Christian walk as one of warfare. Christians war not against individual or collective people, although individuals may be used in this conflict. The core warfare is against Satan and his forces of evil. Peter exhorted his readers in 1 Peter 5:8, "Be of sober spirit, be on the alert. *Your adversary, the devil*, prowls about like a roaring lion, seeking someone to devour." The word "adversary" could easily be translated "enemy." Enemies consist of those opposed to you, who seek victory over you, and the chief antag-onist of every Christian is Satan. Whenever true spiritual warfare flares, no matter the degree to which human agents are involved, trace the path back as far as you can, and you will never out walk Satan's footprints. Paul warned the Ephesians, "our struggle is not against flesh and blood, but against the rulers, against the powers, against the world forces of this darkness, against the spiritual forces of wickedness in the heavenly places" (Eph. 6:12). Paul wrote of "weapons of our warfare" necessary for spiritual battle (2 Cor. 10:4). This warfare motif is evident within the context of these verses: "For though we walk in the flesh, we do not war according to the flesh, for the weapons of our warfare are not of the flesh, but divinely powerful for the destruction of fortresses" (2 Cor. 10:3-4). Adversary, enemy, struggle, weapons of the warfare—each item points to a war in which, like it or not, Christians are frontline participants.

I remember reading these passages when I was a new Christian. I accepted and believed them, but I did not remotely understand them. Why would anyone want to be my enemy? What had I done to deserve enmity with anyone? Jesus instructed us to love, not to hate. How can one be in a war and yet not hate those involved? Of course, this was merely a child's deeply limited perspective, darkening God's counsel by words without knowledge (Job 38:2). Valid reasons exist for the warfare. For instance, Satan hates Jesus with an active, unholy passion. The very existence of the saved in Christ is more than a sufficient ground for Satan's hatred, simply because since Satan hates Jesus, he thus abhors everyone and everything associated with Him. Whenever people are saved, God redeems them "from the domain of darkness and. . . to the kingdom of His beloved Son" (Col. 1:13). Even beyond this is the fact that we whom the Lord has redeemed become eternal demonstrations of God's grace extended through the triumph of Jesus (Eph. 1:3-12; 1 Tim. 1:15-16)—and the enemy that Jesus triumphed over above all else was Satan. This perpetual warfare between God and the forces of evil has been an extended one, already having existed for many thousands of years before the triumphal shout, "It is finished!"

―――――――――――――――

To understand the ultimate spiritual conflict of the ages, we need to go back to the beginning—that is, the beginning as God revealed it. What transpired before Genesis is unknowable unless God discloses it—which for the most part, He did not. What God did choose to disclose are the grounds for the battle, the participants, and the promised outcome.

Genesis 1–2 records the pinnacle of God's creation, namely, mankind: male and female. After this, God rested from His creative activity. Man and woman initially existed in perfect union and fellowship with God and with each other. However, Genesis 3 shows that other creatures of God's creation also existed, and part of that element is evil. The serpent, later shown in Scripture to be the means through which Satan tempted Eve and led her to sin (2 Cor. 11:3), as she in turn led Adam to disobey the word of God, was present too. The sinless couple was no longer sinless; the created ones had rebelled against their Creator. God evicted Adam and Eve from His garden, and "stationed the cherubim, and the flaming sword which turned every direction, to guard the way to the tree of life" (Gen. 3:24).

The account of the Fall of man remains a most tragic revelation from God. After two brief chapters of the Beginning's perfection, events take place in Genesis 3 that changed eternity forever. Especially striking is the entrance of evil to an otherwise "good" creation. God created all things, pronouncing the divine assessment, "And God saw all that He had made, and behold, it was very good" (Gen. 1:31). Man and woman, created in an unsustained holiness, enjoyed perfect fullness and fellowship with the Creator and every aspect of His creation. Then—an enemy enters. Then—the temptation. Then—the Fall. Then—the severe penalties and consequences. Never again on earth would Adam and Eve experience the perfection of their original state after Creation. But where did the evil source come from? Why was it there?

The remainder of the Bible repeatedly depicts Satan as the enemy present—as well as the present enemy (Rev. 12:9). Yet God gives only a few glimpses from Scripture into Satan's past. Even fewer verses show Satan's activities prior to Genesis 3. Ezekiel 28:11-19 offers such clues into Satan's origin. Although designated the king of Tyre in this text, it is evident from the description of this being, coupled with the designation that he was in "Eden, the garden of God" (Ezek. 28:13), that someone other than an earthly king is in view. This being was "the anointed cherub who covers" (or "guards"). While many artists depict cherubs as plump little babies on clouds, the Bible does not. The cherubim are privileged, high-ranking angels of status and power who guarded the Garden of Eden (Gen. 3:24), whose image were part of the Ark of the Covenant (Ex. 25:18-19), and who accompanied God when His glory departed the temple (Ezek. 10:9-19). However, God found unrighteousness in one cherub and cast him away from His holy mountain (Ezek. 28:15-16). The base of Satan's sin was his vaunted overestimation of his essence and identity: "Your heart was lifted up because of your beauty; you corrupted your wisdom by reason of your splendor" (Ezek. 28:17). Paul echoed this same truth centuries later in 1 Timothy 3 when he wrote of the requirements for the overseer that he must not be "a new convert, lest he become conceited and fall into the condemnation incurred by the devil" (1 Tim. 3:6). While God expelled Satan from heaven, both Job 1–2 and Zechariah 3:1-2 indicate that Satan can visit God's heavenly domain, but only at God's intended desire and discretion. Eventually in the Tribulation, Satan will have no access to God, causing him to respond in tantrum-like rage against those who dwell on the earth (Rev. 12:7-13).

If Satan had sinned alone, the pre-Creation account would be tragic enough. Beyond his own sin, however, Scripture indicates that Satan's "tail swept away a third of the stars of heaven, and threw them to the earth" (Rev. 12:4). As we saw in a previous chapter, although we do not have many of the particulars, it reasons that one-third of God's angelic host obeyed Satan rather than God, becoming Satan's angels—better known as demons. These angels are destined for the hell originally prepared for "the devil and his angels" (Matt. 25:41). Anyone doubting the extent of Satan's power to tempt should consider this: holy angels in God's holy presence, surrounded by the majesty and glory of the Godhead and their dwelling place, still were deceived by empty promises and enticements from the evil one. God does not reveal what Satan offered—but whatever it was, it worked. How much more should we—already contaminated by sin in a fleshly body very capable of the lust of the flesh, the lust of the eyes, and the boastful pride of life—fear straying from our Savior by means of similar enticements?

Scripture informs us that both angelic forces, good and bad, remain extremely active in the affairs of humanity. God employs His angels—the ones who did not succumb to Satan's temptation—to execute judgment and carry out His plans (Heb. 1:7, 14). Satan counters by using his demons in attempts to disrupt God's redemptive program. The angelic and demonic hosts are quite numerous. It is not unreasonable to think of both branches in terms of millions or billions—far more than what some may have thought before. Ephesians 6:12 reveals that Satan's legions have a hierarchy of ranks and capacities: "For our struggle is not against flesh and blood, but against the rulers, against the powers, against the world forces of this darkness, against the spiritual forces of wickedness in the heavenly places." We do not have many specific explanations about this verse, but the Bible indicates that Satan's legions are organized into some sort of ranking structure. This verse also gives a graphic picture of the Christian battle against Satan and his angels, as Paul employed a Greek word for "wrestle" that particularly denotes personal hand-to-hand combat. In the Ephesians 6 passage believers do not stand against some mode of thought or philosophical system such as Communism. In some manner Christians wrestle against demonic beings. Probably we have wrestled in this spiritual realm mostly in ignorance, not fully perceiving the nature of the battle. When we go home to be with the Lord we will see aspects of this fight that we may have never identified as originating from Satan. Perhaps the demonic wrestling of Ephesians 6:12 is where most of the discouragement in a believer's faith and walk occurs, as Satan's angels wrestle the saints into spiritual weariness, temptation, and despondency. Paul's admonition is thus to stand firm in the Lord, properly employing the weapons of the warfare God has provided for His beloved (Eph. 6:14-18).

Demons work in unbelievers' lives as well, assisting Satan in keeping people from realizing and receiving the Gospel of Jesus Christ. As 2 Corinthians 4:3-4 reveals: "And even if our gospel is veiled, it is veiled to those who are perishing, in whose case the god of this world has blinded the minds of the unbelieving, that they might not see the light of the gospel of the glory of Christ, who is the image of God." A major means of blinding the masses is through the doctrines that demons espouse (1 Tim. 4:1). These include idolatry and false religions, which are actually foundational bases for demons to operate (1 Cor. 10:20-21). This is why prayer is so essential when witnessing to others. An intense spiritual battle rages on in the hearts and minds of unbelievers, with Satan doing all he can to keep the lost in blindness and bondage. Because of the satanic elements involved, the power of the Gospel and the weapons of the warfare are the only sufficient means for spiritual victory — not human wisdom, philosophy, outward appearance, physical talents nor the power of one's personality and most assuredly not money. While we should readily give a defense for the hope that is within us (1 Pet. 3:15), spiritual victory comes only from the grace and power of God, who makes anyone who comes to Him be "born not of blood, nor of the will of the flesh, nor of the will of man, but of God" (John 1:13). To battle otherwise is to war without the God-supplied armor — a situation in which Satan delights. Christians who do not rely on the full armor of God in spiritual battle stand just as naked before Satan as Adam and Eve once did, and with the same outcome equally assured.

Another reason exists for Satan's enmity against those who love the Lord. Perhaps equal to Satan's hatred of God is his hatred of the redeemed because of this foundational truth, also found in Genesis 3. In the Fall of man, a logical faultfinding digression took place: Adam blamed Eve; Eve blamed the serpent. It would have been most illuminating if God had continued the dialogue and asked the serpent about his role in this sin, but God chose not to do so. We do not know exactly how the snake would have responded, but it would reason that he would answer, "Satan deceived me, too." Scripture does not reveal what Satan had to offer by way of enticement, but it seems he appealed to the beauty of the serpent (Gen. 3:1), much in the same way Satan's beauty led to his own demise (Ezek. 28:17).

But it is in God's stated judgment that we see another clue for Satan's wrath against believers. In cursing the serpent God declared a truth that has far-reaching implications into the deepest wells of eternity: "And I will put enmity between you and the woman, and between your seed and her seed; He shall bruise you on the head, and you shall bruise him on the heel" (Gen. 3:15). Here, at the cradle of mankind's history, God pronounced the demarcations of the spiritual war, as well as the ultimate end and means of victory. While Satan would have temporary victory ("bruise him on the heel"), One from the seed of woman will ultimately win ("bruise you on the head").

The Genesis account does not note Satan's presence when God rendered His judgment—he may or may not have been in immediate attendance. Nevertheless, it reasons Satan would remain close by, even if God had not summoned him to the Garden. His destiny and demise hung on God's pending judgment. Besides, Satan wanted to view his great victory over the human race. Satan did not know everything—or even most things—about God. But from his personal experience he knew that God did not tolerate sin; as a result of this, God's precious couple, including God's own son Adam (Luke 3:38), were now putridly defiled sinners. Satan was aware that God had instructed man not to eat of the tree of the knowledge of good and evil, hearing God warn Adam, "for in the day that you eat from it you shall surely die" (Gen. 2:17). He further delighted in the fact that God could no longer declare, "It is very good" in regard to His previous unblemished creation.

Satan may have anticipated receiving the brunt of God's judgment; however, it still was worth it for him to wreck God's perfection by causing the deaths of the Creator's masterpieces — the only two physical beings of this universe who bore God's own image. Satan would suffer for his sin, but by his unholy reasoning, collective doom greatly surpassed groveling servitude. And besides, he had polluted God's created perfection with very little exertion on his part. Without any major effort he had been able to cause the sinless Adam and Eve to follow his own sinful course of rebellion. Satan promised Eve that she and Adam would have their eyes opened, becoming like God, knowing good and evil (Gen. 3:5). To an extent this part was true; Adam and Eve had their eyes opened to know good and evil. They recognized God was good, but they knew themselves and Satan to be evil. Sin became a perpetual imprisonment from which they could not release themselves. Indeed, Adam and Eve even became part of sin — and darkness (Eph. 5:8). They were not merely victims affected by sin; they added their own transgressions to the mix. Before the Fall, the first couple began their lives unblemished by sin; now they were just as filthy and contaminated as Satan. It reasons that in warped anticipation Satan would await God's wrath on himself and the two defiled human creatures.

Satan most likely would not have known what the divine judgment would be until God revealed it — but God's pronouncement was contrary to Satan's expectation. Two aspects of God's actions surprised Satan, causing him a considerable bewilderment. One act was in reference to Adam and Eve; the other concerns Satan himself. Much to his initial confusion, the enemy witnessed something he has never fully grasped from the day he saw it nor ever will throughout eternity: he beheld God's grace in action. Satan knew God's judgment experientially, as did the rest of the fallen angels. They sinned; God punished. Satan now beheld God's grace for the first time — but only from a distance and only from the vantage point of a curious spectator. Adam and Eve would suffer multiple consequences for their sin, even passing down their state of sinfulness to everyone else born in the normal course of childbearing. Yet they themselves did not die the day they sinned — at least not in the way Satan anticipated. Instead God performed the unspeakable: He passed over their sin for the present time, placing their collected guilt on some innocent animal who had lived in the Garden. In divine grace — not divine wrath — God Himself implemented the first blood sacrifice, clothing the first couple with a covering that vastly exceeded their own futile attempts to cover themselves (Gen. 3:21). Although Satan and the two recipients of God's grace did not understand the depth of God's action—as neither the angelic or demonic hosts currently understand—it was sufficient in God's eyes to cover the sins of Adam and Eve for the time being, and that was all that truly mattered.

It most likely astounded Satan that God had responded as He did, especially since nothing existed with which Satan could make a comparison between God's judgment and God's extended grace. Satan knew firsthand the power of God's vengeance. El Shaddai had driven Satan and his followers out of heaven immediately after they sinned. While loathing his demeaning expulsion, Satan should have recognized that God's reaction was consistent with His holy character. Would God now repeat the process, only this time expelling him from earth instead of from heaven, deporting him into the dreaded abyss of the underworld?

No, God had another plan. This second surprise for Satan concerned his own verdict. God could have rightly and justly secured Satan by imprisoning him immediately, if God had so desired. God needed no intermediary agent to render His judgment, His power being without rival in all creation. However, God chose to use another means to achieve His promised victory, and instead deferred the stated judgment to some undisclosed time in the future. Emerging from the eternal wisdom and counsel of "the predetermined plan and foreknowledge of God" (Acts 2:23), the Godhead resolved that One from the seed of woman would ultimately lead to Satan's defeat and eternal torment, as well as to undo the curse of Genesis 3. Not God the Father in an unapproachable display of power and glory. Neither would this be myriad of angels aligned in battle formation to wage war against Satan and his demons. One—singular—born of woman, from the human race that was made a little lower than the angels (Ps. 8; Heb. 2:7)—and, of course, this would mean they were lower than Satan. One—a promised seed at some point in the future—would defeat the enemy by crushing the head of the serpent.

Satan did not need to wait until David penned Psalm 8 to discern this vast difference between angelic beings and humans. Those of the seed of woman were not angelic creatures of majesty. Adam's race did not shine. They could not appear and disappear at will; they could neither fly nor hover. These were mortal beings, dust-ball creations; they could—and would—die. Angelic beings do not die. Adam's lineage could not even leave the confines of their small planet; that is, if they even perceived they lived on a planet. They could not ascend into heaven; they could not view the expanse of God's creations from the perspective of heaven looking outward. But Satan had done so. Satan had previously dwelt in God's presence. He had witnessed—and even once been a part of—the breathless display of the angelic hosts and he had fully witnessed the incomparable glory of God. As impressive as Adam and Eve were at creation, they still were flesh made from the very ground of a previously lifeless planet. Satan was fully aware of the creatures' limitations and especially of the divine insult that One from this seed would lead to his eternal torment.

Perhaps Satan smirked at the promised victory by the seed of woman. At the very least he breathed a sigh of relief. In spite of whatever confusion may have resulted after hearing God's mysterious verdict, one fact Satan grasped at once: he would not receive God's retributive judgment at the present time. Neither would God confine Satan to a distant prison for fallen spiritual beings. Satan could—and would—be free to maneuver. In fact, perhaps so that no charge could be laid against God claiming He had acted unfairly in behalf of Adam and Eve by granting them grace instead of punishing them as Satan had expected, God also granted Satan special status. With some of the reasons later revealed in God's unfolding plan of redemption, He once more acted in a manner that would have caused us to gasp in amazement if we had been present because it sounds so contrary to our understanding of God and His goodness: *God actually elevated Satan's status after the Fall instead of diminishing it.* We do not know whether God informed Satan of His rendering at this time, or whether God chose some other way to reveal it. But Scripture plainly employs two different terms to describe Satan's high ranking office. In 2 Corinthians 4:4 Paul described Satan as "the god of this world" (literally "age"). Decades earlier in the Gospel of John, Jesus referred to Satan as "the ruler of this world" (John 12:31; 14:30; 16:11). In their deepest meanings, both words describe capacities reserved for the Godhead. However, God in His sovereign wisdom granted Satan temporary exaltation within a realm he most assuredly did not deserve, and he maneuvered only under the sovereign control and restraints of God.

With his judgment deferred to some unspecified time in the distant future, Satan immediately began reassessing his strategy of attack. Before the Fall Satan appealed to Adam and Eve in their innocence. Now he could tempt and test them in their fallen nature, a nature much more lustfully receptive to his multiple enticements. Beforehand Adam and Eve had basked in perfect union with God, themselves, and their environment. Now *God Himself* drives His children out of the Garden, marital friction begins, and the physical earth manifests multiplied effects of God's curse (Rom. 8:18-21). Weeds replace the natural and bountiful vegetation; animals, the very pets of the first couple, given names by Adam himself, become fearful—or ferocious. Even beyond this, God no longer walked with the couple in the cool of the day (Gen. 3:8). As horrendous as the other consequences of the Fall were, this fractured relationship with the Creator cut the deepest. In fact, all other painful effects of sin are merely subsidiary outgrowths of this broken relationship with the Trinity.

If I were Satan, I would have fought to suppress a grin when I heard God's verdict. All things considered, I like my chances. I fear God, but not His fleshly son, Adam, or my first target, Eve. Before they had fallen in—and from—their undefiled spiritual status. Now their world imploded from the ramifications of their own sin. Earlier, Adam and Eve had fallen with merely a nudge, a suggestion—falling in spite of their faultless environment. Previously the couple had not responded properly within the freedom God had granted them. Adam had not protectively watched over Eve when they both lived in pristine innocence. Eve had not relied on Adam when Satan enticed her. Now her desire would be for her husband, but not in the way God originally intended. Now, at their hearts' cores, Adam and Eve had digressed into self-serving self-preservation. Satan would recognize this selfish aspect in his victims because it so mirrored his own reflection more than they who were created in the image of God.

With circumstances such as they were, God's rendering satisfied Satan—although the insult regarding the seed promise registered with him. Armed with his extensive arsenal, his hatred fanned white-hot by his vaunted pride and warped self-estimation, Satan prepared for war. "My demise by *the seed of woman*? Let's see if the seed of woman can survive my onslaught. Or better still, let's see if Adam's defiled race can simply survive living among one another." Already Satan began plotting multiple new ways to make sure the promised seed of woman never had the opportunity to crush his head.

Throughout the Gospels, demons always cowered whenever they encountered Jesus. Demons recognized Who Jesus is, and from their most limited perspective, why He came to earth. Often they addressed Jesus before He addressed them. Usually merely being in Jesus' presence made the demons cry out in fear: "What do we have to do with You, Son of God? Have You come here to torment us before the time?" (Matt. 8:29). Writing after the crucifixion, James noted that demons believe God and shudder (James 2:19). James used the Greek word denoting a bristled-hair type of fear, such as a cat exhibits in extreme fright. Demons know much about the Godhead, and what they know causes them to bristle in terror. They have good reason to do so; all one day will be judged by the Son and deposed to their proper place of eternal torment.

In spite of their fear of God, demons still constantly sin. They never tire of evil; they never repent. No element of good exists in them or their activities. Demons sinned — past tense, in choosing the lies of Satan over the truth of God — and demons sin: repeated, constant, present tense action.

Yet beyond these truths, the Bible indicates that a particular subset of demons transgressed beyond the normal sins of Satan and his angels. Some group of demons rendered an action so heinous in God's estimation that He intervened to remove these demons out of the earthly "playing field" and confined them in tormenting pits of darkness reserved for His great judgment. What did these specific demons do? Why did God react so strongly? Why incarcerate this group of demons but leave vast multitudes of others to work more evil? What could demons do that would be so evil that God would intercede and say, "No more! Enough!"

Three different passages disclose that God has already imprisoned some subset of demons. The passage at hand, 1 Peter 3:19-20, states that Jesus went and "made proclamation to the spirits now in prison, who once were disobedient, when the patience of God kept waiting in the days of Noah." These verses give rise to intriguing matters. Demons are *always* disobedient to the Father, other than whenever a member of the Godhead issues a direct command. What did these demons do that went beyond their continual wickedness that God currently tolerates? In fact, that God chose to confine this group of demons is such a foundational point to Peter, he repeats it in his own death row epistle of 2 Peter. Just a relatively few days before his own death, when most people are prone to write or speak about matters most important to them, Peter once more noted the fate of these same demons: "For if God did not spare angels when they sinned, but cast them into hell and committed them to pits of darkness, reserved for judgment . . ." (2 Pet. 2:4). As before, Peter wrote of some particular sector of demons that God currently confines and punishes, not in reference to the entire demonic masses. In addition to this, Jude 6 describes some subset of angels, in this case demons, "who did not keep their own domain, but abandoned their proper abode, He [God] has kept in eternal bonds under darkness for the judgment of the great day." Again the emphasis is on what God did: seizing, imprisoning, and confining a specific detachment of fallen angels.

Something significant must have taken place. Considering how many events Scripture records only once (such as the account of David and Goliath) the spirits now imprisoned receive much more attention. Two biblical writers make note of this truth. Peter, whom Jesus taught for over three years, considered it important enough and so strategic to his teaching, that he included it in both of his epistles. Even more to the point, *the Holy Spirit* deemed it necessary to be within the eternal Word of God. What could the demonic sin be that was so bad? It was not murder (John 8:44). Neither was it lying (also John 8:44). The sin also could not be inciting nations to war (1 Kings 22; Rev. 16:13-14). False religion and idolatry could not be what God responded to either, since these continue throughout the world (1 Cor. 10:20-21). Some other particular sin must be in view. What was it?

Still, another question lingers. Jude wrote about false teachers and their destiny, so perhaps a reference to God punishing angels who sinned may be encouraging in this context. False teachers will ultimately share the same fate of the fallen angels who did not obey God. But Peter wrote to an entirely different audience with differing circumstances. He wrote to Christians who were suffering for the faith and were deeply hurting. Yet he twice wrote to them about God not sparing angels when they sinned but instead confining them into pits of darkness. Such teaching is fascinating theology, and both references add to — as well as stretch — our theology. Peter's complicated passages make great fodder for a weekly home Bible study or theological debate, but it is not exactly what we would expect for persecuted, suffering saints of the Lord who face a very distinct possibility of being tortured and murdered for their faith.

Peter — and especially the Holy Spirit — must have had a very good reason to include this teaching in both of his epistles. Yet the simple question remains: why?

6

THE COLLUSION

Scripture presents numerous and significant contrasts between angels and demons. Some differences are readily seen such as that the good angels obey God while demons serve Satan, and God's angels retain a standard of holiness while Satan's demons are completely evil. One important distinction, however, may not have been noticed. Throughout Scripture, angels of God have repeatedly demonstrated the capacity to manifest themselves physically in order to be seen and to interact with those of the human realm. Demons have not. From where God placed the cherubim to guard access to the Garden (Gen. 3), to Abraham eating with the Lord and two angels (Gen. 18), to Lot and the residents of Sodom and Gomorrah encountering two angelic messengers (Gen. 19), to Elijah's servant having his eyes opened in order to view the surrounding angelic warriors (2 Kings 6:16-17), to various Old Testament prophets such as Isaiah (Isa. 6:1-2), Daniel (Dan. 9:20-21), and Zechariah (4:1-2), to John the Baptist's father Zacharias (Luke 1:11), to Mary at her annunciation (Luke 1:26-29), to the shepherds viewing a multitude of the heavenly host (Luke 2:8-15), to the early arrivers at Christ's empty tomb (Matt. 28:1-8), to the Eleven present at the Ascension of Jesus (Acts 1:9-11)—God has repeatedly manifested His angels into the world of physical beings. Humans have seen, touched, conversed, and eaten with different angels at various times throughout history. As we saw in a previous chapter, an angel even smote Peter on his side to awaken the sleeping apostle (Acts 12:7-9), smacking him in a literal, physical sense. The author of Hebrews informed his readers that some of them had "entertained angels without knowing it" (Heb. 13:2), again indicating that angels have the capacity to appear as mortals and yet have their true identities undetected.

Demons, however, never visibly display themselves. The simple reason for this seems to be that they are not permitted to do so. For whatever reason, God does not allow demons to manifest themselves in our world in a physical manner as He does with His own angels. Not only do demons never visibly appear, but also throughout the biblical account demons must have a conduit or vehicle through which to speak if they are to be heard (again, holy angels require no such medium). Typically human beings, such as the various demon-possessed individuals presented in the Scriptures, occupy this role of demonic mouthpiece. One of the most fascinating passages in all Scripture is the account of the Gaderene demoniac who encountered Jesus in Luke 8:26-34. The fallen angels within this man begged Jesus to permit them entry into a herd of swine nearby rather than being expelled into the abyss. Why did these demons need the physical bodies of pigs that would straightway drown? Did the restrictions God placed on them necessitate physical beings of some kind in order for them to function as they desired? Did the attending pigs serve as a temporary conduit before the demons afflicted someone else? We will never know the outcome during our lifetime. God grants us only limited glimpses, not full disclosure, all for reasons reserved for Him. The secret things still do, indeed, belong to the Lord our God (Deut. 29:29).

The same physical restrictions apparently apply to Satan as well. Nowhere in Scripture did Satan ever manifest himself physically, including during his temptation of Jesus. Although always visible to God, the only Scripture instances where Satan became observable to people were during God-given visions, such as to Zechariah (Zech. 3:1) or to the Apostle John in the Book of Revelation (Rev. 12:7-9; 20:2, 7-10). Satan roams and walks around the earth (Job 1:7), but does so without his presence being visibly witnessed by the human realm. This is true from Genesis through Revelation. In his initial encounter with mankind, Satan maneuvered by means of the serpent (Gen. 3). Even at the height of his power during the Tribulation, Satan will employ the human agents of the Antichrist and false prophet to carry out his agenda (Rev. 13), while he himself will remain unobserved by the human masses.

As previously noted, Ephesians 6 presents Satan's realm as organized into various ranks and capacities: "For our struggle is not against flesh and blood, but against the rulers, against the powers, against the world forces of this darkness, against the spiritual forces of wickedness in the heavenly places" (6:12). God must divulge such information regarding the demonic realm. Other than wondering about the pervasive effects of sin and evil, we would never know that a demonic hierarchy exists if God did not expose it. Such doctrine requires divine inspiration, not human logic or worldly reason. That demons operate without observation from the physical realm does not mean they are unsuccessful. After all, throughout most of the world's history God generally chooses to work without manifesting Himself or His agents to anywhere near His full capacity to do so. Therefore, we would not conclude that God who is invisible is likewise ineffectual in what He attempts. Actually working beyond the realm of human cognizance gives greater freedom to operate, especially for demonic beings who lust after evil. Those who consider themselves Christians, but do not believe that the adversary exists, by no means insult Satan because such people do not remotely stand in the warfare either.

Scripture reveals some of the areas in which Satan's evil activities take place. The devil and his angels constantly war against individual believers, seeking someone to devour spiritually (1 Pet. 5:8-9). Demons disseminate false doctrine that causes much disharmony in the church and keeps many people away from the grace of God's gospel (1 Tim. 4:1). Satan and his legions place large obstacles to hinder and discourage God's workers (1 Thess. 2:17-18), blind unbelievers to the truth of the Gospel (2 Cor. 4:3-4), and perform other multiple evils that Scripture does not reveal (2 Cor. 2:11) — all achieved beyond the sensory perception of the world's populace.

It is with this background that we consider the puzzling teaching of Jude 6: "And angels who did not keep their own domain, but abandoned their proper abode, He has kept in eternal bonds under darkness for the judgment of the great day." One group of fallen angels in some manner stepped beyond their God-ordained domain and into another. Obviously these are not the same demons who remain active, such as those described in Ephesians 6:12. The demons that Jude refers to no longer play any role in the other affairs of the world. In some way this demonic subset entered an abode different from that of the current fallen angels. Having done so, God intervened and banished them from earth, removing these specific demons from further contact with whatever realm they illegally entered. It is a most engaging verse in Scripture, raising as many questions as it answers. Which realm did these demons enter? Did these fallen angels do this on their own initiative, or did Satan lure them into doing it? Yet even if God revealed the answers to these questions, we would still lack understanding. After all, it is one thing to know broadly what these imprisoned demons did (although how they achieved their entrance into another realm is not explained). It is quite another to know why they did it.

––––––––––––––––

God maintains sovereign control over all His creation. This includes Satan and his domain. While Satan is immensely powerful — Michael the archangel attested to this in Jude 9 — God alone is God, and He has no rivals. God currently imprisons some subset of demons, yet He allows others to continue their evil activities. In a display of His omnipotence God permits Satan and his legions free reign to do much, but they are not free to do all they desire. This separation between active and imprisoned demons helps explain the pleadings of the demons in Luke 8. They were quite aware of the abyss, knowing it to be a place where they would be both confined and tormented. The demons of the Luke 8 account fervently pleaded with Jesus "not to command them to depart into the abyss" (8:31). What is this place, and why did the mere thought of being sent there evoke such horror among the demons?

The abyss shows up in various ways in Scripture. Generally speaking, the abyss can refer in more general terms to either the place or status of the dead. Paul wrote of the abyss in reference to Jesus in Romans 10:7: "'Who will descend into the abyss?' (that is, to bring Christ up from the dead)." However, the word also has sinister connotations and refers to a much more restricted place of torment, particularly for Satan and his realm. The Bible reveals that some demons whom God has previously imprisoned will temporarily be released from the abyss to attack and torment the unsaved during the Tribulation (Rev. 9:1-2, 11). These may be the demons of Jude 6, or they may be some other confined group, the particulars of which God did not reveal in the Scriptures. The Antichrist will also in some way ultimately arise out of the abyss (Rev. 17:8). Ultimately God will confine Satan himself to the abyss for a thousand years (Rev. 20:1, 3) — the same abyss that terrified the demons in Luke 8. It is important to note that the abyss is not hell; Satan will be released from the abyss and soon after be cast into the lake of fire where he will remain forever (Rev. 20:7-10).

Still, this brings us back to our topic at hand. God currently imprisons some set of demons in the abyss. What exactly did this group of fallen angels do? We know from Scripture that they abandoned their first domain, but what exactly does this mean? Even more importantly, why did they do it? Both Peter and Jude write about fallen angels who are now imprisoned (1 Pet. 3:20), who have been cast into hell (literally, *tartarosas* — not the ultimate lake of fire of Rev. 20) "and committed them to pits of darkness" (2 Pet. 2:4), keeping them "in eternal bonds under darkness" (Jude 6). While the word "abyss" is not directly used in Peter's epistles, the language is strikingly similar to references of the abyss in Revelation 9 and 20. All passages refer to bondage, imprisonment by God, removal from activity in the world's realm, and pits of darkness. If the Peter and Jude references do not refer to demons confined to the abyss, then we have no revelation from God concerning these three separate accounts and are at a complete loss in explaining their inclusion in Scripture. If these are references to the abyss, as most conclude, then it only leads to the same questions asked in the previous chapter. While these verses offer a tremendously intriguing lesson in theology, why would Peter send this instruction to churches undergoing intense strain? What did he hope to accomplish by twice referring to it? How does this relate to the rest of his epistles? And why would Jude write the same?

One other significant factor needs addressing: both epistles of Peter refer to Noah. In his first epistle Peter stated, "For Christ also died for sins once for all, the just for the unjust, in order that He might bring us to God, having been put to death in the flesh, but made alive in the spirit; in which also He went and made proclamation *to the spirits now in prison, who once were disobedient, when the patience of God kept waiting in the days of Noah,* during the construction of the ark, in which a few, that is, eight persons, were brought safely through the water" (3:18-20). The second epistle presents basically the same truth: "For if God did not spare angels when they sinned, but cast them into hell and committed them to pits of darkness, reserved for judgment; *and did not spare the ancient world, but preserved Noah,* a preacher of righteousness, with seven others. . ." (2:4-5). This too raises many related questions. What does Noah, or even the people or events associated with Noah's time, have to do with demons now in prison? What is the connection? Peter refers to this in both of his epistles, so it must have played a major part in his logic. But what did he mean by this? And as before, how could this be an encouragement to persecuted and suffering saints of God?

I woke up virtually crippled a few years ago with what turned out to be rheumatoid arthritis. I spent almost a week in the hospital as many doctors attempted to ascertain what was ravaging my body. My feet turned a sickening bluish-black hue, my blood sediment rate sky-rocketed, and then my joints from my feet up to my jawbone became affected. None of the doctors was sure at first how to diagnose the disease accurately. What the doctors did was, in essence, a scientific process of elimination. They would have suspicions of what they thought my ailment was, but when the endless tests and examinations did not support their supposition, they readily abandoned their hypothesis for another. In essence, they first had to see what I did *not* have, so they could steadily move in on what I did have.

The same process is true in biblical research. We must investigate to see what the evidence contains. Various hypotheses are offered. Who or what the spirits now in prison are has received much commentary for nearly two thousand years, and attempts to explain this are numerous and vary significantly. Although not the main purpose of this chapter, at least understanding some of the possible options and rebuttals may be useful in unraveling this mystery. These interpretational options are not all of the ones available, but at least we can see how some have haggled over these verses over the centuries. We need to examine a few possible solutions, but like good detectives, we must sift through the evidence that God has left for us in order to understand this deep mystery. And equally important, if a conclusion does not fit the stated evidence, we must abandon it and search for another one.

One option defines the spirits now imprisoned as the spirits of unbelieving people after they have died. According to this view, these spirits currently await the Day of Judgment. Christ went to them and made a victory proclamation following His crucifixion. While feasible at first consideration, this view has many weaknesses. Initially, it must be addressed how Noah plays into this argument since Peter twice refers to him as living during this time. If the spirits are understood to be the spirits of people who died during Noah's day, then another problem emerges: why did Christ confine His proclamation to one particular group of the dead? Why not preach to all of those who had died from the time when Cain murdered Abel until Christ's own death? Again, if this view is correct, why would such a statement be any encouragement to Peter's original audience?

A second interpretation takes the spirits of whom Peter wrote to be people who did not heed Noah's preaching before the Flood. According to this view, Jesus went and offered this group a second opportunity for salvation. Again, severe problems arise with this. As much as some would like, no biblical basis exists for any additional offer of salvation after one dies; the Bible repeatedly warns that one's lifetime is the only opportunity to receive God's grace. Even if this interpretation is true, why present a second chance for salvation exclusively to this one subset of humanity? Why limit this post-life offer of eternal life to the generation of Noah's day but not to other generations such as those who lived when God judged Sodom and Gomorrah? What is unique about this generation of unbelievers that God decided they warranted a second chance? As before, one other item must be considered: why would unregenerate people receiving a second opportunity for salvation be any solace for the severely persecuted churches of Asia Minor? This would be true whether in reference to those of Noah's day or to those who currently persecuted the believers centuries later. In effect Peter would be counseling the prospective martyrs, "Don't worry about your pending torture and possible death. Those who reject Jesus and slaughter you and your families will have another opportunity to become Christians after they die." While this would be a noble response similar to Jesus praying, "Father, forgive them; for they do not know what they are doing" (Luke 23:34), it is hard to imagine the ones so severely tested would have as their hearts' throb the second-chance-salvation for unbelievers. Consider this as well: if Peter's intent was to inform the readers that those who violently disobeyed God would receive a second opportunity for salvation after they died, it could be reasoned that he would argue against the believers standing firm for Christ, against full obedience to Jesus, and against being faithful even unto death. After all, if everyone receives a second opportunity to receive Jesus after death, why not temporarily abandon the cause of Christ, live a life free from persecution, and then receive salvation after death? This is hard to conceive as Peter's intent, especially since he closes his first epistle with the strong injunction, "Stand firm!" (5:12).

A third approach allegorizes the components involved; that is, the items Peter listed symbolize a deeper, spiritual meaning. Accordingly, some understand the spirits to be human beings who are currently alive but refuse the Gospel. The prison that confines them consists of the prison of their own sins. However, such a symbolic understanding should be approached quite cautiously because of the many problems that arise from it. Initially, if 1 Peter 3:19-20 is symbolic, why limit symbolism only to these verses? Should not most or all of the other chapters of the epistle be considered symbolic as well? Also, Peter wrote to encourage his readers. If he used a veiled symbolism to convey God's truths, how would he know that the readers would glean his intended meaning? Symbolism can be quite nebulous and undefined unless realities exist by which to make a comparison. Peter would chance that the churches would interpret his symbolism in the same way he did, rather than plainly stating his teaching. Because of the dire realities churches faced, it would be a most risky proposition. Also, three other factors work against this view. First, nowhere in the Bible is the word "prison" an established definition of a lost individual's spiritual status. True, the Bible contains such phrases as "set you free from the law of sin and of death" (Rom. 8:2) and "bondage to sin," (Rom. 7:14), but nowhere does "prison" refer to an individual's spiritual status. The Bible does, however, present the abyss as an actual place of imprisonment for demons in Revelation 9 and ultimately for Satan in Revelation 20. To argue for a symbolic use of a literal place is questionable at best. Besides, the demons of Luke 8 certainly considered the abyss to be an actual place; they certainly did not fear being thrown into some deeper sinful condition. Second, this and any other interpretation must harmonize with the dual references to Noah. If this is the proper interpretation, what does Noah have to do with people currently imprisoned by their own sin? Finally, as noted before, how would realizing that people become imprisoned in their own sin be a comfort to persecuted believers? Whatever conclusion one makes must harmonize with Peter's dual purpose to exhort and encourage the suffering saints.

A popular view is that the imprisoned spirits are the people of Noah's day to whom the preincarnate Jesus preached. While Christ preached, He did so by means of the human agent of Noah. Such would be similar to the Old Testament prophets who had "the Spirit of Christ" in them as they heralded God's revelation. Peter attests to this role of prophets in 1 Peter 1:10-11: "As to this salvation, the prophets who prophesied of the grace that would come to you made careful search and inquiry, seeking to know what person or time the Spirit of Christ within them was indicating as He predicted the sufferings of Christ and the glories to follow." According to this view, the wicked generation Peter refers to in chapter three rejected Christ's preaching by means of Noah and are currently imprisoned by God, awaiting the final judgment of Revelation 20.

Perhaps a refresher on what the verses actually state about the spirits now in prison may be useful at this point. First Peter 3:18-20 is one sentence, and these verses must be examined together because they are part of a larger whole. Verses 18 and 19 state, "For Christ also died for sins once for all, the just for the unjust, in order that He might bring us to God, having been put to death in the flesh, but made alive in the spirit; in which also He went and made proclamation to the spirits now in prison . . ." A couple of major factors are extremely important. Initially Peter writes that Christ—not Noah—was the preacher. Also the chronology of the verses must be maintained. Christ was made alive in the spirit *after* His death. In other words the preaching to the spirits occurs *after* the death of Christ, not before it. Whatever took place occurred after the Cross, not by means of someone who lived thousands of years before the incarnation of Jesus. Once more—and always required to be at the forefront—is the repeated question that will not go away: how would this view be a strong encouragement to the original readers of the epistle? It is feasible that the churches would receive some residual encouragement that God will ultimately judge those who reject Him, even as He judged those who rejected the Word during Noah's time; but it does not relate to the readers' immediate fears and dreads. Simply put, they feared the outcome of their own circumstances more than they did the righteous judgment of God on others.

In spite of all the interpretational snags and pitfalls, one fact remains: these verses nonetheless appear in both epistles, are inspired by God, and are intended for a divine purpose. Peter must have had something in mind that he knew his beleaguered readers would readily understand—and divine truth by which they would be strengthened and encouraged in the enormous trials before them. But what was it?

The oldest interpretation, which is still held by many, offers another explanation for the spirits now in prison. Several throughout the centuries have understood the imprisoned spirits to be demons who abandoned their own estate and somehow cohabited with women. This teaching is found not only in Peter's two epistles and in Jude, but also occurs in Genesis 6 as well, where the sons of God took wives for themselves (Gen. 6:2). Because these fallen angels entered into a forbidden realm, God arrested them and condemned them to the abyss.

As bizarre as this may seem to some who have never considered it, this view has substantial support. One significant factor should not be overlooked: Peter expected his readers to understand his meaning. That he included no accompanying explanation supports this conclusion. It would seem that if Peter presented new and unknown revelation to the readers, he would have given sufficient explanation as to what it was. That he wrote so briefly in both epistles indicates that he expected the collective churches to understand his meaning quite clearly.

So how would an early assembly, especially one with Jewish roots or one versed in the Old Testament, understand these verses? That demons once cohabited with women during the days of Noah was actually widely held Jewish theology. In explaining the Genesis 6 account, the Jewish historian Josephus, who followed the teaching of the Pharisees, wrote of fallen angels cohabiting with women. Josephus did not concoct some fantastic new story but rather presented this as somewhat common knowledge among the Jews. Also, several Jewish writings of the day, including the widely read *Book of Enoch*, gave the same account of demons of Genesis 6 cohabiting with women who gave birth to their offspring. While such works are neither inspired nor authoritative, they do present popular Jewish thought that was almost universally held in Christ's day. Peter had much contact with the Pharisees and other Jewish religious leaders; therefore, he would have known about this widely held conviction. If any misunderstanding existed he could have easily cleared this up with one simple explanatory phrase, such as, "Christ went to preach to the spirits now in prison, but not the way the Jewish leaders understand this . . ." That Peter knew this popular view was held by the majority and yet did not respond against it, coupled with the fact that he was aware that his readers knew this view as well, supports that no correction was required.

The standard rebuttal always raised against this view occurs in Matthew 22:30. In the context of Matthew 22 the Sadducees attempted to trick Jesus by asking Him when the resurrection occurred, who would be married to a woman who had many husbands in this earthly life. Jesus explained that no one would be her husband, "For in the resurrection they neither marry, nor are given in marriage, but are like angels in heaven." Since angels cannot marry or are given in marriage, then it reasons that the passages in Genesis 6, 1 and 2 Peter, and Jude cannot refer to fallen angels.

While this verse in Matthew 22 may initially seem to eliminate demons cohabiting with women, a closer examination is needed. Jesus stated that the resurrected dead will not marry, but instead "are like angels *in heaven*." Other angels exist who are not angels in heaven (Matt. 25:41)—Jesus states nothing in reference to them. If anything, Jesus' specificity supports the claim that the spirits imprisoned are fallen angels. If Jesus had only said, "but are like angels," both holy and fallen angels would have been included. So actually Matthew 22:30 states nothing prohibitive in regard to what demons may have done—and may actually support the claim that they did, in fact, cohabit with women.

From the evidence contained in Scripture it seems the best explanation for the spirits now in prison are those who abandoned their own domain and cohabited with women. While God chooses not to explain the particulars of how this transpired, nothing in Scripture—including the often-quoted Matthew 22:30—prohibits this sin from having occurred. That this act happened in the days of Noah harmonizes with 1 and 2 Peter, Jude, and the Genesis 6 account.

While the view that demons abandoned their own domain and cohabited with women is fascinating, we must not lose sight of the bigger picture. Demons *never* work independently of Satan; they never operate outside of his command. In other words, what occurred did not merely happen by accident. Consequently, it would reason that Satan played a significant role in sending the demons out from their God-restricted domain—a domain, incidentally, that Satan himself chose not to abandon. The Bible does not reveal how he convinced them. Did Satan coerce a subset of his angels to cohabit with women? Did his enormous power and authority make his followers cower at the thought of disobedience to him? Did they fear how the Godhead would respond? Maybe Satan relied more on his repeatedly proven method of deception. Did he deceive his minions by promising them exalted status and glory if they successfully fulfilled their mission, or were they most willing to go and required only permission or a nudge? We will never know in this lifetime. We will have to wait until we get to heaven to have God show us.

But whether by coercion or by deception tempered with temptation, a satanic collusion took hold in the spiritual realm of evil; a veiled demonic conspiracy converged to take aim at the spiritually ignorant world. Not all demons would invade the human realm; most would remain behind and continue their evil assaults. Yet a select group of demons would depart from their God-ordained realm and somehow infiltrate earth beyond the bounds that any other demons had ever before attempted. Their purpose was plotted; their strategy had been secured. The stakes were eternally substantial—for Satan's realm, for the human race, and for God's salvation program.

In spite of all this, we are far from understanding the overall story.

The view that demons went and cohabited with women (if that is indeed the correct interpretation) only gives rise to additional questions, somewhat like attempting to stomp out a larger flame that divides into numerous smaller flames. It is one thing to know what these imprisoned demons did (came to earth and cohabited with women)—it is entirely another matter to know why they did it. What was their motivation? What was their goal? Why did it matter if they accomplished what they intended? It seems that it mattered most greatly because God so violently intervened after they came to earth, although He patiently waited until Noah finished the ark. God currently and temporarily endures the on-going sins of the demonic hosts. What was it about this one act that caused God to respond so drastically while He still tolerates multitudes of other heinous acts by Satan's angels?

But even beyond these unanswered questions, one repeated perplexity keeps gnawing at us. One piece of the puzzle sits off to the side, isolated from the others, and refuses to go away: *why did God the Holy Spirit, by means of Peter, consider this teaching on demons so foundational to the extended churches of Asia Minor during their most heated hour of trial and persecution?*

7

THE HELP

Certain sections of First Peter must have seemed harshly contradictory to the initial recipients of this holy epistle. Considering the severity of their circumstances, if the early churches did not know and trust Peter, much of what he wrote would have seemed particularly cruel. First Peter 3:13 is an example of Peter writing something that appeared to clash with the readers' plight: "And who is there to harm you if you prove zealous for what is good?" A natural response by the churches could have been, "'Who is there to harm us!' Is Peter too as insane as Nero? 'Who is there to harm us?' Well, the full force of the Roman Empire will do for starters. They rule the entire world with a strangle grip of power, decimating all armies and nations who oppose them. How much easier will they devour scattered bands of sacrificial sheep among the churches. 'Who is there to harm us?'—just look out your window, Peter; you will have no difficulty finding potential candidates."

An earlier verse would likewise appear to mock those already weak and spiritually wounded instead of comforting them in their despair. In 1:5 Peter wrote that the believers are currently "protected by the power of God," employing the present tense to indicate God's continuous watchful care over them. At no time whatsoever does God cease His divine protection over His own. While this truth offers strong encouragement, the horrendous events and pressures brought about by Rome's expanding persecution against Christians would have caused the beleaguered flocks to wrestle through many internal terrors: "Protected by God—when each night I cannot sleep for fear the government officials will storm my house to arrest me or my family? Protected by God—when I cannot sell my goods or trade in the market place in order to feed my family? Protected by God—when my neighbors ostracize my wife, and my children become the objects of ridicule by other children encouraged by their hate-filled parents to do so? Protected by God—when my son sobs as he shows me where the stone from some unknown assailant burst his scalp, leaving a patch of dried blood? Protected by God—when that madman Nero reigns in Rome, saturating the ground with martyrs' blood? Protected by God—in beatings, torture, and yes, perhaps even martyrdom? Protected by God—when I have to look into my youngest daughter's eyes, hoping against hope that the deeply embedded fear she continually displays is not merely the reflection of the deep fear residing in my own eyes? Protected by God—when I gather my family together and attempt to reassure them that there is no reason to fear, lying to them that everything will turn out all right? Protected by God?"

Although such a response would be logical to those under such a burdensome existence, the recipients knew Peter. They knew he was one of them at heart, not one cloistered away and protected from their present danger. They were amply aware of Peter's life, his own sufferings, his unselfish ministry, and most likely would know of the Lord's prophesied manner of Peter's own pending death (John 21:18-19). Even more importantly, these related-by-faith churches not only knew Peter, they also experientially knew God as well. Though weary and oppressed, though hated by the world, they lived out eternal life— regardless of their current discomfort and increasing fears. These who resided on this earth as aliens were more than conquerors through the blood of Jesus, as He had been more than Conqueror in behalf of them.

So what Peter wrote must have brought a divine solace to them, an anointing oil from the Good Shepherd on some of His most precious sheep. Protected by God?—most assuredly, you beloved of God, and protected to a depth you may never have realized, because quite often God works above and beyond our extremely limited perception. Most of how God protected us will be revealed after this life when we stand before Him in heaven. Yet before the full disclosure, God has left clues about His sovereign protection embedded within His Word. For instance, this same epistle that speaks of God's protection over believers also contains the passage about Christ going to make proclamation to the spirits now in prison. Do these verses have any correlation? Also, since Peter twice referred to Noah when writing about the imprisonment of fallen demons, we need to visit the account of the Flood to attempt to see the connection. Even more so, as did the persecuted Church of the first century, we need to step back and marvel at the depths of God's constant love and protection through our protective Good Shepherd, Jesus Christ.

Ask most people who believe the Bible why God sent the Flood, and the answer will often be a paraphrase of Genesis 6:5-7: "Then the Lord saw that the wickedness of man was great on the earth, and that every intent of the thoughts of his heart was only evil continually. And the Lord was sorry that He had made man on the earth, and He was grieved in His heart. And the Lord said, 'I will blot out man whom I have created from the face of the land, from man to animals to creeping things and to birds of the sky; for I am sorry that I have made them.'" The Genesis account reveals that mankind grew progressively more evil until they reached a point where God delivered a cleansing judgment. Only Noah and his immediate family would survive.

Scripture does reveal that the world became so corrupt that God intervened in judgment, but we often fail to see a broader significance of the Flood, especially when starting with the Flood as the beginning point of the study. Whereas it is true that the inhabitants of the earth became progressively evil, it was nonetheless a process. Centuries, or at least decades, of increasing disobedience added to the cumulative sin of mankind. But instead of beginning with the Flood itself, we need to drop back to the beginning of mankind to see the greater significance. The Flood is a crucial event in the overall battle between God's truth and Satan's lies; but it is only an event, a battle within a much larger conflict. The greater war had already been operative for many years in history past.

When Adam and Eve sinned against God in Genesis 3, God decreed punishments against the various parties involved. To the power behind the serpent, namely Satan, the serpent of old (Rev. 12:9; 20:2), God rendered this verdict: "And I will put enmity between you and the woman, and between your seed and her seed; He shall bruise you on the head, and you shall bruise him on the heel" (Gen. 3:15). Thus God not only established the battle lines, He also determined the ultimate outcome—the seed of woman, that is, One born of a woman, would crush the seed of the serpent. God spoke a statement of fact already true in His sovereign will, not some distant possibility contingent on human assistance or circumstance.

God could have dealt directly with Adam and Eve and Satan, destroying them all — if He had so desired — and casting them into the outer darkness. Instead God in His sovereignty chose to work according to His eternal wisdom. Although not yet revealed in this opening section of His progressive revelation, God knew before the creation of the world that man would fall (Acts 2:22-23). He also knew Satan's destiny (Matt. 25:41). God gradually revealed aspects of His grand design in Scripture, beginning with the verdict of Genesis 3. *One* from the seed of the woman would eventually come at some unspecified time in the future and complete God's judgment against Satan. God chose not to use angels to carry out His judgment. Neither would He use many from the seed of woman; only one would be necessary — He (not "they") will bruise the head of the serpent in a most devastating way.

Put yourself in Satan's position: *You have experienced God's judgmental power firsthand with your own expulsion from heaven. You know that God always tells the truth. In fact, God binds Himself by His own Word. And while you are not strong enough to go one-on-one with El Shaddai, at this moment you have a glimmer of hope concerning your own destiny. God has decreed that it will be through the seed of woman that your ultimate defeat will occur. Although you do not possess the power to defeat God, maybe you can defeat the instrument through whom God would bring judgment. Maybe you can completely destroy the seed of woman from the face of the earth. After all, these human creatures now are just as rebellious in nature as you are. You led them to sin in their undefiled innocence. Now they will be easier targets because of their own fallen nature coupled with myriads of deep-hearted lusts that constantly draw them to sin.*

Beginning from this point onward, the seed of woman became utmost in Satan's mind and in his plots. From now on, his primary objective was to destroy the human seed lineage. It did not matter to him how he destroyed it, as long as something worked. Expecting that one of his multiple strategies would surely lead to the seed's demise, Satan would employ his potent arsenal against them.

While containing many tragedies, Genesis 3 also presents a glimmer of Light for mankind. After all, God Himself maintained a significant stake in this drama between Satan and humanity. God had declared it was through the seed of woman that Satan would ultimately be defeated. He decreed divine truth; He did not present this as a possibility. God chose not to have any supplementary plans if His first plan failed. Consequently, God must protect the seed of woman against whatever wiles and attacks Satan would bring against them — divine protection of which the human realm at this point remained completely unaware. If God does not sovereignly protect the seed of woman, if Satan is able to destroy it, the evil one wins—forever.

Adam and Eve likewise heard that God's promised deliverer would come somehow through means of Eve. How much they comprehended or how much more God made known to them, Scripture does not disclose. It does seem evident, however, that God chose not to reveal the timeframe for the seed's arrival to Adam or Eve—or to Satan. The first couple had no reason to expect it to be thousands of years in the future, having no experiential base of comparison. They were in immediate need, living in—and now as a part of—God's curse. Adam and Eve most likely expected redemption by means of either of their first children, Cain or Abel. Yet if the first human parents expected one of their first two potential candidates to be the deliverer seed, they were horribly disappointed. Cain murdered Abel. One potential redeemer is dead; the other becomes forever disqualified and banished by God.

Thus began Satan's initial tactic of defeating the seed: get the seed of woman to destroy each other. Thousands of years later Jesus made note of Satan's behind-the-scenes role in the Cain and Abel tragedy. In John 8:44 Jesus described Satan as "a murderer from the beginning." Cain murdering Abel is the first recorded murder in history, and it seems from Jesus' revelation that Satan played a strategic role in bringing it into reality. Murder was not so much Satan's intent as it was his means, especially in reference to the seed promise.

All things considered, this first encounter with the seed after the Fall pleased Satan: two seed candidates; two seed disqualifications. From his initial victory Satan could conclude that he was no nearer being threatened by the seed of woman than he had been in the garden. However, events would soon transpire that would ultimately change everything.

Genesis 4 concludes with the birth of Adam and Eve's third child, revealing the renewed hope of the fallen couple: "And Adam had relations with his wife again; and she gave birth to a son, and named him Seth [Hebrew *sheth*], for, she said, 'God has appointed [*shath*] me another offspring [literally, "seed"] in place of Abel; for Cain killed him'" (4:25). As a mother who had lost two sons, Eve strongly desired the advent of the promised seed, hoping that her newborn child would be the appointed one of God. Since the kingdom and authority of Satan depended on the seed of woman not being in a place of potential victory, Satan would readily note the significance of the name. He did not trust anyone alluded to as "Appointed Seed." Even more alarming to him would be Genesis 4:26 that adds another aspect Satan could not ignore: "Then men began to call upon the name of the Lord."

Satan then faced two significant developments in the seed saga that he must address. Instead of the seed murdering one another out of existence, the seed actually expands numerically. But beyond this, some of the seed begin to call upon the name of the Lord. Satan had witnessed God's grace in action firsthand in Genesis 3—and God's grace *always* remains so illogically alien to Satan's mentality, repeatedly confronting him as the most unpredictable component of God's actions. Satan despises God's grace; but even beyond this, he *fears* God's grace. Despite all his efforts, Satan cannot bring himself to reason as God would reason in any realm of grace. Displays of God's grace always cause the good angels as well as the bad to marvel (1 Pet. 1:12)—and though temporarily exalted in his status, Satan nonetheless remains an angel. Although most likely not knowing the outcome of man's prayers to God, humanity calling upon a gracious and loving God *by name* would be a most alarming development to the evil one.

But the event that ultimately moved Satan to action was the birth of one depicted in Genesis 5:28-29: "And Lamech lived one hundred and eighty-two years, and became the father of a son. Now he called his name Noah, saying, 'This one shall give us rest from our work and from the toil of our hands arising from the ground which the Lord has cursed.'" Satan readily understood the significance of this prediction. The ground was not the only thing God cursed—Satan himself shared in the curse. If God used this newborn one to remove the curse, by simple logic, God would likewise use him to crush Satan. Satan did not know if Noah was the promised seed or not, because after all, no "thus says the Lord" accompanies Lamech's proclamation. But Noah might be the promised one—he just might be. One from the seed of woman, whose name and time of appearing God had not yet revealed, would bring about Satan's downfall. Could this baby be that promised one? And while what Lamech stated was not a direct quote from God, it shows the active expectation of at least one man who looked for the fulfillment of the promise that God had made in the garden. Both the curse and the deliverer seed had not drifted from many people's memories. How could they? With every new death, with multiple evidences of a cursed earth, with each tragedy that afflicted the fallen race, the necklace of fallen humanity wove in another bead of misery. Maybe Lamech did receive a word from the Lord. Maybe this was God's battle cry that Satan's reign would soon end as one from the seed of woman would rise up and destroy both him and his kingdom.

Such changes in circumstances would force Satan to act—quickly. He must now alter his strategy. Although he had secured various successes with the human race up to this point, the seed lineage—and the seed promise—continued. Also, people began calling out to the God of grace, even calling on His name, indicating that somehow God made specific knowledge of Himself available. The result was that at least some embraced Him as their God. Now one is born whose father proclaimed at his birth that he would end the curse, giving rest to the earth and its inhabitants. The end of the curse meant the end of Satan's reign and the beginning of his imprisonment and torment. A desperate man will try desperate means when confronted with a life-and-death crisis. So would a desperate ruler of darkness.

The author of Hebrews reveals the total insufficiency of animal sacrifices to redeem mankind from his spiritual bondage. "For it is impossible [not "difficult"] for the blood of bulls and goats to take away sins" (Heb. 10:4). A logical reason exists for this divine impossibility. God created mankind—male and female—in His own image. One aspect of this image was distinction from and mastery over all other animals. "Let Us make man in Our image, according to Our likeness; and let them rule over the fish of the sea and over the birds of the sky and over the cattle and over all the earth, and over every creeping thing that creeps on the earth" (Gen. 1:26). No other animals are created in God's image—only humans. Consequently, by God's divine design, the totality of the animal world collectively sacrificed could never take away one individual sin of even one person, much less the accumulated sins of all time—because animals are lesser creatures. God instigated the various Old Testament sacrifices as a temporary means until the ultimate Sacrifice would come through His Son (Rom. 3:21-26). Such is what the author of Hebrews argues in detail throughout chapter 10. Because this is true, in order for a proper redemption to occur, a one-to-one correspondence must exist. Mankind must be redeemed by one who has the image of God, not by animals who do not.

The same logic applies to humans and angels. Psalm 8 reveals that mankind is currently made a little lower than the angels. Although this status will change in the future ages, at the current time, humans are not on equal footing with angels; angels hold an elevated position. Thus, no angel could ever redeem mankind since no one-to-one correspondence exists. Another obvious problem concerns the eternality of angels; spiritual beings never die as flesh does.

From the collective information that God revealed in Scripture, these truths seem to be the likely basis on which Satan acted. While Satan most certainly did not comprehend redemption, God had pronounced that one from the seed of woman would crush his head. Satan had continually worked to destroy the seed from the face of the earth, yet the seed still continued. The birth of Noah, the possible seed deliverer, forced Satan to drastic measures, whereby he applied a two-pronged strategy. The first strategy involved employing a subset of demons to abandon their God-ordained domain and somehow cohabit with human women. This had never before been attempted by demons; even more to the point, by no means had the Trinity previously tolerated such sin.

God gives only very limited information about what took place. Even less does He disclose how, which very well may be for our own protection. We see only the event and result in Scripture. However, why this happened seems evident from the biblical account: destroy by pollution and defilement the God-designated means by which Satan would be destroyed, namely, the seed of woman. No seed meant no head crushing—and no destruction. The intention, therefore, was not so much sexual lust; the satanic intent was some hybrid mixture that would eventually make the human seed no longer viable. God promised judgment by means of the seed of woman; not by means of another seed from some demonic-human offspring. God bound Himself by His Word; judgment *must* come by the means He stated—and the means He stated was one from the human race. So in an attempt to alter the seed of woman permanently, Satan plotted that God would have to destroy either the seed—and the promise—or else to tolerate some hybrid seed, thus ruining the one-to-one redemption necessary for man.

The second prong of the strategy appears to be more of a backup plan. Simply put, Satan's second plot intended to increase the manifestation of evil to such a degree that God Himself would intervene and destroy the very seed He had created. Either approach carried to its fulness would work; the seed lineage would become perversely polluted, thus abolishing the means through which the promised seed was to arrive. Satan would continue to reign. God's promises would become null and void. Darkness would overtake all light—*forever*.

First Peter 3:20 implies that Satan had initial reason to delight in his efforts. God knows all of Satan's movements, so the demons did not abandon their realm and enter a prohibited one without God's full awareness. However, instead of God acting immediately as soon as the demons first trespassed in the earthly realm, God chose to wait to respond. In reference to the spirits now in prison who were once disobedient, Peter reveals *"when the patience of God kept waiting in the days of Noah*, during the construction of the ark . . ." God did not ignore the demonic collusion or the world's sins—He strategically waited. Neither did God look the other way at the pollution on earth—He patiently waited with divine vigilance. The imperfect tense in the Greek describes something of the duration that God patiently waited—that is, He repeatedly waited over and over.

Genesis 6:3 gives an indication of how long God waited. Immediately after the sins mentioned in Genesis 6:1-2 comes this pronouncement by God: "Then the Lord said, 'My Spirit shall not strive with man forever, because he also is flesh; nevertheless his days shall be one hundred and twenty years.'" For one hundred and twenty years God waited for the right time to respond: enough time for the demonic collusion to increase many times over; enough time for the evil that Satan intended to saturate the earth; enough time for Noah to be born twenty years later and complete the ark one hundred years after that.

If God chose not to reveal His plan to His holy angels, the angelic host must have viewed the earthly drama in mystified amazement. They would have observed the utter brazenness of a cluster of fallen angels abandoning their God-established domain—and yet Yahweh did not respond. They would have witnessed the forbidden cohabitation and the resulting corrupted offspring—and yet God still waited. The holy angels witnessed or sensed evil permeating throughout all the earth in previously unknown proportions. They fully knew of God's pronunciation of the promised judgment by means of the seed of woman, and yet here was the seed line becoming corrupt almost to the point of nonexistence. When God finally responded, what He said seemed to contradict the very promise He had pledged years earlier. In Genesis 6:7 God declared, "I will blot out man whom I have created from the face of the land, from man to animals to creeping things and to birds of the sky; for I am sorry that I have made them." If this was all that the angels or Satan heard, then God stated no exception at this point. The angels expected God to respond, but not in this manner. The demise of the human race would also mean the demise of the seed of woman—and the eradication of God's promise. If God did not disclose His plan, the angels could only stand stupefied, perhaps even fearful of the impossible concept that the vile usurper Satan would win. Perhaps they discussed this among themselves, much as the disciples of Jesus would discuss God's ways thousands of years later.

If Satan heard God's pronouncement of Genesis 6:7, he rejoiced in glee. Yahweh God, the loving Creator, would *Himself* blot from the earth the creation of His own hand, including the seed of woman. Satan did not need to act because, after all, he could not—but God could. Instead of one prong of Satan's attack working, both had worked: the demonic collusion was rapidly overriding the seed of woman, and evil multiplied to the magnitude that God would soon terminate all associated with the earth.

Satan had enacted his plan. The results were perhaps even better than even he had previously expected.

But God had already enacted His plan too, in a much more subtle and substantial manner.

How majestically the writer of Hebrews works through the difficulty of the mandatory one-to-one correspondence needed for redemption. The author repeatedly shows that an animal cannot fully redeem fallen man because it is not man's equal. Yet this correlation goes beyond man and the animal world. God is higher than angels, and angels are higher than man. So how could highly exalted God redeem one who is lower? God accomplished this by humbling Himself to the level of those He came to save: "But we do see Him who has been made for a little while lower than the angels, namely, Jesus, because of the suffering of death crowned with glory and honor, that by the grace of God He might taste death for everyone" (Heb. 2:9). Even more to the point, Hebrews 2:14-15 reveals, "Since then the children share in flesh and blood, He Himself likewise also partook of the same, that through death He might render powerless him who had the power of death, that is, the devil; and might deliver those who through fear of death were subject to slavery all their lives." Almost incomprehensibly, the Son stepped down from heaven into His own creation, choosing to become a little lower than *His own* angels, so that He could fully identify with fallen man. Simply put, He was born into and became part of the seed of woman lineage.

The author of Hebrews reveals even more. In Hebrews 2:16 he writes a most intriguing explanatory statement: "For assuredly He does not give help to angels, but He gives help to the descendant [literally, "seed"] of Abraham." Twice in this verse the author of Hebrews employed the same Greek word for "help." This word can be translated two different ways, and accordingly adds another controversy. The word means "to take hold of; to seize; to take to one's self." Accordingly, the word used this way describes what is called the Son's "assumption" — that is, His taking on a human body. This is how the King James Version understands the word, translating the verse: "For verily He took not on Him the nature of angels, but he took on Himself the nature of man." Other scholars conclude that the word instead has the meaning "to come to the aid of; to help; to assist." Understood this way the verse reads, "For assuredly He does not give help to the angels, but He gives help to the descendant [or "seed"] of Abraham." Debate about which definition is correct will undoubtedly continue. However, the context of Hebrews 2 deals with the incarnation, so the meaning of Christ not assuming the nature of angels but the nature of man may be more prevalent. Nonetheless the idea of help, even — or especially even — help by assuming the human nature is also evident in the passage.

So while both meanings fit the text, we often miss the obvious by arguing the tangents. Whether the emphasis is that Jesus did not take the form of angels or whether Jesus did not help angels, a foundational nugget of truth must not be overlooked — the good angels do not need such help; the bad angels need it, but will never receive it. While this passage does not directly speak about Christ making proclamation to the spirits now in prison, it is another reminder of Christ's great love for mankind. God displayed His most active exhibition of love, not in the angelic realm, but in that of the fallen humanity. Angels — both holy and evil — can view this love only as spectators, not participants, because the Help was not given to them.

And so God has protected us — not only in what He destroyed but also in what He preserved. Not only did God annihilate the effects of the demonic collusion, He also protected and sustained the seed lineage even in the midst of the Flood. Mark this well, beloved: the protection of the seed family and its continuous existence is just as important in the biblical account as the destruction of the evil ones, yet we rarely acknowledge this. For instance, many people who read the Bible love the first four chapters of Genesis, with the grandeur of God's creation and the tragedy of man's rebellion. Yet when they come to Genesis 5, the account becomes much harder to read, being often referred to as "one of those boring genealogies." But God's revelation is never without purpose. Initially, it should be noted, Genesis 5:3 records Adam begetting a son, Seth. The recording in this manner is important. Seth is Adam's third son, not the first. Cain and Abel were the first two, yet Moses omits them from the genealogy. So Genesis 5 diverts our attention. Its purpose is not to give a detailed history of Adam and his descendants; its purpose is to trace the development of the seed lineage. In what some consider "another one of those boring genealogies" thousands of years later in the New Testament, Luke reminds us that God had been working from Eden onward. Beginning with Jesus in Luke 3:23, Luke traces the seed lineage backward in time through David (3:31), through Judah (3:33), Jacob, Isaac, and Abraham (3:34)—each of these seed descendants receiving glorious and expanded promises from God. But even beyond these seed members, Luke walks us back further to "Noah, the son of Lamech" (3:36), in fact, all the way back to "Seth, the son of Adam, the son of God" (3:38). Each name recorded in the genealogy, as well as the many names omitted, adds another copula and story to the seed promise that God revealed back at the Fall of man. And each story adds another reminder of the faithful God who brings all things into completion in the fullness of time (Gal. 4:4).

When my daughter Lauren was a small child rarely a month went by when she did not ask me to tell her about the day she was born. It was her favorite story. She knew it by heart, readily correcting me if I happened to omit even a minor detail that I had included in a previous account.

"Tell me about when I was born, Daddy."

"Well, it began early one Saturday in September in Dallas, Texas. Mommy and I were asleep in bed . . ." We had not received our newspaper for several days, and after many complaints to the newspaper office, the delivery man made sure we that knew our newspaper had arrived by throwing it at the glass doors of our bedroom patio. The projectile newspaper sounded like a grenade exploding, causing Betsy and me to sit up in bed in startled unison. Although we had intended to sleep in that morning, having been jolted awake and unable to return to sleep, we began our activities a little before 5:00 that morning. Betsy was due in two weeks, and many preparations remained before the arrival of our first child.

We did our separate activities. Betsy shopped and prepared the nursery; I studied and then went for a sixteen-mile prayer-run. We attended a party later that Saturday night, and after returning home and going to bed, Betsy informed me that it was time to go to the hospital.

"And that was to have me," Lauren half-asked, half-boasted.

"And that was to have you," I nodded in agreement.

Often Lauren would silently mouth the words of certain parts or phrases most dear to her. This is her love story — and she never grows tired of hearing it.

"Then what happened, Daddy?"

I retold how we drove to the hospital after midnight, and how busy the doctor and the nurses were. I reminisced about that unique time in life when you view your first child, not a sonogram, not a curvature of Mommy's tummy — but a real live child with life and a soul.

"Lauren, I waited by the bed for you to be born. And when I finally saw you, I had never seen anyone so beautiful in my life. From that very first moment, I knew I loved you as deeply as I could ever love any other human being."

Lauren beamed.

I reminded her how she stopped crying as soon as we placed her on Mommy's chest. She reminded me how Nana and Pop Pop drove all the way from Cary, North Carolina just to see her, and how we all would stand at the nursery window just to stare at her.

"Then what happened, Daddy?"

"After a few days you and Mommy were able to go home. So we packed up our things, and then I stopped by to pay the hospital bill."

Although Lauren had heard her story dozens of times, the fact that we actually had to pay money for her to come home to live with us had previously escaped her. She was a little older now and realized she could not buy ice cream from the ice cream truck unless someone around her had the necessary money.

"You mean I *cost* you something, Daddy?"

"It's not past tense, Sweetie — you still do everyday. But yes, Mommy and I had to pay the doctors and the hospital so we could take you home to live with us."

"Well, what would have happened if you hadn't paid for me?"

"Oh, I don't know, I guess you would still be there."

I had spoken my last words in jest, but they were not funny to a four-and-a-half-year-old. I regretted saying them as soon as the words left my mouth. I had unintentionally wounded my beloved little girl. A hurtful fear swept over Lauren as her young child's mind grasped about the most horrendous concept she could possibly conceive: life forever separated from Mommy and Daddy. Our twins had died a few months earlier. Separation was a concept Lauren now experientially knew — and one that she greatly abhorred.

She erupted in a tearful plea, "But Daddy, I don't *want* to live without you and Mommy!"

"Lauren, we knew God had given us this wonderful child, and Mommy and I planned in advance to do whatever was necessary to bring you home to live with us. We knew we had to pay for you before you were ever born. We went to the hospital prepared. We paid what was necessary — and would have paid it a thousand times over — in order to bring you home with us. And you know what? We paid every bit of it — nothing remains for anyone to ever come and take you away from us. You will never hear from that hospital about this ever again."

"But I didn't know this, Daddy."

"You didn't have to, Sweetie. It was our price to pay — not yours."

Sometimes the best response comes when the dialogue stops. A little light flickered within Lauren with this particular retelling of her birth. She had gained a better understanding of how loved — and valued — she was. Lauren hugged me in a protracted embrace as though she would hug right through me. I savored the moment.

Later that night as I tucked her in bed, I could tell Lauren was still mulling over our earlier conversation. I knew she wanted to hear her story again. Now she possessed a deeper base of experience so she could appreciate it so much more. We would discuss her story again, but tonight was not the time. Instead of repeating the story, I wrapped her in a final thought as well as a blanket.

"Lauren, I protected you before there was a you to protect — and I still do."

"Tell me about when I was born, Lord."

"Well, as with Lauren's story, events associated with your birth began long before your actual birthday, beginning, in fact, in eternity past.

"You were to be born in a world gravely burdened with the curse resulting from Adam's disobedience. You would enter a world severely affected by one who hates Me and all those aligned with Me. I have an enemy, and because you are Mine, he and his own actively hate you too."

"Why is that, Lord?"

"It is partly due to their nature—My enemies know only evil and hatred. They wanted to keep you and all others from Me. But a large part of their hatred is due to fear. Long before you were born I made a promise that the redemption of mankind would come from one member of the human race. One promised seed of woman would claim victory over the serpent and accomplish his demise by crushing his head. For centuries the enemy and his legions continually plotted to destroy the promised seed line so that My pronounced victory would never take place."

"How close did they come, Lord?"

"By human reasoning, they came extremely close. By My reckoning, it is as though they never even moved. I am God Almighty, the Beginning and the End. I am omniscient. I knew their devious plan before they even conceived it in their collectively evil hearts, knowing it always in eternity past. Satan convinced some of his angels to infiltrate and pollute the seed line so that the promised One would never come. I fully observed them in all of their evil for one hundred and twenty years, but I tolerated it until your forefather Noah completed the ark, and until I brought the animals to him (Gen. 6:20).

"At that time this was the pinnacle of all of Satan's plots to keep the One promised seed from ever coming. But this was the absolute best Satan and his legions could muster after many years of strategizing. Yet not one element of their strategy surprised Me. I met them at every turn, even using their own actions as a means of punishment against them and the world.

"I destroyed the mixed seed and the ungodly world with the Flood. In fact, I had *already* created My earth many years earlier to be ready for Satan when he attempted this most brazen assault that I knew would eventually come. Not only did I send rain with the Flood, but I also opened "the fountains of the great deep" that I had originally made as part of My creation (Gen. 7:11; 8:2). I did not have to create anything new or react in an extravagant manner. In Wisdom I created the fountains of the great deep many years earlier with Satan's future attempt—and with you—in mind. No one knew they existed except Me. As I later revealed in Proverbs 3:19-20, 'I by Wisdom founded the earth; by understanding I established the heavens. By My knowledge *the deeps were broken up*, and the skies drip with dew.' My windows and fountains stood ready for My intended purpose long before Satan ever conceived his plot. I needed to wait only until the time was right to suit My intent.

"Not only did I judge rebellious man, but I also preserved the seed lineage through Noah and his family, protecting them and bringing them into a freshly cleansed world.

"I punished the guilty demons so severely that no other demons will ever attempt that blatant disobedience again. Besides this, I would never again wait one hundred and twenty years to respond. Even more to the point, I would never tolerate their abandoning their designated restrictive abode.

"Not only this, but I went and made proclamation to the spirits now in prison, pronouncing victory over what they had attempted to disrupt. Their demonic collusion had failed. Not only had the seed lineage continued—the Seed Himself triumphed. The serpent's head had been fatally crushed.

"Satan and his demons gravely underestimated not so much My power, but rather the depths of My love—and the eternal extremes I will go to in order to bring My beloved home with Me.

"I knew you would be coming home to live with Me—and I paid what was necessary for you to be with Me forever."

Like Lauren, I too often mouth the words of certain parts or phrases whenever I hear this love story. Also as a child, no matter how often I hear it, new elements that I never realized before register with me.

"You mean I *cost* You something, Lord?"

"Oh yes, you cost Me dearly."

"But what would have happened if You didn't pay for me?"

"Then you would always be separated from Me. You and the rest of the world's inhabitants would always be under Satan's domain—even after you died—and you would stay eternally tormented in the hell originally prepared for the devil and his angels."

"But I don't *want* to be separated from You, Lord!"

"You need not worry. Satan and his demons will never ultimately harm you again. Nothing or no one can take you away from Me. You are My own. You are destined to be with Me forever—and in a marvelous manner you do not yet fully comprehend, you are destined to be even like Me (1 John 3:2).

"The process of your arrival home is often quite difficult, whether it is the savagery of the Roman Empire, or the ravages of old age, or disease, or the lonely isolation of the wilderness. But these hardships are only momentary; you reside on earth only as an alien. Our relationship—and everything about us—is eternal.

"Your faith is currently being tested by fire—but not your identity. *You are Mine—and I am yours.* Neither death, nor life, nor angels (the bad ones), nor principalities, nor things present, nor things to come, nor powers, nor height, nor depth, nor any other created thing—and that includes you, and that includes Satan—has the power to separate or remove My own from Me (Rom. 8:38-39).

"My beloved child, I protected you before there was a you to protect—and I still do.

"I am Yahweh God, El Shaddai, God Almighty—and I always, *always* keep My word. And I always, *always* accomplish what I purpose."

Blessed be the God and Father of our Lord Jesus Christ, who according to His great mercy has caused us to be born again to a living hope through the resurrection of Jesus Christ from the dead, to obtain an inheritance which is imperishable and undefiled and will not fade away, reserved in heaven for you,

—Who are protected by the power of God through faith for a salvation ready to be revealed in the last time —

In this you greatly rejoice, even though now for a little while, if necessary, you have been distressed by various trials, that the proof of your faith, being more precious than gold which is perishable, even though tested by fire, may be found to result in praise and glory and honor at the revelation of Jesus Christ;

And though you have not seen Him, you love Him, and though you do not see Him now, but believe in Him, you greatly rejoice with joy inexpressible and full of glory, obtaining as the outcome of your faith the salvation of your souls.

—1 Peter 1:3-9

For it is better, if God should will it so, that you suffer for doing what is right rather than for doing what is wrong. For Christ also died for sins once for all, the just for the unjust,

in order that He might bring us to God,

having been put to death in the flesh, but made alive in the spirit;

In which also He went and made proclamation to the spirits now in prison, who once were disobedient, when the patience of God kept waiting in the days of Noah, during the construction of the ark, in which a few, that is, eight persons, were brought safely through the water.

—1 Peter 3:17-20

8

THE EXCHANGE

The utter tragedy of man's fall in Genesis 3 erupts against the divine creation glories of Genesis 1-2. Only two relatively short chapters in the Bible present the world and its inhabitants at peace with itself and its Creator; the severity of man's fall follows shortly thereafter. Everything—and everyone—changed. Imperfection replaced perfection; purity transformed instantly into defilement. Sin. Crime. Disease. Death. War—all active components of a world helplessly degraded by the savage ramifications of man's sin. Even beyond these tragic reverberations, the most severe change was the wedge that sin drove in between the Creator and His creatures. No longer could God and His image-born children enjoy walks in the cool of His garden. Sin separated—as sin still separates. God responded to the Fall in keeping with His holiness. After decreeing His verdict against mankind, the earth, and Satan in Genesis 3, God expelled the first couple from His garden and, in a sense, away from His presence.

What thoughts Adam must have pondered that first night in his newly fallen domain. How quickly his world—and he himself—had changed. How much he had given up—and given over—to the Enemy. We of the human realm do not experientially know perfection with others, with our world, or even within our ourselves. All we have ever known is sin's contamination, being conceived and born into a state of sin (Ps. 51:5; Eph. 2:1-3).

Adam knew. He knew firsthand what he had once possessed. Even more he knew what he had been: sinless, undefiled, holy. For the remainder of his days on earth Adam would always have a base of comparison restricted only to himself and Eve. Adam once enjoyed the perfect union with his God-given bone-of-his-bone wife. Together the two cohabited an environment that contained no trace of sin's death-filled effects. Yet even beyond these blessings—and harmonizing with Jesus' statement thousands of years later that man does not live by bread alone, but by every word that proceeds from the mouth of God—Adam once basked in radiant fellowship with his Father and Creator, a pristine union unrestrained by sin. His other blessings, such as Eve and his environment, were mostly external and temporary. Adam's relationship with God, as Scripture would repeatedly disclose throughout the unfolding of God's revelation, emerges from the inside out—and is eternal.

In the engulfing darkness of the first night away from Eden, a depleted Adam brooded over his plight. If Eve sat by him physically, it would still be as though she never existed. Inner core searchings of this magnitude required sifting through Adam's own heart before considering input from another. An enemy had struck, a devastator had plundered, and together the first man and woman stepped away from God and into the non-retractable arena of sin. While Adam and Eve shared the responsibilities of a married couple, the burden of a fallen world's plight resided uniquely on Adam. Although Eve had first entered into this new realm of disobedience, deep inside, Adam knew he was where he was by his own choice, as a consequence of his own actions. No one had deceived him; of his own free will he had chosen the creature over the Creator (Rom. 1:25). The previously prophesied death resulted just as God had promised—spiritually at this point, with the physical death to follow at some undisclosed time in the future. Now Adam sat in darkness, perhaps a fire or some torch struggled to illuminate his newly darkened world. Yet everywhere fallen man looked—other than at the meager first glimmers of the Light—he saw only darkness. Hope had become a distant memory, not so much in time, but in grasp.

Adam now existed in the midst of a curse that marred every good thing he had once experienced and possessed. The very ground on which he sat, as well as every other aspect of God's physical creation, had already begun to sprout the contaminated fruit of his sin. His marriage immediately changed forever, never returning to the perfect relationship that God had originally intended in Genesis 2. Hardship, toil, worry, and grief would mark Adam all the days of his life, haunting him in varying degrees, as it continues to do so with his collective progeny today. Every day would bring forth new evidences of his fallen condition: some mild, others severe. Adam would eventually learn a new depth of sorrow as his first son Cain murdered his second son Abel, with even this crime ultimately traced back to the effects of his own disobedience to God.

Many know the mammoth weight one carries for the consequences of his own sins; a deeper misery resides within those whose sins ensnare the ones they love—and Adam experienced this darkness before anyone else did. He also carried the weightier burden of having no past experience or example of others from which to learn, or from which to see God's divine working to bring about good even out of the residual embers of tragic sins.

After Adam had lived nine hundred and thirty years (Gen. 5:5), experiencing both the joys and hardships of life, he died physically, as he had initially died spiritually the moment he transgressed against God. This once majestic being, one-half of the pinnacle of God's creation, a component of the handiwork God Himself had pronounced "very good" (Gen. 1:31), ultimately returned to the dust from which God had created him (Gen. 3:19). Yet before this promised end, no matter how good any segment of Adam's life was, he still never retrieved what he once possessed in the Garden. Some people dream—Adam *remembered*. His fallen condition remained a thorn too deeply embedded within his soul for him ever to remove by his own strength or efforts as he sat amidst a new realm of darkness.

Another truth that caused Adam deep sorrow was the exchange of his God-ordained authority for servitude to another. God's original design placed the first couple in a ruling capacity over the inhabited earth: "Let Us make man in Our image, according to Our likeness; and let them *rule over* the fish of the sea and over the birds of the sky and over the cattle and over all the earth, and over every creeping thing that creeps on the earth" (Gen. 1:26). An ironic absurdity, no doubt, later crossed the regal couple's minds: one of the animals over which God gave them authority—the serpent—had played a pivotal role in their demise. A new grief they would continually encounter began its initial residence within them as well: at least one of their beloved animals assigned to their care became instead their sacrifice, offering his life in place of theirs, as God Himself clothed the defiled couple with the skins of the world's first blood sacrifice (Gen. 3:21).

Psalm 8 presents an even more majestic description of God's original grand intention for mankind than even the Genesis account. Millennia later, David, most likely on the graceful hills overlooking Bethlehem, contrasted the visual expanse of God's domain with the frail limitations of man:

O LORD, our Lord, how majestic is Thy name in all the earth,
Who hast displayed Thy splendor above the heavens!
From the mouth of infants and nursing babes Thou hast established
strength,
Because of Thine adversaries, to make the enemy and the revengeful
cease.

When I consider Thy heavens, the work of Thy fingers,
The moon and the stars, which Thou hast ordained;
What is man, that Thou dost take thought in him?
And the son of man, that Thou dost care for him?

Yet Thou hast made him a littler lower than God,
And dost crown him with glory and majesty!
Thou dost make him to rule over the works of Thy hands;
Thou hast put all things under his feet,
All sheep and oxen, and also the beasts of the field,
The birds of the heavens, and the fish of the sea,
Whatever passes through the paths of the seas.

O LORD, our Lord, how majestic is Thy name in all the earth! (Ps. 8:1-9)

While Adam still retained elements of God's authority after the Fall, his present reign only slightly resembled his previous exalted capacity. Not only were his circumstances different, *he* was different. Adam sensed this curse to his deepest being. Through his own choice he had given over his God-ordained authority to another, and exchanged a relationship of watchful love and fellowship with his Creator/Protector for the wrathful tyranny of a ravenous wolf.

Luke 4:6 is one of the most compelling verses in Scripture. Here, in tempting Jesus, Satan offered Jesus worldwide authority, claiming, "I will give You all this domain [authority] and its glory; for it has been handed over to me, and I give it to whomever I wish."

God does not give us any explanatory details in Scripture, which is one reason a verse like this is so intriguing. *Everything* within Luke 4:6 raises questions. For instance, as an initial consideration, is what Satan claimed true? Had the world's domain actually been handed over to him? Satan is a liar from the beginning, his very nature being that of a liar (John 8:44). Yet would Satan be brazen enough to lie in his encounter with Jesus? On the other hand, if the statement is true, another question emerges: who handed over the authority or domain to Satan: Adam or God — or both?

Scripture overwhelmingly bears witness that the earth is the Lord's, and all therein (Dan. 4:17, 25-26, 34-35). The history of the world — past, present, and future — firmly rests in God's hand (Isa. 46:8-10). Even Satan's pinnacle of exercised dominion in the world, the future Antichrist, will ultimately step into history only after Jesus breaks the first seal (Rev. 6:1-2), and God grants him authority to rule over the entire world for a designated period of time (Rev. 13:7).

Nonetheless, while Satan's boast may repulse us, Scripture supports aspects of his claims. As strange as it may seem, Satan initially benefited more from Adam's fall than anyone else, receiving an expanded authority, domain, and rule. Jesus underscored Satan's great authority by three times referring to him as ruling over this world. In John 12:31 Jesus stated, "Now judgment is upon this world; now *the ruler of this world* shall be cast out." Later on the night of His betrayal, after Jesus had dismissed Judas, Jesus spoke again to His despairing disciples, saying, "I will not speak much more with you, for *the ruler of the world* is coming, and he has nothing in Me" (John 14:30). In reference to the new work the Holy Spirit would begin shortly after Jesus' ascension into heaven, He said, "and concerning judgment, because *the ruler of this world* has been judged" (John 16:11). Paul also described Satan as possessing a high status, describing him as "the prince of the power of the air" (Eph. 2:2), and even more to the point, "the god of this world" (or "age") (2 Cor. 4:4). The Apostle John, decades after Christ's victory at the cross, still wrote, "the whole world lies in the power of the evil one" (1 John 5:19). Adam forfeited; Satan grasped — all with God's permission.

When considered, the account of the Fall does not seem just or proper. Satan, the instigator of man's temptation and defiled status, left the judgment scene of Genesis 3 with vastly *more* than he had when he had entered. Whether Satan foresaw how God would respond is debatable. We do not know if Satan calculated his new exalted status before the Fall, or if he expected only God's severe judgment afterwards. However, Scripture repeatedly bears witness to one fact: Satan incredibly gained — and substantially gained — after Adam's fall. In fact, the exchange that occurred is so massive, it seems most unfair. Satan tempted Eve, who in turn ensnared Adam — and mankind collectively fell from their status of holy innocence to debased depravity. The robber robbed, and God permitted *him* to retain what he had stolen. On the other hand, Adam and Eve, along with the serpent, immediately received severe judgments from God Almighty. Yet the Serpent of Old behind the earthly serpent received no present judgment, only a veiled promise of a future demise. Adam and Eve would eventually return to the dust from which God created them (Gen. 3:19). What an exchange for the *magnum opus* of God's creation as their regal status would eventually degenerate into mere dust over which both man and animals would later trod. Adding to the insult is the fact that humans and beasts of future generations would not be cognizant who of ancient past had added their dust residue to the path on which they walked. Long after Adam and Eve died and decayed, Satan would continue to prowl about on the earth, seeking someone to devour (1 Pet. 5:8), exercising his evil power in a world he himself helped to contaminate.

It does not seem fair or just at all. It does not seem like a righteous act of a loving God.

When one contrasts the creation majesties of Genesis 1 and 2 with the dismal realities of Genesis 3, certain questions seep through, some we most likely would not voice in the company of other believers. Perhaps the most nagging questions originate from the simple question, *"Why?"* Why would God allow Adam and Eve to taste perfection and creation glory, and then have them exchange it for a life of contamination, toil, and heartbreak? Why did God react so strongly and severely to Adam's single act of disobedience? Why did one sin result in worldwide devastation and contamination, both spiritually and physically (Rom. 5:15-18)? The horrors of this sin are passed on to the billions born thousands of years afterwards. Adam *chose* sin; we are born into a realm of sin that we did not choose but nonetheless affects everything about us. This also seems out of balance; we conclude it is unfair. Also, why would God not be a better protector of Adam and Eve? We have no indication from Scripture that God warned them of the adversary's presence. Would we allow our children to play within the confines we determined, knowing an evil one lurked who could cause their deaths, and not explicitly warn them of the danger or intercede to protect them? Even if the enemy gained access and brought about such devastation, would we not immediately seek out the culprit and properly punish him for the murder of God's creatures and creation, for ruining the creation masterpiece composed by God? Even beyond these questions remains this one: why would God grant Satan much more domain and authority, knowing that he was the chief instigator of the world's first crime? Why would God shorten man's days, ending it with death, and yet grant Satan multiple millennia to bring compounded heartache and carnage on the world he himself had led into defilement?

Why, God?

We of the flesh generally view spiritual realities from a most limited and uninformed base, usually beginning with ourselves as the point of reference. Since "the world through its wisdom did not come to know God" (1 Cor. 1:21), if God did not reveal Himself and His truth to us, we would never find either, groping about in spiritual darkness as much as Adam did the first night after his fall. Our limited understanding often manifests itself in the very phrasing of our questions. For instance, "Why would God act so severely against *one little sin?*" By framing the question this way, we approach God by elevating ourselves and lowering Him—lowering Him only in our perception, that is, not in His essence.

Let's consider some of the questions. Initially, who determined that the sin of Adam and Eve was "little"? Adam's sin may have been a simple act, but at its heart was a defiant act of disobedience. The creature willingly rebelled against his Creator. Yet even beyond this is a deeply more sobering truth: *one sin resulted in the death of God's Son Jesus.* Would you classify one act that would lead to the brutal murder of your child "a little sin"? Neither would God. If Adam or Eve alone was the only sinner in all of human history, even if sin's ramifications did not produce expanding concentric circles of effects, Jesus would still have had to become flesh in order to redeem them. From the predetermined plan and the foreknowledge of God (Acts 2:23), Jesus had to die to redeem the lost. It would cost the Son His death, as well as His entire lifetime, to accomplish God's plan of salvation. Even before His sacrificial death, Jesus had to live a perfect life in the very midst of a fallen world and endure the most severe attacks from mankind's great enemy. Such He did, masterfully living and dying to redeem and restore the lost of Adam's race: one perfect sacrifice sufficient to cover—and recover—the totality of what Adam had forfeited.

The accomplishment of man's redemption did not occur automatically. Instead it required an exchange for Jesus, one from glory to humility—an exchange for which there is no earthly comparison, since it involved God stepping out of His heaven. As David pondered centuries earlier when looking out at the expanse of heavens, to whom or with what could we compare God or His abode to anyone or anything on earth? Jesus took a divine step down—not up. Thousands of years beyond Adam and Eve's exchange of innocence for defilement, Jesus willingly exchanged His abode in heaven and His equality with God (Phil. 2:5-11) for confinement within the frailties of flesh and blood. He exchanged preincarnate glory (John 17:5) for humble servitude (Mark 10:45), exchanging exalted status as God (Isa. 6; Phil. 2:6), to obedient sacrifice (Phil. 2:8). Jesus exchanged these freely, by His own choosing, as the visible love of the Godhead became encased in a form of Adam's race, living among a cursed people on a cursed planet.

Before considering other related matters, one additional item in Luke 4:6 needs exploring. Satan used the perfect tense when boasting that the domain and the glory of the earth had been handed over to him. The perfect tense is the "done deal" tense in Greek. Satan claimed that what had been handed over to him was a permanent exchange. Was this a lie, or did Satan genuinely believe that the handing of the earth's domain over to him was irrevocable?

Satan may have concluded that the earth and Adam's race was forever in his power, but God never had. The Lamb alone remains worthy to receive permanent glory (Rev. 4–5). How Satan viewed Jesus in His meekness—especially having previously observed Jesus in His preincarnate glory—God does not reveal. But if Satan equated meekness with weakness, he erred beyond all calculation. The transformation of Jesus to a lowly servant was temporary, lasting long enough to crush the head of the serpent, lasting long enough to redeem Adam's fallen race. Jesus' victory shout, "It is finished!" began a long series of its own concentric circles, much like Adam's sin, only in the reverse direction. Jesus' victory began expanding circles of victory, of salvation, of glory—of reclaiming what Adam had handed over to the enemy. Because Jesus triumphed over sin, death, and Satan, all of the parties affected by the Fall in Genesis 3, including inanimate objects, await a God-ordained exchange at the consummation of the age.

A predetermined exchange awaits the initial "victor" in the Garden. One day, at Christ's return, Satan will hand over his usurped status of power to one of confinement, and ultimately to one of eternal torment (Rev. 20:1-10). No longer will he hold the designation "the god of this world" (2 Cor. 4:4) because that "age" will have passed—as well as its "god." One day Satan will receive the brunt of the hell originally prepared for him and his angels (Matt. 25:41). As previously noted, contrary to popular belief, Satan does not presently, nor ever will, rule over hell. Hell is the place where Satan will receive the full reckoning of the weight of his sin. The most brazen and rebellious humans at least have only one life for which to give an account to God. Satan must do so for *all* his sinful activities from his expulsion from heaven up through his imprisonment in the lake of fire. Not only has no one else has ever sinned more in volume than Satan, no one else has sinned with as much awareness of God's grandeur and glory. No one else has ever sinned against such Light. Simply put, no one will suffer more in hell than Satan—or come even remotely close to doing so.

From an eternal viewpoint, therefore, it becomes evident that God's judgment is fair and just. Earth is temporary; hell is eternal. What shall it profit a man—or Satan—if he gains the whole world and loses his soul? What circumstance of earth could be valuable enough to enjoy for a time if the outcome is God's fiercest wrath throughout eternity? From this perspective, God's reactive punishment against Adam and Eve is far more grace-oriented than His allowing sin to go unchecked for an extended period. God dealt severely with mankind, but His most devastating judgment awaits the Serpent of Old. Only this time God will not clothe the offender's nakedness, nor does He offer any hope of the Light to rescue and redeem. No sacrificial Lamb steps in Satan's place to redeem this one who would never accept Him even if God made the offer of grace to him while he agonized in hell. Satan prefers his own realm, even in torment, than that of God's in any capacity. It may not make sense to us, but, as before, we have God's image within us, and we cannot fully reason with the capacity that the Evil One does.

Although we do not see this now, the earth will one day have the effects of the curse of Genesis 3 removed, exchanging its present corruption for renewed glory. Romans 8:19-21 reveals that while man's Fall corrupted *everything* associated with the earth, Christ's glorification of His own will extend to the farthest earthly realm: "For the anxious longing of the creation waits eagerly for the revealing of the sons of God. For creation was subjected to futility, not of its own will, but because of Him who subjected it, in hope that the creation itself also will be set free from its slavery to corruption into the freedom of the glory of the children of God." So at some designated time in the future,

God will restore to the earth the primeval majesty it briefly enjoyed. Yet beyond this blessing, even as God makes those in Christ new creatures (2 Cor. 5:17), God will one day create a new heaven and a new earth (Rev. 21–22), similar in some ways to the old ones, but better, purer, recreated—and above all, full of glory.

The sin-scarred body of Adam's race, initially crowned with honor by God, will also receive unspeakable benefits of Christ's victory, exchanging the mortal for the immortal (1 Cor. 15:50-53). No matter the degree to which the outer man decays (2 Cor. 4:16), those saved in Jesus have a resurrection body promised by God (2 Cor. 5:1-6). Though momentary light affliction continually bombards those beloved of the Lord (2 Cor. 4:17), this onslaught is only temporary, although often the affliction seems to us to be neither light nor momentary. Those in Christ currently have eternal life; one day we will likewise receive a body which sin and death will have no access. Even more to the point, one day a body will be specifically created so that we can enjoy pure fellowship with the Godhead, fellowship infinitely more expansive than the limited one Adam knew.

So ultimately, in God's grand design, the second Adam, Jesus (1 Cor. 15:45), will undo the curse and the calamities brought about by the first Adam, regaining all that was lost—and more. Eternal life in fullness will replace death and separation. The cursed earth will receive the grand remaking God intended. Satan will encounter the full force of God's wrath; the promised victory first glimpsed in Genesis 3:15 will finally be fully accomplished. Eternally damned; eternally separated; eternally removed from the glory of God, and after Revelation 20, Satan will never again pose a threat to those of Adam's race, nor mostly likely will his name ever be mentioned.

We, whom Christ has redeemed from the curse, long for that day of victorious restoration. With every death of those we love, with our own failures both physically and spiritually, with our own sinfulness, with the perils of the world's events, with the coming apostasy promised before Christ's return, we ponder our present status in much the same way that Adam did that first night. But our course differs from Adam's: we live on the other side of the cross with much more Light revealed than Adam had. We know how, and even more importantly Who; God has chosen not to reveal when. So we stand firm. So we go on in faith. So we look anxiously for His return, as God's children have looked for since Christ's ascension: "For our citizenship is in heaven, from which also we eagerly wait for a Savior, the Lord Jesus Christ, who will transform the body of our humble state into conformity with the body of His glory, by the exertion of the power that He has even to subject all things to Himself" (Phil. 3:20-21).

Yet as blissful as the elements associated with Christ's return are to reflect on and desire, one other divinely-decreed exchange awaits us — an exchange, when once fully perceived, leaves us longing in breathless anticipation.

Genesis 1:26-27 and Psalm 8 describe the authority that God originally intended for mankind. Hebrews 2:8-9 explains how Jesus ultimately fulfilled the requirements of Psalm 8: "For in subjecting all things to him, He left nothing that is not subject to him. But now we do not yet see all things subjected to him. But we do see Him who has been made for a little while lower than the angels, namely, Jesus, because of the suffering of death crowned with glory and honor, that by the grace of God He might taste death for everyone." What Adam could have possessed eternally, Jesus ultimately receives. And with Jesus being Jesus, He joyously shares the fruit of His own victory with those whom He has redeemed.

But the exchange Jesus offers goes vastly beyond even this truth of restoring God's original designation of mankind's earthly reign. God currently reserves magnitudes more for those who love Him.

The Bible offers us only glimpses of what God gives the believer in Jesus Christ. Some we can partially perceive; others we will understand only when we stand before God. Some truths we can better contemplate by way of comparison. For instance, as previously shown, 1 Peter 1:12 indicates that angels desire to look into, or to investigate, things relating to a believer's salvation. Part of this is no doubt due to the fact that no angel ever received God's grace and forgiveness. Yet another aspect is evident as well: angels understand that believers will receive rewards vastly expanded beyond their current worldly domain. Though temporarily made a little lower than angels, the redeemed in Christ will one day be exalted even beyond the sphere that angels currently occupy. Paul writes that in heaven Christians will be granted a judging capacity over angels (1 Cor. 6:3). The Word promises that even now believers are blessed with every spiritual blessing in the heavenly places in Christ Jesus (Eph. 1:3). For the time being we take the assurance that God has granted us such a privilege. One day we will understand and receive the full meaning of this. Paul, to whom God granted a preview of heaven, concluded, "For I consider that the sufferings of this present time are not worthy to be compared with the glory that is to be revealed to us" (Rom. 8:18). This verse comes after the promise that we are now God's children, "and if children, heirs also, heirs of God and fellow heirs with Christ" (Rom. 8:17).

Revelation 2:26-28 explains some of the exchange that awaits the children of God. To the one who overcomes Jesus promises:

> And he who overcomes, and he who keeps My deeds until the end, to him I will give authority over the nations; and he shall rule them with a rod of iron, as the vessels of the potter are broken to pieces, as I also have received authority from My Father; and I will give him the morning star.

It is one thing for Adam and Eve to rule over the earth before the Fall; it is quite another to rule with Jesus after the Fall. Actually Jesus quotes from Psalm 2, a Messianic psalm that promises that He will rule the nations. Yet the Savior takes His own psalm about Himself and expands it to include His children.

As wonderful as this will be, there is still more.

In the final promise to the overcomer in Revelation, Jesus increases the domain in the previous promises. It is one thing to rule with Him on earth; it is quite another to rule with Him in heaven. Unless it had come directly from the Word of God, we would consider such a statement pure blasphemy: Jesus Himself promises, *"He who overcomes, I will grant to him to sit down with Me on My throne, as I also overcame and sat down with My Father on His throne"* (Rev. 3:21). We will spend the remainder of eternity with Jesus, fully understanding all that is involved in this one promise from our Savior.

Heirs, fellow-heirs, blessed with every spiritual blessing in the heavenlies, ruling with Jesus—all beyond all earthly comparison.

But as hard as it is to believe, there is still much more offered by the Lord! One simple promise remains.

What could possibly be compared to ruling with Jesus on His throne? Perhaps the matchless elevation of believers is best summarized in the divine promise of 2 Thessalonians 2:14: "And it was for this He called you through our gospel, *that you may gain the glory of our Lord Jesus Christ.*" What an incomprehensible promise; nothing else anywhere remotely compares with this one promise. We should note that no article exists in the Greek text, which means the verse could be rendered, "that you may gain glory of our Lord Jesus Christ." We will receive some of Jesus' glory, but not all of it, as is only fitting. Perhaps the varying measures of Christ's glory correspond to the degrees of rewards for believers. Nonetheless, receiving any of the glory of God vastly surpasses any element available on earth. Fallen, sin-filled, and cursed humanity, exchanging their depraved defilement for the eternal glory of Jesus—as the Godhead has continuously yearned for with a holy-heated passion.

The glory of Jesus gained by the redeemed stands in staggering contrast with the domain originally granted to Adam and Eve. After the creation of man and woman, God granted the first couple the authority on earth. When Jesus conquered Satan and his domain, His victory expanded to all of heaven and earth (Rev. 4-5). After all, Satan originated from heaven, and currently occupies the space between heaven and earth for his activities. The Bible presents him as "the prince of the power of the air" (Eph. 2:2). Part of his domain consists of "the spiritual forces of wickedness in the heavenly places" (Eph. 6:12). Jesus conquered that realm completely—and then delights in sharing His deserved domain with His brothers and sisters. His victory—our reward. No exchange in any other realm can compare. What Jesus freely gives is billions upon billions times more than Adam and Eve originally possessed. Simply put, Jesus almost infinitely exchanges and enlarges the domain He gives to those who love Him. Earth is merely a microscopic speck in our own solar system, much less in the countless solar systems throughout space. The collective solar systems are most likely mere specks when viewed from heaven's vantage point, and their combined glories are dark holes when contrasted with the glory of the Lord that He freely shares with His own. Sin debased us; Jesus will exalt us. Satan pulled mankind downward; Jesus raised us up—up even unto Himself and into Himself.

God originally crowned mankind with glory and honor, giving His children reign over His earth. But that was all that God had granted for the time being, revealing no authority for mankind anywhere else: no promised heavenly blessings; no initial word in regard to heaven; no prophecy of reigning with Him; no affirmation of receiving His glory. Yet after Christ's triumph, God freely bestows this and so much more to those in Jesus, abundantly giving to these what Satan so lustfully desired, but could never attain. At the end of the age God will expand the authority of the redeemed to include the limitless domain of Jesus, a domain so vastly beyond our comprehension that no adequate comparison presently exists. Perhaps putting it as simply as our childlike minds can understand, Jesus' domain includes everything and everywhere that God created. This He gives—*with Himself*—to all who simply ask Him in faith, and believe He is able to do what He promises.

Not only will God immensely expand our realm of authority and rule, He will also recreate us into all that we truly are in Jesus Christ. One day God will remake us in the incomparable glory—glory originating from His own essence. "Beloved, now we are children of God, and it has not appeared as yet what we shall be. *We know that, when He appears, we shall be like Him, because we shall see Him just as He is*" (1 John 3:2).

Adam's one sin—universal depravity.

Jesus' one sacrifice—sufficient redemption for all who call upon His name for salvation.

We of Adam's race—multiplied sin upon sin, countered by grace upon grace—made into new creatures in Christ.

The Earth—temporary, defiled, passing away—to be changed into a new heaven and a new earth.

We whom God makes into new creatures—eternally united with God through Jesus Christ—are fellow heirs with Jesus over His entire domain. Actually when considered from what Jesus already possessed, Satan's offer of worldwide dominion to Him in Luke 4 was a mere speck of dust in the totality of God's expanse. But Jesus had to succeed so that He could bring you and me along with Him—and bring us into the very presence of God.

Is it any wonder Paul that would pray in Ephesians 1:17-21, asking "that the God of our Lord Jesus Christ, *the Father of glory*, may give to you a spirit of wisdom and of revelation in the knowledge of Him. I pray that the eyes of your heart may be enlightened, so that you may know what is the hope of His calling, what are *the riches of the glory of His inheritance in the saints*, and what is the surpassing greatness of His power toward us who believe"? As a reminder of the believers' expanded domain Paul continued, "These are in accordance with the working of the strength of His might which He brought about in Christ, when He raised Him from the dead, and seated Him at His right hand in the heavenly places, far above all rule and authority and power and dominion, and every name that is named, not only in this age, but also in the one to come."

Come soon, Lord Jesus!

For this reason, I bow my knees before the Father, from whom every family in heaven and on earth derives its name, that He would grant you, according to the riches of His glory, to be strengthened with power through His spirit in the inner man;

So that Christ may dwell in your hearts through faith; and that you, being rooted and grounded in love, may be able to comprehend with all the saints what is the breadth and length and height and depth, and to know the love of Christ which surpasses knowledge, that you may be filled up to all the fulness of God.

Now to Him who is able to do exceeding abundantly beyond all that we ask or think, according to the power that works within us, to Him be the glory in the church and in Christ Jesus to all generations forever and ever. Amen.

— Ephesians 3:14-21

And I saw a new heaven and a new earth; for the first heaven and the first earth passed away, and there is no longer any sea. And I saw the holy city, new Jerusalem, coming down out of heaven from God, made ready as a bride adorned for her husband.

And I heard a loud voice from the throne, saying, "Behold, the tabernacle of God is among men, and He shall dwell among them, and they shall be His people, and God Himself shall be among them, and He shall wipe away every tear from their eyes; and there shall no longer be any death; there shall no longer be any mourning, or crying, or pain; the first things have passed away."

And He who sits on the throne said, "Behold, I am making all things new."

And He said, "Write, for these words are faithful and true."

— Revelation 21:1-5

And he showed me a river of the water of life, clear as crystal, coming from the throne of God and of the Lamb, in the middle of its street and on either side of the river was the tree of life, bearing twelve kinds of fruit, yielding its fruit every month; and the leaves of the tree were for the healing of the nations.

And there shall no longer be any curse; and the throne of God and of the Lamb shall be in it, and His bond-servants shall serve Him; and they shall see His face, and His name shall be on their foreheads.

And there shall no longer be any night; and they shall not have need of the light of a lamp nor the light of the sun, because the Lord God shall illumine them;

and they shall reign forever and ever.

— Revelation 22:1-5

9

THE POSITIONING

J esus had previously designated the Twelve minus one as His apostles (Matt. 10:1-4), divinely commissioning them for authoritative positions in His soon-to-be-born Church. While granted God-given authority as leaders, even now to their core they remained disciples (Matt. 28:16) — learners from their Master — and would continue to be throughout their earthly lives and even throughout eternity. At this point their Teacher still had very much yet to instruct His earnest students before He departed from them and returned to the Father.

So much had transpired in the last few days. Divine truths and prophecies displayed in rapid-fire succession in the presence of many witnesses. Each monumental event or discourse would be discussed repeatedly and studied throughout the age, as they still are today: the grand preview entry of Messiah into Jerusalem, the discourses with the religious opponents, the private training of the Twelve, the Passover meal, Gethsemane, the arrest, the trial, the crucifixion, and the resurrection.

Acts 1:3 presents a summary statement covering the time from the resurrection of Jesus to His ascension: "To these He also presented Himself alive, after His suffering, by many convincing proofs, appearing to them over a period of forty days, and speaking of the things concerning the kingdom of God." Within this one verse, God divulges three substantial truths that we do not find elsewhere in Scripture. The first is that Jesus appeared to His disciples, Luke employing a rare Greek word that means "to be visible" or "to appear." The implication is that Jesus appeared to them and then departed from them, as He did with the two disciples on the road to Emmaus, who after having their eyes opened, recognized Jesus, "and He vanished from their sight" (Luke 24:31). The second divinely revealed detail is that the timeframe from the resurrection to the ascension was forty days. Coupled with the first truth of His appearing, this is important. Jesus did not stay with His disciples the entire time; He repeatedly appeared and disappeared, often leaving them alone with themselves — and in a new way, alone with Him — for undesignated days. The Bible presents several different resurrection appearances that took place during this approximately six-week segment. There may have been more, but if so, God chose not to reveal it, so it is best to limit this to what Scripture has revealed. The third truth from this one verse reveals that the content of Jesus' teaching was "speaking of the things concerning the kingdom of God" (Acts 1:3), which of utmost importance, was the content of His first public message in Matthew 4:17. Only this time the teaching on the Kingdom of God did not include "is at hand" — the King was going home before He returned to reign.

Each sentence spoken or act witnessed from the cross to the ascension would take all eternity to learn the extent and nuances God revealed about Himself and His holy program. Still within the cluster of the resurrection appearances that Scripture records, one particular session stands apart from the others. All of the manifestations are significant, yet one remains extremely important because the Godhead repeatedly emphasizes it. However, casual readers of the Bible who generally skip over this one account often miss significant clues that God purposely left in His Word. As before, we will also discover that identifying the clues leads to additional questions — and again to a deeper mystery.

On three separate occasions the Bible points to one designated meeting between Jesus and His disciples that would transpire at some point after the resurrection. The first reference to this predetermined meeting happened before the crucifixion, immediately following the Last Supper. Matthew 26:30 records that after Jesus and His disciples sang the closing Passover hymn, they proceeded to the Mount of Olives. It was at this point Jesus somberly revealed to His followers in a verse we have already studied, "You will all fall away because of Me this night, for it is written, 'I will strike down the Shepherd, and the sheep of the flock shall be scattered'" (Matt. 26:31).

Continuing where He left off, Jesus attaches a most important detail in the next verse: "But after I have been raised, I will go before you to Galilee" (Matt. 26:32). Here, then, are Jesus' simple directives to His disciples, and the first designation of where He would be after His resurrection. Galilee was the early home of the majority of the apostles — and of Jesus Himself. It was also the region in which Jesus had done the bulk of His earthly ministry. Galilee was approximately sixty miles north of Jerusalem, where Jesus and His disciples were that night. Travel from Jerusalem to Galilee was generally a two to three day journey, depending on how hurried one was and the route chosen.

The disciples, however, could not mentally abandon Jesus' first words that they all would fall away that night because of Him—especially Peter. He and the others loved Jesus. Abandoning Him now was the furthest intent of their hearts. The subsequent verse records Peter's boast that, "Even though all may fall away because of You, I [emphatic in the Greek] will never fall away" (Matt. 26:33)—distancing himself from the others whom Jesus had just addressed. By default Peter claimed that he was stronger than God's written Word, affirmed by the Incarnate Word, that *all* would not fall away that very night. Jesus in turn prophesied that before the cock would crow Peter would deny on three separate occasions that he even knew Jesus. Peter restated the sheer absurdity that he would fall away, insisting he would rather die in place of Jesus than ever to abandon Him. The other disciples immediately added their voices to this ignorantly boastful mantra.

Yet Jesus' word remained: "I will go before you in Galilee." With the trepidation of that dark evening and the hastening of the crucifixion activities and subplots, the disciples could easily overlook Jesus' specific instruction. Nothing in the account shows that they asked Him anything about seeing Him in Galilee. We can sympathize with these heart-crushed disciples if they passed over this seemingly inconsequential statement, such was the pathos of the present moment. Yet Jesus fully intended to go before them in Galilee as He had previously stated.

God was so intent on having the disciples leave Jerusalem at some forthcoming point and meet Jesus in Galilee that it becomes part of the initial Resurrection Day dialogue between the women at the empty tomb and the angelic witness sent by God. In response to the great fear that these female disciples displayed, the dazzling angel began: "Do not be afraid; for I know that you are looking for Jesus who has been crucified. He is not here, for He has risen, just as He said. Come, see the place where He was lying" (Matt. 28:5-6). After viewing the bodiless sepulcher, the women received instruction on what to do next: "And go quickly and tell His disciples that He has risen from the dead; and behold, *He is going before you into Galilee*, there you will see Him; behold, I have told you" (Matt. 28:7). Mark's parallel passage reveals one additional item of interest, "But go, tell His disciples *and Peter*, 'He is going before you into Galilee; there you will see Him, just as He said to you'" (Mark 16:7). Possibly since Peter had just days ago attempted to remove himself from the "all" who would betray Jesus, the Risen Savior addressed Peter separately from the other disciples, perhaps as a mild rebuke. Another reason may have been more likely: this designation could have encouraged Peter that the Lord was by no means finished with him, despite Peter's repeated denials of even knowing that Jesus existed.

Before moving on we need to note a most significant item within this text. As we have noted, the word *behold* is a very important marker in the Bible. Sometimes translated as "lo," we mostly rush over this little word; however, we never should. *Behold* denotes emphatic notation. It could be translated, as "Mark this carefully! Pay attention! This is important!" At the very least, we should always read this with an exclamation point attached: "Behold!" This greatly differs from the melodious "lo" that we often read aloud in the English texts that seems to smooth the text. *Behold!* is intended to grab our attention, directing us to something important that is about to be said.

The twofold use of "behold" in the angel's proclamation to the women at the tomb not only added a certain importance to the statement (*"Behold!* He is going before you into Galilee," *"Behold!* I have told you"), but may have verbally slapped the original recipients of this divine mandate back into the conversation. Normally, viewing an angel whose "appearance was like lightning, and his garment as white as snow" (Matt. 28:3) would have been one of the most startling events of these women's lives. But to be the first to see the abandoned tomb—where death was literally conquered by Life—was more than they could readily compartmentalize. Their racing minds would most likely not absorb what the angel said unless he added a certain emphasis, which he did: "The Savior is alive! Behold! He is going before you into Galilee. There you will see Him! Behold! I have told you."

The women reacted as most of us would. The parallel account in Mark 16:8 tells how they "went out and fled from the tomb, for trembling and astonishment had gripped them; and they said nothing to anyone, for they were afraid." Matthew 28:8 adds that these faithful ladies of the Lord responded obediently to the angel's command, stating, "And they departed quickly from the tomb with fear and great joy and ran to report it to His disciples."

And then, in the midst of their adrenaline-fed run to make the announcement, the resurrected Jesus encounters and greets them. The adoring women responded with leaping-heart love, and coming to their Savior, they "took hold of His feet and worshiped Him" (Matt. 28:9). Then, instead of a revealing discourse by the Resurrection and the Life, whereby He disclosed new and profound doctrinal truths, the Bible records only one sentence that Jesus spoke: "Do not be afraid; go and take word to My brethren to leave for Galilee, and there they shall see Me" (Matt. 28:10). This third account differs in that although the previous two were pronouncements of what would take place, now it becomes a command: "Take word to My brethren to leave for Galilee."

Scripture thus presents specific instructions on three separate occasions about the disciples journeying from Jerusalem to Galilee to meet Jesus. Each admonition came at momentous events: after the Last Supper and just moments before Gethsemane, by the angel to the women who had visited the empty tomb, and by Jesus Himself at a first post-grave appearance. The reunion in Galilee obviously had tremendous significance for Jesus' training of His disciples—yet few note that such an encounter ever occurred.

But here is something odd. We would think from the multiple instructions of Jesus and the angels that Galilee would be the place where the resurrected Lord would first manifest Himself to His disciples. Yet by the time the disciples had journeyed to Galilee, Jesus had already appeared to them at least a few times. Luke 24:13 states that after Jesus appeared to the women at the tomb, He next appeared to two unnamed disciples who "were going *that very day* to a village named Emmaus, which was about seven miles from Jerusalem." This is important because later, on that first Resurrection morning, Luke 24:33-34 discloses: "And they arose that very hour and returned to Jerusalem, and found gathered together the eleven and those who were with them, saying, 'The Lord has really risen, and has appeared to Simon.'"

Even though the Eleven are addressed in Luke 24, it is evident that when the two disciples who conversed with the Lord excitedly reported what they had witnessed, Simon Peter was not present that very moment. They would have no need to say to the others that the Lord has appeared to Simon if Peter was in the room. He may have stepped out of the room, or his Lord and Master may have given him other orders to go and do something else. Years later, in writing the most extensive chapter in the Bible about the absolute importance of the resurrection, Paul gave this resurrection appearance order: "and that He appeared to

Cephas [another name for Peter], then to the twelve" (1 Cor. 15:5). Jesus granted Peter a special and singular meeting with Himself. God does not offer any additional information regarding when Jesus first appeared to Peter, but it would be so rich if He did. It was another resurrection appearance, somewhere in or near Jerusalem, but not in Galilee.

The Luke account of what occurred that very day continues as the road to Emmaus disciples told of the astounding events that they had witnessed: "And they began to relate their experiences on the road and how He was recognized by them in the breaking of the bread" (Luke 24:35). Then to add divine support to their testimony, Jesus "Himself stood in their midst. But they were startled and frightened and thought that they were seeing a spirit" (Luke 24:36-37). John's description of this first appearance of Jesus to His apostles gives these details: "When therefore it was evening, on that day, the first day of the week, and when the doors were shut where the disciples were, for fear of the Jews, Jesus came and stood in their midst, and said to them, 'Peace be with you'" (John 20:19). This is the same portion of the Bible that records, "Thomas, one of the twelve, called Didymus, was not with them when Jesus came. The other disciples therefore were saying to him, 'We have seen the Lord!' But he said to them, 'Unless I shall see in His hands the imprint of the nails, and put my finger into the place of the nails, and put my hand into His side, I will not believe'" (John 20:24-25).

So instead of in Galilee, Jesus appeared to the eleven minus Peter and Thomas on Resurrection Sunday in Jerusalem—not in Galilee in the north. A second appearance occurs in Jerusalem a week later: "And after eight days again His disciples were inside, and Thomas with them. Jesus came, the doors having been shut, and stood in their midst, and said, 'Peace be with you'" (John 20:26).

An additional appearance of the Lord does take place in Galilee, but this is not the meeting so designated at the resurrection. John 21:1 states, "After these things Jesus manifested Himself again to the disciples at the Sea of Tiberias [Galilee], and He manifested Himself in this way." This is the chapter that tells of Jesus eating with His disciples and of His threefold questioning of Simon Peter as to whether the stumbling disciple really did love Him. So going to Galilee must have some other significance other than initially beholding the resurrected Lord. Yet since Scripture points to this one designated meeting three times, it would reason that the Godhead wants us to mark it as well.

Conceivably, Jesus had the disciples meet Him in Galilee in order for them to retrace some of their steps with Him, and by doing so to relive some of their greatest memories of the Messiah's words and works. Even now, though by no means mature, they were better vessels than they were only days before, especially since they had received a preliminary bestowment of the Holy Spirit when Jesus first appeared to them (John 20:22) and opened their mind (singular in the Greek) so that they might understand the Scriptures (Luke 24:45). Everything that had occurred with their walk with Jesus now became fresh to them, each step bearing witness through new-faith eyes. "There! By that tree, Jesus had healed two blind men. On this slope the living Word of God spoke the living Word of God to the assembled masses. In this village, a man received back alive his previously dead daughter." The apostles probably encountered the road that led to the hated Samaritans, a road they had once avoided—but one Jesus purposely walked to fulfill a divine appointment with the woman at the well (John 4). They probably would have avoided the Samaritans once again, but not so much because of the disdain they previously held for the people. The salvation of the masses was not their present concern. They too had their own divinely ordained rendezvous with Jesus. At this juncture in their spiritual walk, any other activity would be only an annoying distraction.

And so they journeyed to the place where Jesus had repeatedly called them. Perhaps we too should assemble with the Eleven in Galilee. Hopefully we can likewise learn what Jesus so strongly desired to show His original disciples—as well as His other disciples throughout the ages.

The newly commissioned and confused Moses had multiple questions for the unknown God who encountered him by means of the burning bush. One of the foremost mysteries in his mind concerned God's identity. In Exodus 3:13 Moses asked how he should respond when the sons of Israel asked the name of the God who had sent him. God replied, "I AM WHO I AM. . . Thus you shall say to the sons of Israel, 'I AM has sent me to you'" (Ex. 3:14). Moses did not ask the significance of this reply from God, but the revelation of God's name by no means answered his questions. Even today scholars continue to debate the deep nuances within God's answer. Most emphasize the pre-eternal, self-sustaining aspects of this name based on the Hebrew verb "to be" and correlating with the Old Testament name YHWH or Yahweh. To the Jews, I AM, or YHWH, thus became the most sacred name. For one to use—or by their estimation, misuse—this most hallowed of names was considered a blasphemous act worthy of immediate death. Many Jews to this day still substitute Elohim in place of the sacred name YHWH or I AM.

As the centuries passed and the course of history continued, the nation of Israel rose in prominence, declined into exile, and returned to the land given them by God. Those who acknowledged that the God of Israel is also the God of all creation would still treat the I AM name of God most reverently. Yet it challenged the faith of the faithful to see God's hand operative in bondage-weary Israel. This divinely designated times of Israel's subservience paralleled the rise of Gentile domination. Simply put, beginning with the Babylonian exile, the Jews lived in "the time of the Gentiles" (Luke 21:24). Gentile rule proceeded from Babylon to the Medo-Persian empire, to be followed by the rise of Greece under the command of Alexander the Great, and finally during the time of Christ's incarnation, Rome. Gentile power and influence affected every area of Israel's life, including its language. Greek became the *lingua franca* (common language) of the day, which is one reason why God chose to present the original New Testament in Greek; it would be widely received and understood at that time.

The Greek parallel for the Hebrew YHWH or I AM is *ego eimi*. The first part of the phrase is translated "I," and is where we derive our word "ego;" the second part was simply the verb form for "I am." The verb *eimi* alone could be translated as a generic phrase such as, "*I am* hungry;" if *ego* was added in front of it, the phrase emphasized who was doing or saying this, such as "I am hungry." The words used together could also carry the connotation of the Hebrew I AM name of God, so a fastidious Jew would be extremely careful not to utter this divine attestation and description of the Holy God. It should be noted, however, that much of this came from the tradition of man rather than from the commands of God. For example, when Moses asked how he should answer when the Hebrew people asked, "'What is His name?' What shall I say to them?" God instructed Moses, "Thus you shall say to the sons of Israel, 'I AM has sent me to you'" (Exod. 3:14). Nothing in the passage indicates that God ever intended for Moses to refuse to speak aloud this designated name; nothing in the text indicates that Moses reasoned that he should concoct a substitute name so that he would not offend God. Nevertheless, tradition was added and it often replaced the original commands of God. A faithful Jew would *never* utter the name I AM nor tolerate anyone else who would, if there was anything he could do to stop it.

Imagine then how Jesus would be received whenever He used this holy name for God. The first instance where Jesus used *ego eimi* or I AM is one we generally do not observe. Note how different the implication is when this phrase is used, especially in reference to God's name. In Matthew 14, after feeding the 5,000, Jesus forced the disciples to get into a boat on the Sea of Galilee and to depart for the other side. Instead of making it to the other shore, a fierce storm arose so that their lives were in peril. In the midst of the raging storm, Jesus approached the terrified disciples who were in the boat, as He calmly walked on the sea that He Himself had created. In the previous verse the terror-stricken disciples shrieked, "It is a ghost!" Jesus responded, "Take courage, it is I [literally, the "it is I" is *ego eimi*, I AM]; do not be afraid" (Matt. 14:27; Mark 6:50; John 6:20). Stated differently, an expanded paraphrase would be, "Take courage, I AM (Yahweh) — and I AM is with you, even as Moses stood in the presence of I AM. Stop being afraid." Jesus did not reveal His earthly identity as He approached the frenzied disciples; He disclosed His essence, instructing His disciples in this visual object lesson concerning His deity. The disciples' understanding progressed, just as Jesus had desired: Storm! Ghost! Jesus! God! They received Jesus into their boat, and Scripture records the first instance where this God-selected assemblage worshiped Him (Matt. 14:33). Such worship is either right or wrong — holy or sinful — but it cannot be both. This either stands in obedience of the first two of the Ten Commandments of having only one God and worshiping Him only — or it is all a lie. Galatians 4:4 records that Jesus was "born under the Law," consequently the Law was just as binding on Him as it was on any other Jew. No middle ground exists. We should note that Jesus did not rebuke His disciples for their act of worship.

A public encounter with the Pharisees in John 8 gives another instance of Jesus employing the divine name of I AM/*ego eimi*. Notice the subtle changes in two earlier verses in this chapter where *ego eimi* is used. Jesus declared to the Jews who were present, "I said therefore to you, that you shall die in your sins; for unless you believe that I am [*ego eimi*] He [note the italics; "He" is added to smooth the English translation], you shall die in your sins" (John 8:24). The Pharisees may have rightly understood Jesus to use God's name, which would be considered by them to be blasphemous, but not necessarily use this in reference to Himself. What Jesus said could be accurately translated as, "Unless you believe God . . . [*ego eimi*] . . ." The Jewish opponents may have thought, "What a buffoon. Of course we believe in God." The same phrase could likewise be understood in John 8:28: "When you lift up the Son of Man, then you will know that I am [*ego eimi*] He, and I do nothing on My own initiative." By the Pharisees' estimation, Jesus had tread extremely close to blasphemy, but enough leeway existed in the context for what Jesus said that they would be unclear exactly to whom or about what Jesus had spoken.

If any uncertainty remained whether Jesus referred to Himself or to God—or to Himself as God—all doubts evaporated shortly thereafter. Later in the same chapter, in response to the Jews who ridiculed Jesus' statement that He had seen Abraham, Jesus declared, "Truly, truly"—used by Jesus to underscore the veracity and solemnity of what He was about to say—"I say to you, before Abraham was born, I am [*ego eimi*]" (John 8:58). This statement was clear; it was bold. No doubt remained shrouded under linguistic nuance. What Jesus claimed was either divine truth or satanic blasphemy. The Jews believed the latter. That they clearly understood Jesus' intended meaning is seen in that they immediately picked up stones to stone Him. But it was not yet His hour, or the prophesied manner of His death—and I AM passed out of their very midst (John 8:59).

How much more illuminated then become the "I AM" sayings in John's Gospel because each one begins with *ego eimi*. "I AM the bread that came down out of heaven" (6:41) becomes somewhat like a biblical pun: "God—the bread of life that came down out of heaven." Elements of Christ's deity harmonize seamlessly as deeply as one desires to take them. "I AM—the light of the world" (8:12). "I AM—the door" (10:9). "I AM—the good shepherd who lays down His life for the sheep" (10:11). "I AM—the resurrection and the life" (11:25). "I AM—the way, and the truth, and the life" (14:6). "I AM—the true vine" (15:1). Each statement is true about Jesus; each statement is true about God, as the Holy Trinity can never be divorced completely from one another.

Still one more account in John's Gospel contains an *ego eimi*—I AM—episode. This particular instance offers us a front row seat of the majestic Jesus in sovereign control of all matters relating to His pending death. In the approaching hour of darkness, the Good Shepherd, having loved His own unto the end (John 13:1), gave His collective flock one more visual lesson before His trial and crucifixion.

Peter, James, and John had just witnessed a portion of the horror of Gethsemane. Together with a blood-smeared Jesus they rejoined the other disciples. In the short distance away Jesus and His increasingly fearful, pre-scattered flock could see hundreds of torches making their way from the Temple area toward the Mount of Olives. Judas, accompanied by a cohort of Roman soldiers and officers, the chief priests and Pharisees (John 18:3), moved forward to arrest Jesus. If God granted us spiritual eyes to see, at the forefront of this mob we would see Satan, for as Jesus had revealed earlier, "for the ruler of the world is coming, and he has nothing in Me" (John 14:30). Satan had already entered Judas (John 13:27). So in a very real sense, when Judas approached, Satan approached.

Satan's hour of darkness was at hand. The Shepherd would soon be stricken—the sheep would momentarily flee in terror.

John discloses the divine bravery that Jesus displayed. Knowing all the things that were to come upon Him, Jesus went forth to meet His oppressors (John 18:4).

"Whom do you seek?" Jesus asked, as He—not they—initiated the encounter.

"Jesus the Nazarene," was the mob's answer.

"I AM— (*ego eimi*)" Jesus stated in reply.

As before, English translations often render this verse, "I am *He*," with the "He" is usually italicized, rightfully indicating that it is not part of the literal text. John too seems to focus on Jesus' use of this divine name in answering whom the mob sought. Before revealing the effects of Jesus' response, John wrote, "And Judas also who was betraying Him, was standing with them" (John 18:5). John had good reason for noting Judas' presence. The pronouncement of God's name affected Judas—as well as Satan who indwelt him—as much as it did all the assembled enemies: "When therefore He said to them 'I AM—(*ego eimi*),' they drew back, and fell to the ground" (John 18:6).

By the mere power of His spoken name, the opponents of Jesus—including both physical and spiritual enemies—drew back and fell to the ground. Divine power manifested in subdued control, in no way exercised in its full force, or the world itself would have been instantaneously consumed. Satan and his demons would have immediately known the Source, although the ignorant human agents would not. Satan and his legions had already experienced a similar display of the Word of God's power when He had expelled them out of His own heaven. The disciples most likely marveled in stunned bewilderment.

God's observing angels would have expected no less. In the darkness of the betrayal, the Light of the World demonstrated to His disciples—and to His opponents—a visual preview of Philippians 2:9-11: "Therefore also God highly exalted Him, and bestowed on Him the name which is above every name, that at the *name* of Jesus every knee should bow, of those who are in heaven, and on earth, and under the earth, and that every tongue should confess that Jesus Christ is Lord, to the glory of God the Father."

Jesus could have continued this display as long as He desired, but His divine demonstration at this time would be instead in humble submission to the Father, rendering His oppressors helpless. Jesus once more asked whom the arresting party sought. The voices of the blind once more communally bleated, "Jesus the Nazarene," perhaps while either wiping the moistened dirt off their newly-stained clothes, or leaning away from Jesus, expecting to fall backward to the ground again.

Jesus replied in another almost biblical pun that was lost on the human agents—even His own—but not on His spiritual enemies. "'I told you that I AM— (*ego eimi*); if therefore you seek Me, let these go their way,' that the word might be fulfilled which He spoke, 'Of those whom Thou hast given Me I lost not one'" (John 18:8-9). Hours earlier, when Jesus informed His disciples that they all would fall away that night (Matt. 26:31), He utilized a Greek word that means, "to cause or make to stumble." Actually Jesus used the future passive to describe what would take place: "they will be caused to stumble." The disciples did not stumble of their own accord; they had been made to stumble in fulfillment of Scripture. This was so Jesus could stand alone against the forces of darkness, so His divinely-shepherded flock could learn the vastness of Messiah's strength and love—as well as their own utter weakness and failure without Him.

At the second issuing forth of I AM, Jesus could have again immobilized the mob merely by the power of His name, from the first member of the cohort all the way back to the last soldier at the end of the ranks who may not have even heard Jesus' first answer, but who nonetheless fell to the ground. But God Incarnate allowed the ignorant guard to stand; He permitted Himself to be bound. Jesus placed Himself in Satan's hands to do as the evil one desired in his designated hour of authority. At no time whatsoever was Jesus a helpless victim, even as His terrorized sheep ran furiously away from the Light and into the protective confines provided by the darkness.

Still beyond these rich nuggets of scriptural truth, one last instance exists where Jesus used I AM— (*ego eimi*) to instruct His disciples. This particular I AM occurs only once in all Scripture, and it took place when Jesus gathered His disciples to Himself after His resurrection— in Galilee.

At some point between the resurrection and the ascension, "the eleven disciples proceeded to Galilee, to the mountain which Jesus had designated" (Matt. 28:16). We do not have enough details to know the particulars. In John 21:1, Jesus had already manifested Himself in Galilee. This is the account of Jesus eating with the disciples on the beach and later His threefold questions to Simon Peter (21:1-25). Did they stay in Galilee because of their fear of the Jewish authorities in Jerusalem, or did they return from Galilee to Jerusalem, perhaps to encourage the fledgling flock left behind? It would be nice to know, but we do not presently have this disclosed. However, in Matthew 28 they obviously were not in Galilee because "the eleven disciples proceeded to Galilee" (Matt. 28:16). It is important to note that although this is the end of Matthew's Gospel, the ascension of Jesus does not happen at this point, rather occurring some time shortly after this meeting somewhere near the Mount of Olives, opposite Jerusalem, towards Bethany (Luke 24:50). The disciples would rendezvous with Jesus in Galilee and later subsequently return to Jerusalem. Although Matthew's account deals specifically with the Eleven, many scholars reason that this appearance in Galilee is also the time Jesus "appeared to more than five hundred brethren at one time" (1 Cor. 15:6). Matthew 28:17 states, "And when they saw Him, they worshiped Him; but some were doubtful." It would not reason that Jesus, having appeared to the eleven minus Thomas, having noted the doubting apostle's proclamation, having later appeared to the eleven with Thomas, with Jesus offering the one who wanted the opportunity to feel His wounds, and having eaten with them on the beach, that the Eleven alone would gather "but some were doubtful." Probably the reference is to some of the other five hundred assembled.

Still, while the five hundred would play important roles in the early days of the church, and for whatever reason Jesus granted each to see Him after His resurrection, their stories must wait to be revealed at the judgment seat of Christ. The primary focus of Jesus at this point was to prepare the Eleven for their new ministry—and to prepare them for His approaching departure away from them and back to the Father.

None of the disciples was the same as they had been last year, or even a month before. The resurrected Jesus had repeatedly appeared and taught them. Still, to grasp that they had been the ones out of millions of human candidates to walk, eat, learn from—and love—God in the flesh still caused them to shake their heads slowly in disbelief—not disbelief about Him; disbelief that by God's grace each had been selected as one of His chosen ones (Matt. 13:16-17). They no longer boasted about which was the greatest disciple. Peter had denied in public—they all had denied in private. Everyone abandoned Jesus at His arrest. Confused. Panicked. Scattered. Sifted. They *all* had betrayed Him in some way, not only Judas. Jesus, however, never abandoned them, having loved His own until the end. His initial appearance to them after His death commenced with the divine pronouncement, "Peace" (John 20:19-21). The Good Shepherd began not only binding their wounds; He also strengthened that which was weak. Jesus did not make these men better; He made them new. They would become the human vessels designated to take up the baton of the Christian race after Jesus departed from the earth. Each one had a divinely designated course—as well as a cup to drink—and each would in turn hand the Gospel treasure over to others who would repeat the process, and so it continues today until the Lord returns in glory.

Coming by twos or threes, perhaps by themselves, they assembled at some designated point to journey to Galilee. If they left from Jerusalem, which seems to be the inference from the text, they may have gathered where the Last Supper had been served. Would they remind the others of what Jesus had said, or would each one simply sit where he had sat that night? It would not be surprising if each was lost in his own musings, everyone of them repeatedly moved to the point of tears with every remembrance of some word, some hand gesture, some look from the Savior. The two vacant seats of Jesus and Judas would have been visual reminders of the past few days and could not be looked on long without the resurging accompanying tears.

Perhaps instead they gathered at Gethsemane, directly across from Jerusalem, where John noted that Jesus "had often met there with His disciples" (John 18:2). If the disciples did assemble at Gethsemane, they could view Jerusalem approximately a quarter mile in a straight line across from them—and perhaps even view Golgotha. Maybe Peter, James, and John revealed to the others some of the agonies of Gethsemane; perhaps they pondered these in their own hearts, their own failure too fresh to relate quite yet to others. If they did gather at Gethsemane, the Eleven could see in the general direction where Judas had hanged himself, and shuddered to think about numerous episodes that they had shared with the prophesied traitor, all the time unaware that he never had truly belonged to the Lord.

Everything they heard, saw, and smelled reminded them of some aspect of the last three-and-a-half years of their lives. The Temple would be in view, with its streams of worshipers and religious activities. The Feast of Pentecost approached, one of the three great national feasts of Israel. How ironic—as the deeper spiritual truths always are—that the majority of Israel busily scurried about to prepare food, drink, as well as the offerings for the various Temple sacrifices, while the Bread of Life had come down from heaven. He who gives Living Waters to those who ask had already been slain in the predetermined plan of the Godhead, and He had tabernacled in their very midst.

But in a matter of days the Lamb of God would be going home. Soon, as Jesus had disclosed on the night of His betrayal, He would go to prepare a place for them (John 14:2-3). The concept of a place that Jesus would prepare for them would be warmly encouraging in the upcoming years, especially during times of bleak discouragement and darkness. But that night, and still to a degree now, all that these who so loved the Lord would hear is that Jesus would return to heaven—alone—without them.

Perhaps Jesus had informed the Eleven of the precise day of His ascension as Elijah had with Elisha (2 Kings 2:1-3)—perhaps not. Jesus had freely spoken of His return to heaven and may have continued to do so during His post-resurrection discourses. The Eleven would not view this pending event as Jesus would. Try as they might, the thought of Jesus returning to the Father would not be considered good news; in fact, it was just the opposite. His disciples had collectively and individually failed in His presence, often repeatedly. How could they possibly hope to fare any better after His absence? Jesus' ascension to the Father also meant His personal departure from among His own. The apostles would not grieve this event as they did the agonizing crucifixion, but they would continually ache for the promised reunion for the rest of their lives, and they would dread His departure as they would dread the pending permanent departure of a beloved friend, such as when Jonathan and David parted (1 Sam. 20:40-41). Each disciple, other than John, would have to wait until he went to be with Him in heaven to behold His face and see His smile again.

Jesus understood this and, as always, had already prepared for such—weeks before His disciples began their designated journey to Galilee.

After the repeated emphasis on the disciples meeting Jesus in Galilee, one would think that He would offer another discourse similar to the Sermon on the Mount, revealing additional divine truths this side of the cross—this side of His victory. While He no doubt said more, what Scripture does record is abruptly short, consisting of only two short sentences. "All authority has been given to me in heaven and on earth. Go therefore and make disciples of all the nations, baptizing them in the name of the Father and the Son and the Holy Spirit, teaching them to observe all that I commanded you; and lo, I am with you always, even to the end of the age" (Matt. 28:18-20). All things considered, after His threefold insistence that the disciples go to Galilee, we would expect much more to accompany this statement.

Of course, the two sentences that Jesus spoke are monumental, being the basis for most of the evangelical ministries throughout the world, and they remain the hallmark for many churches and denominations. Based on His total authority in heaven and on earth, Jesus issued what people usually call "The Great Commission" focused around the main verb "to make disciples." All that surrounds this—going, baptizing new believers in the name of the Trinity, teaching them to observe all things Jesus had commanded them—are participles explaining the accompanying activities associated with making disciples.

However, the conclusion of Matthew 28:20 is just as important, if not more so, than the previous segments of the sentence. For the most part, we usually treat this last phrase as something attached to what we consider the more important teaching of the Great Commission, focusing more on the mandate to take the Gospel to the world—Jesus did not. He began His concluding phrase with "lo," which, as we saw earlier, is the same Greek word for "Behold!" used elsewhere throughout Scripture. Again, it would be similar to someone clapping their hands together rapidly with two sharp claps saying, "Listen! Pay attention! This is important!"—which is so much more arresting than a casual, mellow reading of "lo." Although the Gospel mandate is eternally important, this last phrase, not the previous part, is what Jesus emphasized.

It would seem quite appropriate that Jesus would again employ *ego eimi* at this crucial juncture. His statement would make sense: "And behold, I AM with you always, even to the end of the age," or the extended meaning, "And behold! God with you always, even to the end of the age." With all the previous uses of *ego eimi* by Jesus, the disciples would be greatly comforted by this truth: the resurrected and exalted Lord would be with them as long as days existed. Not once would they ever be alone; at no time would His watchful care of His own ever cease. In a sense the Savior promised to be with them in some capacity as He had been ever since their first encounter with Him over three-and-a-half years before.

Jesus did use the divine self-designation of *ego eimi*, but He used it in a manner He had never done in all the previous accounts in the Gospels. This one instance of *ego eimi* — (I AM) stands apart. Jesus Himself and a messenger angel ensured that the disciples would be with Him in Galilee to receive this foundational revelation. Three times Scripture points to this one lesson with Jesus, drawing us to consider its importance. Jesus still summons all who read and obey His Word, likewise directing us to our own designated meeting with Him so that we do not miss this crucial statement. Behold! The Savior has also gathered us to Galilee! Behold! Jesus has something to teach us, too!

Matthew 1 contains the account of Joseph receiving divine revelation concerning the Son whom Mary would soon bear. An angel in the divinely-given dream instructed Joseph to name the yet-to-be-born baby "Jesus, for it is He who will save His people from their sins" (Matt. 1:21). Matthew further explained the significance of this truth by quoting the Messianic prophecy of Isaiah 7:14: "Now all this took place that what was spoken by the Lord through the prophet might be fulfilled, saying, 'Behold [Look! Pay attention!], the virgin shall be with child, and shall bear a Son, and they shall call His name Immanuel, which translated means, "God with us"'" (Matt. 1:22-23).

In the outworking of God's redemptive plan, this prophesied presence of God was vastly different — and so drastically needed — from His previous manifestations. In the Old Testament, God's presence was sometimes visually demonstrated, as when God descended on Mount Sinai or when the Shekinah Glory filled His Tabernacle and later filled His Temple. That God would indwell the Tabernacle and the Temple is beyond adequate words of human description. However, God's special presence within these two designated holy places also meant a sense of removal and separation: while God

Himself resided in the highly restricted Holy of Holies, the people dwelt outside and away from Him. So although God was present, He was veiled and, in a sense, removed from His people. Only God's designated high priest could enter into the very presence of God, only once a year on the God-ordained Day of Atonement. As long as God's presence dwelt in the Holy of Holies, no one could enter under any circumstance and live. Eventually because of repeated blatant sinfulness of the soon-to-be exiled Jewish people, God abandoned His Temple during the days of Ezekiel (Ezek. 8–11).

During this subsequent time of decline, God granted His prophets increasing revelation about the One who would eventually be born. The Messiah would come, redeem and reign—and yet be a Man of Sorrows, rejected by His own, as the sacrificial Servant of Yahweh. So while the prophecies told of One to come, for centuries He had not yet arrived, as the world lay in a darkness many could sense but could not comprehend its depth or magnitude.

After four hundred years of divine prophetic silence, the Promise of God would soon enter the world as a baby. The Greek translation of "God with us" in Matthew 1:23 gives a graphic picture of the divine progression, being literally translated "with us God." No more centuries of silence—God is with us. No more separation—God is with us. No more stumbling in spiritual darkness—God is with us.

And now, at the conclusion of the Book of Matthew, God is returning home.

The theological reality is that the Word became flesh and dwelt *among* His people—immensely different from the dwelling of the Old Testament. The human reality for the disciples was that Jesus would soon leave them. While Jesus would return the Victor, it would seem to the disciples that the departure of the Light would make the world as dark an abode as it was before His arrival. From the disciples' perspective, if Immanuel meant "God with us," then Jesus' return home would mean "God was with us"—His perceived absence making His presence past tense.

And so Jesus gathers His disciples for a most strategic lesson in their spiritual training. The disciples all had Jewish backgrounds and knew the respect placed on the unspeakable I AM name of God. Because they had to develop and grow in their faith and understanding of the person and work of Jesus, the disciples most likely would have winced whenever Jesus had previously used *ego eimi*—(I AM), fearing that He would greatly offend the religious leaders. But by this time they had repeatedly heard Jesus employ this term in reference to Himself as God, and they could comprehend its significance much more clearly than they could at the beginning of His ministry.

When the designated gathering to Galilee finally took place, Jesus began His teaching session by reminding His followers of His total authority in every realm. "All authority has been given to Me in heaven and on earth" (Matt. 28:18). The last instance when the disciples had heard Jesus evoke *ego eimi* (I AM) was at His arrest, and it would be fresh in their minds. Before their eyes the power of the Word of God had repelled His opponents backward in a small display of His vastly restrained power. This coupled with His resurrection would make much more sense to them now. However, His power was not the pressing question of their heart—separation from Jesus was.

Jesus, in turn, commissioned His believers regarding future ministry, one that would ultimately encompass the utmost parts of the earth, even unto all the nations. The disciples would eventually cultivate this same mentality—but not now. They were Jewish born, bred, and trained, and the designated ministry to all the Gentiles would begin in earnest only after many years. Even after the ascension, Pentecost, and the founding of Christ's Church, God still had to prod Peter by means of a threefold vision in Acts 10 to go to the Gentiles. That each of these men would play a pivotal role in the foundation of the faith and future ministry, especially to the Gentiles, was not their main concern at the moment—separation from Jesus was.

Jesus knew this. He knew their hearts, and He knew their heartaches. He continued with His teaching. "And behold!" [Note what I am about to say! Pay careful attention!] I AM with you all the days, even to the end of the age." However, this one time Jesus altered His declaration.

In Matthew 1:23 Immanuel is translated "God with us," or literally in the Greek, "with us, God." What Jesus now said was progressive in nature—*and* encompassing. Instead of merely saying, "I AM with you," He splits the "I" and the "AM" in the Greek. Literally, what Jesus said was I (*ego*) with you AM (*eimi*)—"I with you AM." Christ took His beloved disciples—those present and those in the future—and placed us within Himself, within God's holy name. The disciples who had repeatedly heard the *ego eimi* (I AM) statements of Jesus would readily mark the difference, although a fuller comprehension of this indivisible union would come over the years. Perhaps after beginning with the opening "Behold!" [Mark this! Pay attention!], Jesus used hand gestures to illustrate His spoken truth, as He would in a few days by lifting His hands and blessing them at His ascension (Luke 24:50). Not to step beyond the bounds of Scripture — and we will have to wait until heaven to see exactly how Jesus told them — but if Jesus did employ any hand gestures, they might be something along the lines of forefinger of the right hand lifted, as religious leaders of that time and beyond were apt to do when making profound statements. "I" — placing both hands on His heart, a heart that had long since incorporated those of all time who would love Him. "With you" — moving His arms forward in an encircling, encompassing manner. "AM" — bringing His hands back to His heart, bringing into His arms those He so lovingly and powerfully embraces.

I am sure some who are reading this will say, "No, that's going too far. The words in Matthew's account are just there. The arrangement does not matter. It is reading way too much into the text." Perhaps they may be right. Nevertheless, beyond this final verse in Matthew's gospel, there is much support for seeing the encompassing of Jesus' own in a manner completely unknown to them before. For instance, we need to remember the threefold insistence from God that the disciples go to this setting. We need to mark that this is the only place in the entire New Testament where this phrase exists. We need to note that at bare minimum Jesus used the emphatic for in the Greek when stating, in essence, "I (Myself) am with you." We need to note that Jesus placed His "Behold!" at this point, not at the beginning of the verses. Yet even beyond that, there is more: Jesus was merely teaching them — again — what He previously began to teach them on the last night before the Lamb of God gave His life as a ransom for many.

Entire books have been written about John 17. So much gold lies within it. We will limit ourselves to the matter at hand, walking past unmined treasures in this longest of Jesus' prayers recorded in the Bible. In His final group teaching of the Twelve-minus-Judas until after the crucifixion Jesus repeatedly drew attention to God's name. Five times within the English text and four in the Greek, Jesus specifically refers to the name of God. For instance, John 17:6: "I manifested Thy name to the men whom Thou gavest Me." *Name* in the Bible often refers to the whole person or to the person's true essence, such as in John 1:12, "to those who believe in His name." It is also noteworthy that while there are numerous names of God in the Old Testament

(Yahweh, El Shaddai, Adonai, etc.), Jesus employed the singular word "name," not the plural "names." The use of the singular could express the oneness of God so that all the names collectively depict God's name in a unified concept, or it could be a reference to one particular name of God. If the latter were the case then, by what we have already studied, the name I AM would certainly be the one Jesus manifested to both His disciples and to His enemies.

The emphasis on the name of God in this prayer continues. John 17:11: "And I am no more in the world; and yet they themselves are in the world, and I come to Thee. Holy Father, *keep them in Thy name, the name which Thou hast given Me*, that they may be one, even as We are." Jesus does not merely say, "keep them" or "protect them," but asks for God to do it in His very name, the very name that was given to Jesus by the Father. In fact, in the next verse Jesus reveals something the original listeners and we would not know unless He revealed it: "While I was with them, *I was keeping them in Thy name which Thou hast given Me*; and I guarded them, and not one of them perished but the son of perdition, that the Scripture might be fulfilled" (John 17:12). Jesus concludes this sublime prayer of wonder and glory by adding one final time, "and I have made Thy name known to them, and will make it known; that the love wherewith Thou didst love Me may be in them, and I in them" (John 17:26).

The last phrase in John 17:26 is eternally important: "and I in them." Jesus had already developed this previously unheard of concept in earlier verses: "I do not ask in behalf of these alone, but for those also who believe in Me through their word; that they may all be one; *even as Thou, Father, art in Me, and I in Thee, that they also may be in Us*; that the world may believe that Thou didst send Me. And the glory which Thou hast given Me I have given to them; that they may be one, just as We are one; *I in them*, and *Thou in Me*, that they may be perfected in unity, that the world may know that Thou didst send Me, and didst love them, even as Thou didst love Me" (John 17:20-23).

The requests that God the Son made unto God the Father are incredible! As we saw, the apostles at that time lived under the Law (Gal. 4:4); they were trained in the Torah. *Nowhere* in the Old Testament is there the concept that one could approach the unapproachable God except on the Day of Atonement, and then only the high priest *alone* coming with the God-ordained sacrifice. Here is the reason that what Jesus said would have been so staggering to those who initially heard Him: go to the Old Testament and see if you can find *one* prophecy that Messiah would be in anyone. For instance, the sublime Messianic prophecy of Isaiah 9:6 states, "For unto us a child is born" (KJV), not, "Into you a child is born." The Messiah was to sit on David's throne (Isa. 9:7) and rule over the world (Ps. 2:6-7; Zech. 14), having received an everlasting kingdom from the Ancient of Days (Dan. 7:13-14). Psalm 110:1 shows the Son will be seated at the right hand of God, waiting for His enemies to be placed as a footstool for His feet. The High Priestly Prayer of John 17 would be the first time His followers heard what must have been considered strange—if not impossible—as the question of birth asked by Nicodemus in what later would be recorded in John 3. How can the Messiah, whom they had handled with their hands (1 John 1:1), somehow be *in* them? This was earth-shattering divine revelation, and unless Gethsemane and related events were at hand, no doubt several questions would have been asked to the One who had prayed that they would be in Him—and in God the Father as well.

So alien would have been these concepts that instead of being in His presence, as when attending the temple sacrifices, believers would actually be *in* God Himself—loved, honored and respected—and, not only that, but Christ Himself would be *in* us, just as the Son is in the Father and the Father in the Son. Gone is the separation! See the Temple veil ripped from top to bottom! The Holy of Holies becomes open—by God Himself—and we have *bold* access to the Father through the Son.

Thou in Me, and I in Thee—that they may also be in Us.

The Great Commission is a manmade designation or "title". Perhaps a more accurate title would be "The Great Positioning."

The concept that Jesus began in His prayer in John 17 becomes developed more fully later with additional divine revelation. The apostle Paul fully understood this teaching, perhaps better than any other human who ever lived. Being "in Christ" was a reality for Paul, not merely some ethereal theological term. Because of Jesus' I AM statement in "the Great Commission," being "in Christ" should become much more vivid for us. In Romans 8:1 Paul declares, "There is therefore now no condemnation for those who are *in Christ Jesus*." The transforming reality of being in Christ is further seen in 2 Corinthians 5:17: "Therefore if any man is *in Christ*, he is a new creature; the old things passed away; behold, new things have come." And on and on the references go.

"And behold! I—with you—AM."

I AM at the burning bush becomes the I AM born in Bethlehem.

I AM the Resurrection and the Life becomes the life-giving source for all who believe and receive in His name.

I AM the Good Shepherd is also the I AM who continuously engulfs His sheep within Himself.

I AM the Light of the World Who shines His Light on and in our darkness.

I AM the Alpha and the Omega is also the I AM who will never desert or forsake you.

"And behold! I — with you — AM always, even to the end of the age."

Of this church I was made a minister according to the stewardship from God bestowed on me for your benefit, that I might fully carry out the preaching of the word of God, that is, the mystery which has been hidden from the past ages and generations; but has now been manifested to His saints, to whom God willed to make known what is the riches of the glory of this mystery among the Gentiles, which is

Christ in you,

the hope of glory.

— Colossians 1:25-27

But God, being rich in mercy, because of His great love with which He loved us, even when we were dead in our transgressions, made us alive together with Christ (by grace you have been saved), and raised us up with Him, and seated us with Him in the heavenly places,

in Christ Jesus,

in order that in the ages to come He might show the surpassing riches of His grace in kindness toward us

in Christ Jesus.

For by grace you have been saved through faith; and that not of yourselves, it is the gift of God; not as a result of works, that no one should boast. For we are His workmanship, created

in Christ Jesus

for good works, which God prepared beforehand, that we should walk in them.

— Ephesians 2:4-10

I do not ask in behalf of these alone, but for those also who believe in Me through their word; that they may all be one;

even as Thou, Father, art in Me,

and I in Thee,

that they also may be in Us;

that the world may believe that Thou didst send Me.

And the glory which Thou hast given Me I have given to them; that they may be one, just as We are one; I in them, and Thou in Me, that they may be perfected in unity, that the world may know that Thou didst send Me, and didst love them, even as Thou didst love Me.

Father, I desire that they also, whom Thou hast given Me, be with Me where I am, in order that they may behold My glory, which Thou hast given Me; for Thou didst love Me before the foundation of the world.

O righteous Father, although the world has not known Thee, yet I have known Thee; and these have known that Thou didst send Me;

And I have made Thy name known to them, and will make it known; that the love wherewith Thou didst love Me may be in them,

and I in them.

—John 17:20-26

10

THE GLORY

By its very nature, holiness habitually stands in contrast to evil. Holiness by its mere presence reveals evil, even as light invades the hidden realms of darkness. When Satan and the soon-to-become demons sinned in God's abode, they needed no ferreting out or unmasking; they stood exposed in spiritual nakedness, their darkness being quite evident to all. Satan's darkness would be easily identifiable to the Father of lights (James 1:17), who dwells in unapproachable light (1 Tim. 6:16), and whose very essence is light (1 John 1:5). In the midst of a dark and fallen world Satan may temporarily disguise himself as an angel of light (2 Cor. 11:14), because the world at large has no true basis for comparison, and with its darkened spiritual mind quite often erroneously designates Light as darkness and darkness as Light. But the holy angels of God would never confuse the two. Angels of Light readily detect darkness whenever they encounter it. When contrasted with the engulfing glory of God's holiness, the darkness emanating from Satan and his demons after their own original sin would be as readily observable as Adam and Eve's self-clothed attempt to conceal their sin had been to their Creator—and would have caused Satan to abide most awkwardly in God's holy habitation.

The holy angels of God would have viewed God's new creation of Genesis 1–2 by the same contrasting distinctions between God's Light and Satan's darkness. From the heavenly perspective they would have easily identified the Light of God's holiness surrounding the innocent newly born planet. In Job, God challenged Job by asking, "Where were you when I laid the foundation of the earth . . . when the morning stars sang together, and all the sons of God shouted for joy" (38:4, 7)? In this passage God revealed how the angelic realm marveled at God's hand-iwork, reflexively responding in adulation to the Father of Glory and

His creation, both beatific beyond our imagination. For a passing moment the earth exhibited only the hallmark of holiness, being completely devoid of any defect from sin.

Unless God disclosed to His angels what He was about to do, which does not seem probable, these same angels who recently shouted with joy at creation would watch in increasing alarm as this same darkness recently expelled from heaven now approached and entered God's Eden. They would observe the indwelling of the serpent by Satan—the first record of a spiritual being taking residence within a physical one. They viewed the temptation; they saw man fall, trading his God-given purity for debasing corruption. After the Fall the holy angels of God would watch in hopeless desperation as darkness permeated the earth until it completely engulfed every aspect associated with the planet. Having once witnessed God's creation perfection, the advent of evil to a place previously undefiled would have been most noticeable—and most alarming—to the holy angels.

God's angels had properly expected the divine expulsion of all darkness from heaven after Satan's rebellion. Now earth was likewise defiled. The angels understood that the Holy Father *must* judge the contaminated inhabitants of the newly polluted planet, much as He had within His own heavenly abode. Since God had already severely judged Satan at the initial rebellion, the angels no doubt expected an intensified second judgment against the evil one. Instead, God pronounced judgment and then departed—but Satan remained. And much to their amazement, instead of witnessing the seizure and immediate punishment of Satan, God's angels viewed the multitudes of dark legions take their strongholds in various ranks around the surface of the earth (Eph. 6:12), with their leader Satan now reigning as "the prince of the power of the air" (Eph. 2:2). Not only had the planet and its inhabitants become defiled in darkness, this darkness itself encircled and encased it much as the atmosphere envelops the earth in its entirety.

Before the increased capacity of darkness, however, the spectator angels would have also viewed God's Light approaching darkened Eden. Much to their speechless bewilderment, instead of God's full wrath rightly and immediately being unleashed on the two human contaminants, two lesser lights shown beside God; two little lights were created, reflecting God's true Light in a diminished yet unmistakable measure. The angels never would have viewed this combination before: sinful beings who somehow nonetheless possessed and reflected God's holiness. When God removed His visible presence from earth for the time being, the two little lights remained, standing in utter contrast to the new deep darkness of their environs. Little lights who would begin the seed lineage promised in Genesis 3:15: little lights whom God clothed with the righteousness of the first blood sacrifice. Over time the angels would witness the light multiply and expand, but more often than not, they would view darkness almost completely overwhelm the light.

Perhaps equally as mystifying as God's unforeseen grace given in the Garden was His lack of perceived action in Genesis 6. The angels saw darkness rage in a manner they had neither experienced nor expected, darkness of such magnitude that it seemed to devour all traces of Light. As sin increased, the Father patiently endured it, but never would darkness completely rule the earth. God Almighty had so mandated, and it must be done according to His Word.

The angels would certainly note whenever God furthered His redemptive plan by means of His revelatory Light. They would have heard the discourses between God and Abraham, as the promised seed lineage narrowed in scope to one people who were yet to exist. They would have beheld the birth of the covenantal Jewish people, as well as their later bondage in Egypt. God's angelic messengers would have perceived a new expression of God's Light in Moses' encounter with the Angel of the Lord at the burning bush. The angels would have further witnessed the Shekinah glory of God fill His tabernacle during the days of the wilderness generation, and then later indwell His temple built by Solomon. Unmistakably clear to the angelic realm would be this glory presence on earth—not the full manifestation of His glory, they realized, but far grander than any previously displayed to mortals. The angels would have watched in sadness centuries later as God slowly and reluctantly removed His glory, hovering first over the Ark of the Covenant, then the temple threshold, and finally over the Mount of Olives (Ezek. 10; 11:22-23). The temple would not have the special Light of God's presence in its midst again until Mary and Joseph took the baby Light of the World into the rebuilt structure.

God's angels would have witnessed the scattering of God's covenantal people in the Babylonian exile, with very little light evident other than the illuminating Light of the prophets' voices. Soon, however, even that prophetic light would grow dim for a time. For a period of about four hundred years, increasing darkness existed as God offered no more revelatory light. The most visible light during this stage of the world's darkness was the prophetic Light of God as the

Old Testament was approaching its end—and the Light of God that prophesied of a Coming One who would shine in the midst of darkness (Isa. 9:2).

Then in the fulness of time—the conception. Heaven's Light became the Light of the World. The light of God's star in the heaven appeared, signifying to both the heavenly and earthly realm that a Star had risen from Jacob's house; a Scepter raised in Israel (Num. 24:17). The angelic multitude added their praises (Luke 2:13-14)—and their reflective light—in adoration and praise beyond what they had celebrated thousands of years earlier at creation. But the true Light came into a world engulfed in darkness. He came unto His own, but His own did not receive Him (John 1:11). Although many loved and accepted the Light, more did not than did. Eventually, the Light received indescribable attacks against Himself: the hour of darkness beginning at Jesus' arrest (Luke 22:53); the darkness of assembled evil at Calvary—and finally, the darkness of God's very presence that resided over the cross.

How utterly dark the darkness surrounding the earth must have appeared to the angelic beings who watched the torturous death of the Light. How dark fallen man's domain and future must have seemed to the angels who shared the Father's unfathomable grief.

Rumblings. Distant rumblings and reverberations felt long before the appearance of any visible form. For thousands of years these demons confined in pits of darkness, a darkness even deeper and more restrictive than their own deep darkness, felt the approach of someone or some thing. Having abandoned their previous domain, these fallen angels had long ago entered into the confines of darkness far removed and isolated from the outside world. This subset of demons, participants in the demonic collusion of Genesis 6, received God's judgment earlier than the remaining demons would. Imprisonment was not God's ultimate judgment, the dreaded lake of fire of Revelation 20, but it was the inescapable abyss of darkness: an abhorrent, ghastly place of intense torment and suffering. As far as we know, other than these and the demons that will be released in Revelation 9 (which we will find out when we get to heaven whether or not the ones to be released during the Tribulation are the same as those of Genesis 6, 1 Peter 3, 2 Peter 2 and Jude), no other demons currently reside in the abyss. God may have sentenced other fallen angels there throughout history, but if He did, He chose not to reveal it in His Word.

If God had permitted us to have it, the account of the demons' seizure and confinement after the events of Genesis 6 would have been most illuminating. Was Satan present to witness this judicial act of God? If so, Satan's reaction would have remained consistent with his base character. If Satan attended his angels' imprisonment, he stood by helplessly, either impotent or else unwilling to attempt a rescue of his fallen lessers. By no means would he ever have considered offering his freedom in place of theirs, redemption of others remaining such an alien concept to one so thoroughly evil. Satan certainly would have felt no compassion or compunction as God executed His verdict, only intensified wrath, as he will later exhibit in the Tribulation (Rev. 12:12).

Perhaps instead Satan was absent at the demons' incarceration, choosing not to witness another segment of God's righteous judgment. He may have feared being too close to the holy wrath of God since it offered a preview of the divine retribution that awaited him if the seed promise of Genesis 3:15 ever became a reality. Either way — whether Satan was present or not — the last sight the demons viewed before their confinement to pits of darkness was the absence of any rescuer or redeemer to come to their aide. Though perversely evil and debased, in a sense these demons also had been deceived and betrayed. They currently endure their divinely wrought judgment devoid of the primary instigator of their crime against God. One day they will all reunite in the eternal torment originally prepared for them and their master (Matt. 25:41; 2 Pet. 2:4; Rev. 20:10).

God sequestered these demons away from the rest of the world, making them unaware of the events and developments that had unfolded in the human arena. If the demons in the Luke 8 account represent the mentality of the other demons (which they most likely do), no other demon would communicate with those imprisoned, even if they could, because no demon would be bold enough to venture to the abyss. The fallen angels in the Gospel accounts shuddered at the thought that Jesus might order them into the abyss; it seems certain that they would never attempt to go there on their own initiative. Hypothetically speaking, even if they could stealthily visit the abyss without God's notice (which, of course, is a complete impossibility) Satan's angels could do nothing once they arrived. So secure is this divine stronghold, Satan and his entire forces assembled at the door of the abyss would pose no threat of releasing its occupants. An angel of God in Revelation 9 will one day receive a key from God Himself in order to unfasten the abyss during the Tribulation. Without this key, the lock to the abyss cannot be opened. One must either receive the key from the Father Himself, or else be strong enough to wrest it out of His hand. Neither option was remotely possible for Satan.

So these demons wait in an abode of torment, surrounded by the deep darkness that results from the absence of God's glory. Having been removed from any contact with earth, their information ended with their imprisonment when God sent the flood (Gen. 7). They exist in torment in the abyss with a most restricted understanding of the out-workings of the program of God. Perhaps they waited expectantly for Satan to rescue them. They may have waited for some other colluded demonic scheme to release them. If so, they waited in vain, seething in slow-boil wrathful anger that mirrored that of their master, in whose image they had become permanently recreated.

Finally, in the distant darkness—rumblings. The demons would immediately detect this strange effect on both them and on their confines. Maybe they concluded this was the anticipated force of Satan's legions as they approached the abyss to release its inhabitants.

Then, a distant Light approached their darkness. Power exuded to the confines of the abyss—much, much more power than the demons had ever experienced before, even at their initial imprisonment. At some point, whether sooner or later, the imprisoned demons understood: Light, not darkness, approached. Eventually, every demon confined to the abyss realized that this was not a rescue or release. Divine Glory and Power Himself made His way toward them.

The imprisoned demons would recognize the Second Member of the Godhead as He displayed the divine characteristics they had witnessed before their fall: "Clothed in a robe reaching to the feet, and girded across His breast with a golden girdle. And His head and His hair were white like white wool, like snow; and His eyes were like a flame of fire; and His feet were like burnished bronze, when it has been caused to glow in a furnace, and His voice was like the sound of many waters . . . and out of His mouth came a sharp two-edged sword; and His face was like the sun shining in its strength" (Rev. 1:13-16). But beyond these attributes of the Light were the curious yet unmistakable wounds of the Lamb (Rev. 5:4-6). These visible wounds would be the most significant difference observable to the demons from their previous encounters with the Lord—and by far the most puzzling—but their curiosity would not embolden them to ask of their origin in the presence of the Power they so greatly feared.

Peter wrote that after Jesus' death He "went and made proclamation to the spirits now in prison, who once were disobedient, when the patience of God kept waiting in the days of Noah" (1 Pet. 3:19-20). God did not choose to reveal the full content of Jesus' proclamation to the inhabitants of the abyss. We will get to hear the original from the lips of the Savior Himself when we get to heaven. But from the clues God left in Scripture, a logical paraphrase of some of the content of Jesus' proclamation can be deduced:

"Remember this, and be assured; recall it to mind, you transgressors. Remember the former things long past, for I AM God, and there is no other. I AM God, and there is no one like Me, declaring the end from the beginning and from ancient times things which have not been done, saying, 'My purpose will be established, and I will accomplish My good pleasure'" (Isa. 46:8-10).

"You in your wickedness colluded with the Evil One to prevent the birth of the Promised Seed of Woman who would crush the serpent's head from ever becoming a reality (Gen. 3:15). I declare to you today that the seed lineage the Father first pronounced in the Garden continued long after the Flood was a distant memory to mankind. The seed genealogy persists even to this very day, in spite of every effort of darkness to the contrary. The Seed first promised by Yahweh lives on – while you remain confined in pits of darkness. The primary reason that the Seed lives on is that God Almighty does not give help to angels, but He does give help to the seed of Abraham (Heb. 2:16), a progeny of the seed lineage you never met. Thus the lineage from which the One Seed would come remains: nourished, protected, fully capable of bringing forth the One who will give rest to the cursed earth and regain what Adam originally lost.

"You left your domain for that of another – the Seed did as well. Since the children share in flesh and blood, the Promise of God likewise also partook of the same, that through death He might render powerless him who had the power of death, that is your leader the devil – the one whom you will eventually share eternal torment with in the lake of fire. The Promised Seed entered the world of fallen man for the express purpose that He might deliver those who through fear of death were subject to slavery all their lives (Heb. 2:14-15).

"Similar in many ways to you once abandoning your own domain to cohabit with Adam's race, I Myself now enter your abode – not from heaven but from earth. You entered the world of flesh: the Promise of God did as well, but in a way sanctioned and predetermined by the Trinity (Acts 2:23; 1 Pet. 1:18-20).

"Not only did the seed lineage continue and not only does God give help to the seed – I AM the Promised Seed of Woman (Gen. 3:15)! I AM the

Promised Seed of Abraham (Gal. 3:16)! Although I existed in the form of God, I did not regard equality with God the Father a thing to be grasped. Instead I emptied Myself, taking on the form of a bond-servant, being made in the likeness of human kind (Phil. 2:6-7). You offered death and imprisonment — I AM the Bread of Life come down from heaven, offering Life to all who will receive Me.

"My victory over you and Satan was not so much so I could render you powerless — that option was readily available at your first rebellious act of disobedience. I won so I could rescue and redeem My own so deeply ensnared in the bondage of sin. Multiplied millions through the ages worship Me freely — and I joyously give to My own the abode and positions of authority far beyond what you ever attempted to usurp. Those I redeem will even sit down with Me on My throne (Rev. 3:21), ruling over the nations with the same authority granted Me (Rev. 2:26-27), all because I overcame everything that darkness had to muster — and I stood firm! I will soon return to My rightful place beside the Father (Ps. 110:1). But even more so, I will soon return for and with My own (Rev. 19:11-16).

"The Seed eternally triumphed because I AM the Promised Seed of God — and I have crushed your head forever!"

The reactionary wretched howling of the newly enlightened demons still reverberates off the distant walls of the abyss long after the Light departed and the darkness returned.

The resurrection of Jesus was not the final display of Light to the angelic world. It was magnificent and unparalleled, but it was by no means the last. God had much more to present, especially at Jesus' homecoming. One day God will show us in detail the precise moment of embrace when the well-pleasing, beloved Son returned to His proper abode with God the Father and God the Holy Spirit—while myriads of myriads and thousands of thousands of attending angels responded in extended worship (Rev. 5:11). Until then we can no more comprehend the reunion than we can comprehend the full scope of heaven.

During His earthly ministry Jesus spoke freely of His return to the Father. In fact, in John 3:13 Jesus made the first allusion to His ascension by contrasting it with His coming to earth: "And no one has ascended into heaven, but He who descended from heaven, even the Son of Man." Who currently knows other than the Godhead precisely when the child Jesus knew He was God's Son, but John 3 is the first instance where He revealed His pre-existence with God the Father in heaven. Accordingly, Jesus could tell his heart-broken disciples on the night of His arrest, "Let not your heart be troubled; believe in God, believe also in Me. In My Father's house are many dwelling places; if it were not so, I would have told you; for I go to prepare a place for you. And if I go and prepare a place for you, I will come again, and receive you to Myself; that where I am, there you may be also" (John 14:1-3). At His resurrection appearance to Mary Magdalene, Jesus instructed her, "Stop clinging to Me, for I have not yet ascended to the Father; but go to My brethren, and say to them, 'I ascend to *My* Father and *your* Father, and *My* God and *your* God'" (John 20:17). Even at this point Jesus began preparing His disciples for His return home to the Father, but did so now in a sense of shared brotherhood: "My Father and your Father, and My God and your God." The approaching ascension was merely a first fruits preview of a grander one of which they would one day be participants. After a period of forty days (Acts 1:3), Jesus returned to the Father just as He had promised.

Yet the ascension was more than merely Jesus returning home to heaven. It was a victory parade of heavenly proportions. The ascension showed both the completely finished work of the Messiah—*and* His accepted work by the Father. The wonderful Messianic Psalm 110 states this in its first verse: "The LORD says to My, Lord, 'Sit at My right hand, until I make Thine enemies a footstool for Thy feet.'" In a goldmine section that we must pass over for the sake of time, Jesus used Psalm 110:1 to silence His critics in Matthew 22:41-46. The author of Hebrews best shows the importance of the finished work of the Messiah by writing: "And He is the radiance of His glory and the exact representation of His nature, and upholds all things by the word of His power. When He had made purification of sins, He sat down at the right hand of the Majesty on high; having become as much better than the angels, as He has inherited a more excellent name than they" (Heb. 1:3-4).

Paul reminded Timothy of the eternal importance of the ascension. In 1 Timothy 3:16, he quoted what many understand to be a hymn of the early church:

"And by common confession great is the mystery of godliness:
He who was revealed in the flesh,
Was vindicated in the Spirit,
Beheld by angels,
Proclaimed among the nations,
Believed on in the world,
Taken up in glory."

With all that had transpired leading up to Jesus' ascension, that He was "beheld by angels" may very well have included the entire angelic realm, both holy and evil. But the last phrase, "taken up in glory" is often overlooked. Actually, what Paul wrote was that Jesus was taken up *in* glory, not *into* glory—and there is a difference. This phrase emphasizes not so much that Jesus returned to the domain or realm of glory that awaited Him in heaven, which He did, as other verses testify (John 17:4-5, 22-25). Rather the last part of 1 Timothy 3:16 discloses that Jesus' ascension itself was another display of glory—that is, He displayed glory while He was taken up. We generally do not consider the ascension a manifestation of God's glory, as was the Shekinah glory filling His temple or the glory that was revealed at the Transfiguration. After all, the ascension itself was a relatively brief event for the disciples who witnessed it. Luke recorded the incident with only one sentence in Acts 1:9: "And after He had said these things, He was lifted up while they were looking on, and a cloud received Him out of their sight." Although still young in the faith, the disciples understood that Jesus' ascension was a temporary event, as they immediately began looking for His promised return for them.

Perhaps because the ascension ultimately set the stage for the Lord's return is why the Transfiguration made much more of a lasting effect on Peter. In his last epistle before his pending death, the one event in the life of Jesus that affected Peter the most was Jesus' Transfiguration, not His ascension: "For we did not follow cleverly devised tales when we made known to you the power and coming of our Lord Jesus Christ, but we were eyewitnesses of His majesty. For when He received honor and glory from God the Father, such an utterance as this was made to Him by the Majestic Glory, 'This is My beloved Son with whom I am well-pleased'—and we ourselves heard this utterance made from heaven when we were with Him on the holy mountain" (2 Peter 1:16-18). Maybe for Peter the ascension was something that Jesus did, and the Transfiguration previewed who Jesus really is in essence, and it was an uncovering that Peter could never remove himself from for the remainder of his life.

God in His Word considers the ascension to be a display of His glory; we should consider it as well. Perhaps if we view Jesus' ascension from a different perspective, we can better understand the glory displayed there. Perhaps we too can step back and to a degree witness Jesus being "beheld by angels . . . taken up in glory"—and marvel anew at the glory of God.

Paul described Satan as "the prince of the power of the air" (Eph. 2:2). Later in the same epistle he described an aspect of the demonic host as "the spiritual forces of wickedness in the heavenly places" (or literally, "in the heavenlies") (Eph. 6:12). Like so many other statements in Scripture, limited information usually gives way to multiple questions. It is one thing to know that Satan currently resides as "the prince of the power of the air" — it is entirely another to understand even remotely what this means or why it is important.

That Satan reigns in the sphere of the air does not mean that he has no contact with earth — quite the contrary. When God questioned Satan, asking him where he had been, Satan replied, "From roaming about on the earth and walking around on it" (Job 1:7). Also, in writing that the Christian struggle is not against flesh and blood, Paul employed a Greek word for "struggle" in Ephesians 6:12 which means hand-to-hand combat. Even though Satan's domain consists of the atmosphere in some unique way, it is from the air where he readily gains his access to the planet's inhabitants.

But still, when you think about it, why would God reveal to us that part of Satan's domain consists of the atmosphere that surrounds the earth? It does not affect our struggle, does it? Does it make us any wiser or better able to fight the Christian fight realizing that Satan is the prince of the power of the air? Yet God saw fit to include this revelation in His Word, so this doctrinal nugget is something He desires us to know.

One answer as to why God revealed Satan's domain is that by delineating the various realms, a sharp division emerges. Satan retains a vaulted position over the earth, but his subservient position to the Godhead becomes markedly visible. Paul revealed that years earlier he had been "caught up to the third heaven" (2 Cor. 12:2). Some scholars conclude the three sections consist of earth, Satan's abode in the atmosphere and beyond, and God's abode in the highest heavens. Each realm is distinct from the other: earth is below Satan, temporarily held by his power (1 John 5:19), but heaven remains far, far above him. While this is beneficial to understand — if it accurately depicts the threefold division and may be an aspect of Paul's thought — another reason may exist as to why God included that Jesus was taken up in glory.

Since the holy angels could distinguish between holiness and evil, much as we can between clouds and the clear sky, they would see the earth smothered in evil from the Fall onward. Evil encompassed the planet in its entirety. At no place did earth offer any hope that certain parts remained unaffected by the darkness of evil. How majestic, then, would have been the ascension of Jesus with His attending angels watching. With Satan being the prince of the power of the air, and the whole world lying in his power (1 John 5:19), then the reverse is true as well. Since darkness engulfed the entire earth, when Jesus returned to the Father—when He was raised in glory—He had to travel through the very midst of Satan's designated domain. At His ascension Jesus blasted through the domain of darkness that Satan and his demons held over earth. No struggle or fight was required as the Glory of God returned home in divine power. If this had been a war scene in a movie, then Jesus triumphantly returned to the Father right through the very heart of previously occupied enemy territory. As one ex-gang member whom I once had in class blurted out in a worshipful response about this verse: "He took back the turf!" Indeed Messiah—I AM—did.

Who knows, other than those in the spiritual world, but that the space where Jesus ascended to heaven may have remained open to this day, a visible reminder to both holy and evil angels of the complete victory of Jesus. Perhaps even the residual effects of the Savior's passing leave an irreparable gap before the demonic host. If God the Father tore the temple veil in half at the death of Jesus, how much more would the domain of darkness be torn when the Son returned in triumph? Jesus did not need to tear away the darkness in order for Him to ascend—it was not so much an active tearing away by God as it was the disassembling of the evil powers as the exalted Jesus ascended home in glory. As we saw in a previous chapter, Paul put it this way: not only were our sins forgiven at the cross; Jesus disarmed His spiritual agents that day as well. Colossians 2:13-15 states: "And when you were dead in your transgressions and the uncircumcision of your flesh, He made you alive together with Him, having forgiven us all our transgressions, having canceled out the certificate of debt consisting of decrees against us and which was hostile to us; and He has taken it out of the way, having nailed it to the cross. *When He had disarmed the rulers and authorities, He made a public display of them, having triumphed over them through Him.*"

The rulers, powers, the world forces of darkness, or/and the spiritual forces of wickedness in the heavenly places did not have to be moved out of the way. No one had to inform the demonic hosts that they needed to vacate the premises so the conquering King could return home. As the demons who previously had received the Godhead's judicial proclamation at their expulsion from heaven, these beings knew Power (1 Cor. 1:24) when they were in His midst, and they were as easily repulsed by Power as when the human agents were flattened by Jesus' use of I AM at His arrest (John 18:1-6).

How enlightening it would have been if God had revealed where Satan was as Jesus our Lord was raised in glory. Was Satan present? Did he make eye contact as Christ the King passed? Did Satan bow the knee in partial fulfillment of Philippians 2:5-11? One thing remains certain: no part of his domain would Satan of his own accord willingly give back to Jesus. But why did Satan and the demons not attempt to restrain Jesus? Why did they not forbid Him passage through their territory? We know why: because disarmed rulers and authorities have no means available to them. The collective forces of darkness could never have slowed or deterred Him, not even for a microsecond. The Glory of God can never be dispelled or restricted whenever God chooses to display it; otherwise, one would have to be stronger than God—and that is simply not possible. The Son—the Seed— returned as Conqueror through the very midst of Satan's demonic realm, was seated and accepted at the right hand of the Father, waiting until His enemies—including Satan—are made a footstool for His feet (Ps. 110:1).

What a divine irony had transpired over the ages. Satan originally purposed in his heart, "I will ascend to heaven; I will raise my throne above the stars of God, and I will sit on the mount of assembly in the recesses of the north. I will ascend above the heights of the clouds; I will make myself like the Most High" (Isa. 14:13-14). No, only the Son would ascend to the Father's right hand. In quoting Psalm 110:1, the author of Hebrews asks, "But to which of the angels has He ever said, 'Sit at My right hand, until I make Thine enemies a footstool for Thy feet'" (Heb. 1:13)? What Satan so lusted after, Jesus temporarily released by His own free will. Our Savior, "who, although He existed in the form of God, did not regard equality with God a thing to be grasped, but emptied Himself, taking the form of a bond-servant, and being made in the likeness of men. And being found in appearance as a man, He humbled Himself by becoming obedient to the point of death, even death on a cross. Therefore also God highly exalted Him, and bestowed on Him the name which is above every name, that at the name of Jesus every knee should bow, of those who are in heaven, and on earth, and under the earth, and that every tongue should confess that Jesus Christ is Lord, to the glory of God the Father" (Phil. 2:6-11).

The holy angels of God who had long before observed the first sin in heaven had waited for this triumph for thousands of years. The reactionary worship of heaven's occupants still resounds off the limitless walls of eternity. One day we also will add our voices to the angel choir, singing, "Worthy is the Lamb that was slain to receive power and riches and wisdom and might and honor and glory and blessing" (Rev. 5:12), and "To Him who sits on the throne, and to the Lamb, be blessing and honor and glory and dominion forever and ever" (Rev. 5:13).

Worthy is the Lamb who was "revealed in the flesh, was vindicated in the Spirit, beheld by angels, proclaimed among the nations, believed on in the world – taken up in glory" (1 Tim. 3:16).

I pray that the eyes of your heart may be enlightened, so that you may know what is the hope of His calling, what are the riches of the glory of His inheritance in the saints, and what is the surpassing greatness of His power toward us who believe. These are in accordance with the working of the strength of His might

Which He brought about in Christ, when He raised Him from the dead, and seated Him at His right hand in the heavenly places,

> *far above all rule and authority and power and dominion,*

and every name that is named, not only in this age, but also in the one to come.

– Ephesians 1:18-21

For it is better, if God should will it so, that you suffer for doing what is right rather than for doing what is wrong. For Christ also died for sins once for all, the just for the unjust,

> *in order that He might bring us to God,*

having been put to death in the flesh, but made alive in the spirit;

in which also He went and made proclamation to the spirits now in prison, who once were disobedient, when the patience of God kept waiting in the days of Noah, during the construction of the ark, in which a few, that is, eight persons, were brought safely through the water.

And corresponding to that, baptism now saves you – not the removal of dirt from the flesh, but an appeal to God for a good conscience – through the resurrection of Jesus Christ, who is at the right hand of God,

having gone into heaven,

after angels and authorities and powers had been subjected to Him.

—1 Peter 3:17-22

Through Silvanus, our faithful brother (for so I regard him), I have written to you briefly, exhorting and testifying that this is the true grace of God. Stand firm in it!

Peace be to you all who are

in Christ.

—1 Peter 5:12, 14b

Also available from

Kress Christian
PUBLICATIONS

The Cup and the Glory: Lessons on Suffering and the Glory of God
Greg Harris

One with a Shepherd: The Tears and Triumphs of a Ministry Marriage
Mary Somerville

Christian Living Beyond Belief: Biblical Principles for the Life of Faith
Cliff McManis

Meeting God Behind Enemy Lines: My Christian Testimony as a U.S. Navy SEAL
Steve Watkins

A Biblical Critique of Infant Baptism
Matt Waymeyer

Revelation 20 and the Millennial Debate
Matt Waymeyer

Free Justification: The Glorification of Christ in the Justification of a Sinner
Steve Fernandez

God's Plan for Israel: A Study of Romans 9-11
Steve Kreloff

God in Everyday Life: The Book of Ruth for Expositors and Biblical Counselors
Brad Brandt & Eric Kress

Notes for the Study and Exposition of 1st John
Eric Kress

Commentaries for Biblical Expositors
Dr. Jim Rosscup

The Gromacki Expository Series (by Dr. Robert Gromacki)
Called to Be Saints: An Exposition of 1 Corinthians
Stand Firm in the Faith: An Exposition of 2 Corinthians
Stand Fast in Liberty: An Exposition of Galatians
Stand United in Joy: An Exposition of Philippians
Stand Perfect in Wisdom: An Exposition of Colossians & Philemon
Stand True to the Charge: An Exposition of 1 Timothy
Stand Bold in Grace: An Exposition of Hebrews

www.kresschristianpublications.com